THE GROWING PAINS OF *Peter*

THE GROWING PAINS OF *Peter*

BY TERRY ATKINSON

NEW LIVING PUBLISHERS
164 Radcliffe New Road, Whitefield, Manchester M45 7TU
England

British Library Cataloguing in Publication Data
A catalogue record for this book is available
from the British Library.

ISBN 1 899721 00 2

Scripture quotations are from the King James Version
of the Bible, unless otherwise stated.

Produced and printed in England for
NEW LIVING PUBLISHERS
164 Radcliffe New Road, Whitefield, Manchester M45 7TU by
Nuprint Ltd, Station Road, Harpenden, Herts, AL5 4SE

This book is dedicated to all those
who pass through growing pains in
their quest for maturity.

CONTENTS

CHAPTER

1

Introduction

The Growing Pains of Peter is not set in some historical fashion. The Chapters are not written in sequence. I have sought to bring historical fact into the book, at the same time, adding a spiritual dimension to enlarge and make it appealing to everyone, because primarily it is a book about human nature reacting under the Divine gaze. It is made up of the richness and diversity of the dealings of Jesus with Peter, almost as clay in the hands of the Master Potter. When the clay collapses the Potter does not throw it away. When the piece of clay begins to wobble the Potter begins again. Adding a little here and there He seeks to win and, from that messy lump, there arises true form and imagination. The Potter has conquered. The piece has taken shape and is patterned by the gentle pressure of the fingers of the Engineer of earthenware. What was in the Mind is in the mud as it rises into a new creation.

The life of Peter is as that Galilean clay—slippery, wet, muddy yet, through grace, made fit for the palace of a king. Many times spoiled and unyielding it is never abandoned. None of it is wasted. Even when it seems doomed to failure, that failure was used as a door into another opportunity.

This book seeks to reveal how Peter felt when he made mistakes and was involved in glaring errors. He is always, in a sense, walking on water or sinking into the unknown, finding Jesus Christ in that unknown and seeking to make that fact known to the human heart. The love of Christ has a greater capacity when Peter is leaning the hardest, it is the most gentle at these times. When he falls, he bounces back. It is as if, when he slips, he slips on the steps of the throne to land on that throne! Though he falls seven times he rises seven times. The way down is the way up for him. He returns with reborn vigour. The way out is the way through. He must not climb over or out of the Hand which is lovingly preserving and shielding him for that would be to create a door where there is no door.

Jesus, through Peter, is seeking to bring back all that Adam lost when he was involved in the Fall in the Garden of Eden. The complications of the human heart and character are fully seen and met in Jesus. Very often God in Christ has to bring Peter back to the starting point, to the drawing board. There has to be a re-assessment and re-investment.

Although the book is not particularly chronological it has an order of happenings in the life of any believer. In Peter you will see yourself. In *The Growing Pains of Peter* there are scenes and happenings which are relevant to all. History and theology come alive as we read. Sometimes as we watch holiday programmes on television we are heard to mutter 'I have been there', as we recognise names and places. We are filled with nostalgia, memories and immediate recognition of past experiences. In Peter you will see reflected the sins of the fathers, the immaturity of the child, the zeal of youth, the maturity of the middle aged and the solid wisdom of old age. There are troubled times and peaceful moments, revelations, advice and help. We begin to comment... 'If I had been there... if I had been Peter, I wouldn't have done that... that was the wrong thing to do'. This is the coward's and the dreamer's way out. It is easy from a quayside to criticise a sinking ship. You were there in Adam when he sinned, and you were there also in the dilemmas of this son of Jonas. Peter is as one in the witness box under cross-examination. He tells the truth, the whole truth and nothing but the truth—and God does help him, even as He helps us through life.

Peter is a shadow of all the Old Testament Prophets with the different aspects of character as found throughout the pages of Holy Writ. There is a place for every one of us in Peter. There is that in Peter which we chose to do. There is that congenital twist in all of us. In him we live, speak and have our being. Peter is still the chief spokesman on human nature. What he has to say today is still relevant because we are dealing with human hearts and lives. The opening up of his life as revealed in the atmosphere of the presence of the Lord of Glory is the opening of Pandora's Box. Peter is still an authority on the fiery trial, the conflict within. When I am in sore distress and have a great need then I can bring Peter into my room. I can allow him to visit me in my sickness, turn the light low, let him straighten my pillow and tuck me in, for I feel that my life is in his shadow. He is the understanding human, the human face of the disciples. He does all this as I open the door of my Bible and he walks through and becomes my Mentor. As the loaves and the fishes were blessed by Jesus then handed to the disciples, Peter was one of them. He passed that multiplied miracle to others.[1] His life has miracle bread and fish with it for us to feed on in order that we might be fully satisfied. There will be many hampers left to gather up the fragments.

There are many illustrations in the life of Peter. There is the journey of Abraham in Genesis 12. There is the aggressive faith of the Patriarch, the selling of the Birthright by Esau, the twists of Jacob's nature in Peter as he stands in the Garden of Gethsemane with drawn sword, even as Moses did in readiness to smite the rock.[2] I hear afresh the call of Deborah to 'rise up as a man in Israel and conquer' (Judges 4:14). The tears of Jeremiah and the lamentation of Lamentations are here.[3] He is as one of the spies who went to spy out the land of Canaan. Here is a Joshua, with sword in hand leading the people on into something new and deep. There is a little bit of the Jacob struggle, and there is also the Kingly nature of David. There is the leadership of deliverance as found in the Book of Judges, and something to sing about as in the Psalms. There is something so rich in love as in the Song of Songs. Peter is a true Jonah, a runaway from God at times who is brought back to his commission in John 21. The Prophet's mantle covers him. The Priestly ministry lies across his path. The Kingly nature is brought to the forefront to help in time of need and, when we have said all about this little rock we are brought back to the fact that he was a man. He has clay feet. He was a man called, a man challenged, a man changed, a man chosen, but at the end of it all he was a man, a man in the making. As Jesus and Joseph laid their hands on a piece of wood and transformed it into a wheel or some other object, so did

Jesus lay His hands on Peter. The materials were different but the outcome was the same, to create for use, to fit into the area for which it was created. To live a life for God fully expressing that life and being as God had created it. We can walk in his shoes. We can wear his garments. We can go where he went and learn as this Apostle in the making learned—from the voice of Jesus, sitting like Mary at the feet of Jesus. Peter, like the Master, has left us footprints to follow, a voice which, though dead, yet speaks. He, like Masters Ridley and Latimer, have lit such a light as will never go out. When a person believes on Jesus Christ and, through conversion, becomes a Son of God, the shoes of Peter are left outside his door for him to walk in. Like the old Indian saying…we travel for three days in another's moccassins before we understand them. Peter's shoes are left in such a position that they point towards the Cross and towards Heaven.

At times when you see the life of a great person on film, scenes are shown as life passes and through the art of modern camera work it looks as if, in just a few moments, the person goes from babyhood to grandad. It isn't like that in the spiritual life. It is frame built upon frame, here a little, there a little, losses and gains. We have such scenes in the life of Peter. Scenes which are almost stills, models sitting waiting for the camera to make its faithful sound and see the flash, or posing for the artist to begin his long task of transforming paint into picture, making the colour live on the canvas. Van Goch would add his own blood and spittle to his paint palette to get the right texture and the colours would have a light in them which they would not have contained without the blood. Jesus, when He died, added blood, sweat and tears to the paints of life. Without Him we are as paint squeezed by the hand of a child from out of a tube, the paintbrush flung to the floor, a daubed mess with no design or story to tell. We are like the world before God stepped in without form and void.[4] We read the Word of God and it reads us. We look at it, and it looks at us. We peer into its hidden meanings and interpretations, even whilst it does the same to us. Peter had the privilege of working alongside the Word which was made flesh.[5] The living voice of Jesus was there to instruct and to direct, to cherish and to warm, calling, pleading, lifting, helping.

This Galilean had often used his voice in the family business of fishing, calling, commanding, challenging, changing. A command from Peter and the ship took a different course, the voice bringing home safely. That voice, such a voice, is ours, through the Holy Spirit.

'The entrance of your word gives light' (Psalm 119:130). 'Entrance' means the turning of the soil (see Dr James Strong, analytical concordance). As Adam was created from the soil of the earth. The name Adam means the red earth—so Jesus is creating Peter from the soil by the words, actions and deeds as presented in His ministry and seen as the Majesty of Christ throughout his life. When Jesus steps onto the soil like some Roman Legionnaire claiming the land it brings forth thirty per cent, sixty per cent and a hundredfold....[6]

The Hebrew Dictionary will tell you that the root of the word 'entrance' means 'to carve, to broaden, to begin'. As the chippings fly light goes to that very place. A Hebrew greeting is 'May the God of Israel enlarge you'. The basic meaning of Jesus, traced back to Joshua, is that which enlarges. As in the Acts of the Apostles something has begun which never comes to an end. Peter could never say that he was the finished article. He was always in the 'Finishing School'. He is going on to perfection, to maturity, describing the fully grown piece of fruit or mature wine. The finished work will be seen in Heaven. As the sculptor chisels at the marble there are pieces which fall off and light passes between those pieces and the actual model. We see this happening in the life of the disciple who follows Jesus. Every happening can be a tool of the trade. The rough edges need smoothing until the tip of the finger can be run gently along the surface without being stabbed through with splinters.

To help us in our weaknesses God has allowed us to lift the curtain and take a glimpse into every room in the life of Peter. He has been placed in the Word of God not as a pillar of salt but as a figure of faltering faith, a ladder which never quite reaches to the top of the wall. Faith, though under pressure, does prevail and against all the odds, it conquers. Some things may disturb us, other things we are called to witness and they encourage us. If he can do it, then I can! If he can come through, then I can! He is the prototype of all believers who have the artistic temperament at large in their makeup. Probably not the best type! There is survival equipment left for us in this one. Jesus was a Master Craftsman. Each trained craftsman in some carpentry firms have their own model or object of recognition. With some it is a mouse, a lion, a frog, and, from that one symbol it is possible to tell the name of the craftsman. In the life of Peter it is possible to see Jesus standing in every corner. The design of Peter's life is the designation of Jesus Christ. Jesus, placing gleams of glory into the inner and darker parts of Peter's life. He becomes a more sure person. Little wonder that, when he stands to his feet in Acts 2, they all listen to him with bated breath. With Adam it was an outward creation but with Peter it is within. With this disciple it was inward, a dealing with the Galilean temperament and emotional disposition, rectifying the affections and placing them onto something which would outlast time. From the emotional to the Eternal...from sinking sands to Solid Rock.

Jesus is the key of wisdom, righteousness, sanctification and redemption. He was the key to open doors in the life of Peter, and then to close them as a shepherd might before journeying onwards.

It reminds me of the Doctor who had a village practice and who carried with him on his visits a large bunch of keys, not one of which fitted his own door. The keys belonged to all the old people of the village, and he was able to let himself in to see them whenever they were sick.

All the keys of the life of Peter are in the hands of Jesus. He never loses any key. He might hide it or place it out of reach. 'God holds the key of all unknown, and I am glad'. Jesus was the key and all the keys to the education and direction of Simon the Apostle. He opened every door to Peter and brought him into 'April', from the Latin 'that which is open'.

When Holman Hunt was preparing to paint his famous picture 'Christ the Light of the World', he spent three years painting in the moonlight in an orchard in Surrey. He did this so that the light would be right, so that the colours would not just stand together but blend together. Jesus spent three and a half years with Peter. In that time He was blending everything together until a whole picture emerged, framed in the New Testament for us. As we read the Word of God that picture hangs in the gallery of our heart. The Museum of the Moment captures it for us and as we look at Peter we are amazed at the grace of God. The arrival of good and the blending together of the purposes of God as fibres twisted together provide strength for weakness. When we compare Peter's life with our lives we are even more amazed that the grace of God still operates today it brings us to a realisation and fulfilment of the saying, 'I am not what I ought to be...I am not what I should be...but I am not what I was!'

In Peter we have a living person, thinking, acting, speaking, doing as a human would. If we say of Peter, 'he was only human', then we must say of Jesus, 'He is Divine'. Where these two hiatus meet there is a blending into the oneness which salvation brings. All the time Jesus spent helping the son of Jonas was never wasted. Jesus put into Peter the essentials for ministry. In later years as Peter tours preaching and teaching and even writing, that richness received is passed on to others. Cephas, in saving himself, he saved others also. That which was within him was taken and used to encourage others. The sword, gleaming and unsheathed, cuts all before it and makes a way for others to follow in the battle. He could comfort with the same comfort that he was comforted with. As he carries the light he not only illuminates the pathway for those following, he also illuminates his own way. Peter is a foundation stone which has been laid, with Jesus as the Chief Corner Stone and we all lay side by side in that building of God. I am glad to be a part of *The Growing Pains of Peter*.

Notes

1 Matthew 14:17–19
2 Numbers 20:11
3 Jeremiah 9:1
4 Genesis 1:2
5 John 1:14
6 Matthew 13:8

2

The Galilean

No person in the Scriptures appeals to human nature more than Simon Peter. Any national costume would fit him perfectly. He is at one with the roughest of characters and he finds a place among the disciples of Jesus Christ. All have a place in Christ and all have some form of pattern in Peter. This Galilean lump of stony, gritty clay represents the prickly, thorny side of human nature. There is about him that which is barbed, but wait a while and see the power of God produce the rose among the thorns, for the Rose of Sharon has many flower heads and a fragrance which is surrounded by nettles. There is that brusque, uncouth, unbridled part of human nature, red in tooth and claw, sometimes wayward, other times walking on water, either up on the heights of the mountain or wanting to walk away and leave it all. He is similar to an unbroken colt, and the succeeding years are spent training him in many a trial.

Discovering human nature

If you would discover what human nature is really like then you must draw alongside Peter. Come with a big heart and a listening ear, with a readiness to live and learn. Peter opened up human nature before the eyes of Jesus Christ, and Jesus would gain understanding through the actions of Peter. He would see how we can all move to extremes, how there is a complex nature within us, at times rational and at other times totally irrational, at times doubting and at others believing; sometimes receiving, sometimes retreating. The rock and the sea is a good description of the dual nature of Peter. He was not afraid to walk in the dark, not afraid to jump into the dark, swelling sea and raging storm. The names given to him explain his life…Jonas—fluttering dove…Simon—hearing…Peter—rock. Jesus welded all these together into one whole man. From these frailties a man of God emerged. Much of the teaching and influence of Jesus into Peter's life was to reveal how to live and how to live rightly as we follow the Master.

No matter how often Peter fell he rose again. There was no hiding place for him entering as he did the gaze of the All-seeing eye of Christ. Private was made public for us all to look and learn from. The walk and the word of Jesus became the walk and word of this man in the making. We all long for, we need, another human, one who has made it, to help us to ascend the evolutionary spiral. We sit, eat, sleep, write, talk with Peter. He is part of us in our humanity. He is a living person within each one of us, our friend, our neighbour, the man next door. Peter is involved in that which was built, not for time, but for eternity. Through him we can look beyond our own horizons into a better future. He is left neither sinking beneath the waves nor locked up in prison. There is that within me and thee, reader, which, if helped by Jesus Christ, can walk on water, can climb mountains, is capable of believing and of great acts of faith! It can be that our very shadow passing by can be the source of healing, of chasing evil spirits back to their condemnation. There is that within us that needs putting to sleep until a gentle angel steps forth who will displace and disown any and every demon.[1] Even as the sun peeps from behind a cloud on a December day we can appear and be a blessing, and leave something behind, as the Israelites were commanded to do when they had reaped their corn fields.[2] How God deals with us reminds us of Jeremiah in the Potter's house and the lessons God was revealing through the spinning wheel and the working hand. First one thing and then another appears from the unpromising lump of clay. It is not the clay which determines the shape but the hand of the Potter. The clay cannot shape, hide, or moisten itself, it can only yield. Early sewing machines were decorated so tastefully that they would be acceptable into the pattern of things in the home. The lace and the flowered materials would not make it look out of place. The clay relies on a power outside of itself, even as Peter did. 'Without Me you can do nothing,' you are nothing (John 15:5).

Human nature illustrated

Jesus used many things to illustrate human nature; salt, light, birds, donkey and Peter. Some are products of pain. Their environment has made them what they are. Jesus makes all believers into what He is, not what they are, nor what their circumstances demand. It was and is a stepping out into a new world, a guided tour with Jesus as the Guide.

To discover what human nature is really like, listen through this book to the conversations Jesus had with Peter. What passes between them is as cords of love being placed around the heart. There is the forging of something Eternal and fruitful. You must be the silent listener to every conversation. You must face the salty sea and listen to Love's lips preach the sermons prepared just for you. The winds may be contrary, against you, but in the Will of God they will be made to work for you. Sometimes you will toil all night and take nothing. You, like Peter, will be tempted to deny the Lord. Your speech will betray you. You will be rigorously tested, sometimes to breaking point. Whatever Peter is, he is a good man. Like Peter, there will be glimpses of glory at the wedding and in the Mount.[3] With the son of Bar-jonah we must always come to Christ as if we are coming to school. We are in His class! He has the curriculum under His control. The choice of topic is His choice. It may be studying the lily of the field, or the birds of the air. We must come with a large net for there are many fish to catch when Jesus is casting the net.[4] The net is so full, it is teaching of life so rich. The net of human thinking is likely to break under the pressure of the teaching. Jesus only ever took Peter to the point of learning— enough water just to walk upon, and then to begin to sink. Wise men look to His star,[5] but Peter represents a lesser star, a shaded light so as not to hurt our eyes, a glare that does not shrivel us to a cinder. When we look at this servant, when we gaze into the mirror of his life the image we see is ourselves. When we see Peter we see clearly his faults, but when we gaze at ourselves we see through a glass darkly.

The potential in human nature

From the most uncongenial soil a plant of rare worth, the delight and prize of the scientist botanist is reared. Jesus would see and understand his flaring nature, how he could blow hot and cold without ever leaving the fire. At times there is the wild rushing actions of the unstable. The Jesus who sat on a donkey which had never before been sat on, controlled the donkey's wild stubborn nature and He can also take care of an army of Peters![6] Heaven will be full of those who have travelled the same way as this Apostle. For all who follow along the path which is winding along the Galilean lake, having Jesus as Sovereign means letting Him be dressed in the authority which clothes His Royalty. We say YES to Him in everything. To fully obey Jesus is to dress Him as Sovereign.

There is a complex nature in the Galilean. History, background, experience, culture, temperament, all these spades have dug into this geographical area where Peter was raised as a child and where Jesus found him.

In one European country on a certain day the people throw pots and clay vessels into the air, and fling stones at them to shatter them, releasing a living pigeon from within the vessel. Jesus did that for Peter. At times Peter is not afraid to leap into dark tempestuous waters, black cauldrons. He steps over the side of the boat. He was the only one to do it. He is the only man, apart from Jesus Christ, who ever walked on water! He is just as extreme when making extravagant claims or denying Jesus—and a bird's beak rebukes him by being true to its nature.[7]

When we read the life of Peter in the Gospels or the Book of Acts, we are reading of a disciple, not written by Peter, but inspired by the Holy Spirit and filtered through the minds of other men, some of whom were his contemporaries. They are not the diaries of a doubting man, they are more of a manual on how to piece together that which occasionally falls apart. It is from the life of Cephas and his denial of Jesus that we have received the Americanism 'Petering out'. In our modern day, everytime someone 'Peter's out' it contains a message for us all. We need to motor on. If we do 'Peter out' we end up on the hard shoulder, sometimes in danger, and lost. We become a nuisance and an obstruction to others who are wanting to move ahead. Peter occasionally became the fish out of water, the bird out of the nest. Yet it was this same disciple who gave Jesus the answer as a revelation from God when asked the question 'Whom do men say that I, the Son of Man, am?' (Matthew 16:17). The reply was given as an arrow from the heart. This man, this follower was in touch with Heaven! The names given to Peter explain his character, his strengths and weaknesses, abilities and inabilities. Simon, son of Jonas—the son of the fluttering dove which always flies before a coming storm. Simon, meaning hearing. It is remarkable how often Jesus uses this name when He wants anything to really sink into Peter's heart. Peter, the little rock. The presence of Jesus welds these names together and the diversity becomes a unity. There had to be a combination in the rock for the ability to respond and to fly. Peter had to learn to hold onto the messages of Christ as if they were written in solid rock yet at the same time to fly with that same message like a dove. One hard and resistant, the other soft and gentle. Who but God could combine the two to operate side by side, despite being opposites?

Human nature is impressionable

Whatever we are born with naturally, Jesus unveils through Peter, that human kaleidoscope. Deficiency is turned into efficiency as it is tuned into truth. Out of his rich encounters Peter writes his epistles. He was so influenced by Jesus that many times he quotes verbatim what Jesus said. He can write with authority about fiery trials. He pens those lovely words 'Joy unspeakable and full of glory' (1 Peter 1:8). Also, 'Whom having not seen yet ye love. He writes of precious blood, precious promises, precious faith. 'Unto us, He is precious' (1 Peter 1:19; 2:7; 2 Peter 1:1,4). This gold has come from the fires he passed through as a follower who had to be turned first into a disciple and then an apostle. He has dipped his pen into the inky waters crushed from the rock. Taking charcoal from the fire he uses it as a pen, writing with compassion, understanding and humility.

Much of the teaching and influence of Jesus in Peter's life is more than fragrance from a blossom blown in by the wind. It sought to transform him. All the potential in him was stretched, pulled and developed into the full stature of a godly man. The scroll is rolled open and we are allowed to witness this development in stages.

The party visited the Sculptor's Studio, and had a good look at the work of the artist. A month later they returned and could not detect any difference. 'What have you done since we were here?' they asked. The artist replied, 'I have taken a little off the nose, straightened the ear, added certain touches here and there.' 'Those are but trifles,' one of the party commented. 'They may be trifles to you, but trifles make perfection,' retorted the artist.

It took many years for Christ to produce in Peter that which would find its way into his epistles and writings. Peter illustrates the fact that, despite our failures, Jesus never rejects us.

At the resurrection of Jesus the first words, almost before the stone had rolled away, were 'Tell the disciples, and Peter' (Mark 16:7). It was as if time had begun again for Peter. His life and ministry commence and conclude with this phrase which Christ uses to fully describe this Apostle of not only love but also do, dare and die! Peter doesn't allow smells and adverse circumstances, lack of food or discouragement to dissuade him. He is in touch with Heaven yet with his feet on the earth. His ear is open to the voice and the vision of Heaven.

At the end, his emblem becomes a bunch of keys. Keys which came out of locked situations but which, through conquering in Christ, were given to Peter. There are keys for you, where you are. Don't look at the locks, start seeking the keys. Keys discovered in dilemmas were the way out, sometimes, through the power of God and prayer. There were locks in Peter's life which only Jesus could open and when He did, He gave the keys to Peter. How good when we pass through the crisis with courage! We bring the keys with us. The keys of the Kingdom are not given that they might hang from a key ring, they are to be used to challenge locks and closed doors.

Peter illustrates the impetuous side of us, the side which acts first and thinks later, usually much, much later! There is a place for the penitent Peter, doing Peter's penance, at the feet of Jesus. From those scarred, sacred feet all ways lead to Heaven, branching out from the Way. Jesus takes hold of part of Simon and makes it part of Christ. The parts of the puzzle of life are pieced together so dexterously that it is impossible to tell where they are joined. Jesus seeks to secure and illuminate until we know that He only has the words of Eternal Light, Light which illuminates the hillsides of our wandering ways, thoughts and deeds. To whom else can we go?

Human nature is brave

Peter never feared a challenge. Second wind to him was when first wind was still giving easy breathing! 'Look before you leap' was reversed in Peter. The doubt is not whether he will accomplish it, but when it will be finalised. Napoleon, when informed that a battle was lost, would look at his watch and say, 'There is time to win another one'! This one of the twelve is, at times, like the men Jesus spoke about, seeking to build a tower yet unable to finish it, or going to battle and not counting the troops needed for victory.[8] It wasn't the winning or losing which counted, but the opportunity presented which appealed to the Galilean nature. He was a beast of instinct, not of calculation. It was never cool, calm and collected, never still tongue and wise head. These had no part in the make up of this dashing disciple. He was as free as the wind which, according to John 3:8, blows where it is and comes and goes quickly. He was the opposite of law and commandment. William Burton was a name much revered in the Congo, now Zaire, in the 1950s. The family crest of the Burton family was a greyhound, and William Burton's name in the native language meant 'the dasher forth'. Very often, even at a good age, he was seen cycling around the forests of his much loved country of adoption. He was a very wise man, filled with grace and knowledge.

Human nature requires training

Peter the son of Jonas knew the schooling of family life. He was not far removed into some angelic mode of operation. He was touched with feelings and emotions, his face sometimes wet with tears. He goes in and out amongst the family. He is the father figure in the family. He operated his father's fish business with his brother.[9] He was a Galilean with a thick Galilean accent. He was a fisherman of Bethesda,[10] probably the fishing quarter of Capernaum. He was brought to Christ through the witness of his brother. They were kindred spirits and easily influenced one another. Andrew appears to have been the more placid of the two, an anchor in a swelling tide. Andrew had first been influenced by John Baptist. There was a whole circle of influence and discovery from John 1:40, the first introduction, we have prayers, precepts, epistles, sermons, miracles, journeyings and conversions in plenty. There is height, depth, length and breadth of character discovery. Jesus never assassinates character. What is within is developed and matured, as wine being turned from vessel to vessel until it is pure, then left until maturity seeps through every mouthful. Every step with Jesus is a step to Heaven. Jesus is always there by his side, using sometimes a word of encouragement, other times one of rebuke; a miracle, a conversation, or teaching seated on the mountain listening to the exposition of Matthew 5. There are such deep uncharted waters in Peter. Jesus needed to walk on these waters. They had to be gathered up in the tears of Christ. Large vessels take a lot of making. Every craft God makes He wants it to be unto honour. A chance meeting becomes a life-changing experience. A walk with Peter's brother is a walk into the heart of Jesus. When Peter reached the place where Jesus was he found the door open wide for him and 'Welcome' written on the mat. That one word, that look, the smile, the gracious appearance all did something to melt the heart of Peter, as sunshine poured from the radiancy of Christ. He did not come to Jesus as a lamb to be butchered or a dove in flight to be shot. He came, as we all do, to be lifted, loved, covered and cared for all the days of our lives. For the rock to be broken and the precious metal or jewel to be released. He needed to be led out into new pastures of love from above. As a ship or fishing boat would go into some covert or bay during the time of storm, so Peter came to Jesus Christ. Jesus destroys the worst and brings out the best. What is weighed in the balances and found wanting is placed in the scales by the Lord, and an equilibrium is reached. Just by coming to Christ. No man ever came to Jesus and went away the same. The only sameness is that he still walks on two legs. He has within him that deposited by a far reaching hand, the opener of the heart and the toucher of the heart strings. He is transformed into the Cross-bearing man, the Holy man, the helpful man, the man among men. From one of his own kind to one of God's kind. He is God's man for the Church. He becomes part of the new thinking, part of the new army of ambassadors for Christ, an Elder and a Senior, part of the little flock of God. Peter, after stumbling, rises again on the wings of eagles, discovering the Everlasting Arms underneath. There are greater times than raw discipleship ahead. There are pioneering days into Apostleship. In his frustration one man was once heard to say: 'God I wish you had never made me!' A voice replied, 'I haven't—yet!'

Human nature needs much prompting

There seem to have been three calls in the life of Peter—first, to be the friend of Jesus (John 1:39), secondly, to be a disciple (Mark 1:16), and then to be an Apostle (John 21:15). Friendship deepens into Discipleship, and produces Apostleship. Notice there is a 'ship' on the end of every word. It meant that Peter was going somewhere, he was going into the regions beyond, with his Master. Cephas, like a little ship on a large sea going from port to port and place to place with the Gospel message.

The three names of Peter represent stages in his development and the use of the names is significant. When Jesus comes to him in John 21:15, He refers to him as Simon Peter. Hearing is placed before rocklike character. 'Are you really listening to Me in love, Peter?' The first meeting of Peter with Jesus gives us an insight of wood brought to the Carpenter of Nazareth, Galilee, Jordan, Bethsaida, Jerusalem and anywhere He comes to work.[11] Among working men Jesus sought to deepen friendship into something more, into a future relationship. Family brotherhood was increased to include Jesus, the Brother of all men and the Saviour of mankind. It increased until, in Revelation 5:11 John sees the family of God which no man could number.

Many of the great men of Scripture were found as working folk. Men like Moses, Elijah, Elisha, Amos and Jeremiah made a way to allow God into their circle of business. The monotony, the circle of everyday was broken for Simon when Jesus came to his house. Suddenly, nets and fish became less important and Jesus Christ filled the horizon of every vision. A large new area of operation and great goals were fixed for all who met with the Man of Galilee.

The nets were superceded by the Gospel and Jesus would make Simon a fisher of men. He who was influenced would influence others. Peter would stand up and stand out in the crowd. His shadow, the mere shadow of a man, a man abiding in the shadow of the Almighty, would be made to count as a ready dispenser of healing virtue. His shadow becomes a shelter from the heat and the rays of the day, an enclave from sin and sickness. The shadow of Peter was more than a match for the weapons of Satan.

Peter didn't seem to grasp that Jesus loved Jew and Gentile until the sheet was let down and Peter's prejudices disappeared underneath it. When it was raised, Peter was converted to Gentile preaching. The size of that sheet told how large hearted he would have to be. There are moments in *The Growing Pains of Peter* when it seems as if the Apostle will never appear out of the dark shadows. God brings His principal men onto the stage of life just as the lights are switched on and the curtain is raised on Christ's model man for a model role, freely giving what he has received. Waters flow over the same stone year after year until it is shaped enough to sink lower and then, when it is the right size the Master Builder comes to collect it. There is room in the Plan for the pebble, but not for the cinder or for the boulder.

According to 1 Corinthians 9:5, Peter was a married man, living with his mother-in-law. It is a good thing when your faith touches other members of your family. Peter saw his relative raised from the grip of fever, lifted from its delusions and raging fires. Yet even in a normal relationship there is that which is missing unless Jesus Christ is a family member. If there is love in a family, Jesus will heighten and strengthen that love, given the opportunity. Blood may be thicker than water, but love is larger than life if that life be in Jesus. The family on earth must reflect the family in Heaven.

Human nature is given to change

Josephus, the Jewish Historian, tells us that the Galileans had a nature of change. They loved change and challenge. They delighted in disturbance. They were quick of temper, always prone to follow even if they didn't know where they were going. Providing they felt that the leader did, then they followed as string tied to the shoe. The results did not matter, as long as they were led charging into battle. Never mind the war! Here is a battle to be fought! Peter stands in the Identification Parade and he is recognised. He has all the marks of a Galilean. It isn't the smell of fish which betrays him. He is the one tapped on the shoulder. This is the man from Galilee. The description fits as a hand to the glove. He lived his true humanity to its full capacity, crying like a baby when found out in denial.[12] To the rough Galilean exterior Jesus came. The changes wrought take time, time, time and a half. It is not as light which travels at 186,000 miles per second, which has passed around the earth seven times within the tick of the clock. Jesus never wanted to make Peter simply into a lighthouse, but into a house of light, life, laughter and love, from one stage of glory into another. Through change and the constant application of Christ's teaching, Peter is changed from an unstable, uncertain man into a Christian leader of the finest quality, the silk of Christianity. 'Can any good thing come out of Nazareth?' Can any good thing come out of Peter? The answer is Yes. The beggar is taken from the dunghill and seated among Princes (1 Samuel 2:8). The picture is of the beggar sitting on the camel's dung at the side of the road. Someone throws to him a wealthy jewel. He sat down a begger and he rises up a Prince. The crown falls from the King's head, the beggar grasps it and, standing up with it, he is a Prince. Even in the Old Testament Tabernacle the glory of God was covered by goat and badger skins. It is the glory revealed in Peter which Moses wanted to see in Exodus 33:18. That nature of God. God showed His acts unto the children of Israel, but His 'ways' unto Moses. The sun, moon, stars are all of different glories and there is a glory about Peter. Treasure in a vessel of clay. It is the glory which comes from the hand of Jesus, shining as one thing is changed to another, the chicken from the egg, or the frog from the spawn.

James Hastings in his Dictionary of the Bible points out that many notable leaders came from this same mould and area. National leaders and thinkers, warriors such as Deborah, Barak, Amos, Hosea and Jonah. All came from the same school, proving that there was more than fish, boats and storms in this strata. God in Christ came and saw none of the materialistic things. He saw material for men. What fine vases and porcelain or bone china could be brought from this clay? You may split a rock. One man throws it away, finds no jem held within its stony fist. The other man takes the same piece, penetrates it and finds platinum. Not to a palace Jesus came, not to a throne, but to a manger and to the sweepings of the stable floor. He found a future ambassador in the sea sweepings on the shore of Tiberias.

The Talmud, in describing the Galileans, noted... 'They were ever anxious for honour and gain, quick tempered, easily aroused, soon turned into a mob...emotional, easily aroused by an appeal for adventure...loyal and true to a cause, even in death...always there, even when theirs was a lost cause.' This describes Peter from skull to sole.

Human nature is temperamental

The area of Galilee where Peter lived and worked, was subject to fierce and sudden stormy squalls. Fierce driving winds rushing down the gorges on the hillsides, racing into the open area of water, onto the glass surface of the lake. Peter's life could be just like that, one moment capable of great revelations, the next wanting to rebuke Jesus.[13] This made the brother of Andrew a man of action, sometimes without unction. He was as those who charge into situations forgetting to take with them the necessary equipment for the eventuality of a fall or slip. His emotions dictated his actions, then later his brain would catch up with his mind. He seemed to put a garment on, going through the neck-hole first! Christ had to do such a work on the rock, shaping, rebuking, challenging, telling, consoling and designing until beauty appeared, not as outward adornment but as that fastened deeply in the heart. Fire had to be placed in the metal, then under the hammer held by the black-smith's hand. It is the taking of the white hot metal and the plunging of the same into cold water which hardens it to resist bending and buckling. Peter was being turned into an Apostle. Just as the shadows follow the course of the sun until they disappear with it, so Jesus was covering the whole of the life of this man. God calls us and then He makes us, shakes us, breaks us, forms us into what He has called us to be. God never says, 'You are', but 'You shall be'. On earth it must always be 'You shall be' (John 1:42). There is a Prophecy spoken over every life. God is fulfilling His words: 'Behold I make all things new'. Something of the flinty strong and determined nature of Jesus must be placed in us. We have been called to be saints. The Eternal nature of the Son of God must be found fully formed in the sons of men.[14] This sameness and oneness must become part of the Peter pattern. It is God's working which places Peter at the head of the army when the Apostles are paraded before us.[15] The more Jesus saw the more He uncovered, and the more He loved. He discovered areas in the life of Peter, deep and strong, reserved parts, and then He flooded them with the love of God. Where and when this disciple slipped and fell there was the love of God, at the beginning and at the end of every slippery slope. Jesus saw greater riches in Peter than ever the rich young ruler possessed.[16] There was something of the alabaster box content in Peter's life which was waiting to be broken and released. It was through the dash and the dare, the risk and the fall of Peter, being part of the inner circle consisting of Peter, James and John, that Jesus developed the greater part of a more noble and resilient life.

There were depths in Peter, deeper than the well of Samaria. The Emmanuel drew from that depth. Jesus brings to the surface all manner of riches, riding on grace. He does it that we might be more than just impressed. He does it in order that we might be influenced into the inspiration of New Life in Christ.[17]

Notes

[1] Acts 5:16
[2] Leviticus 23:22
[3] John 2:11; Mark 9:2
[4] Luke 5:5,6
[5] Matthew 2:2
[6] Matthew 21:2,7
[7] John 18:25–27
[8] Luke 14:28–32
[9] Matthew 4:18
[10] John 1:44
[11] John 1:40–42
[12] Luke 22:62
[13] Matthew 16:22,23
[14] Hebrews 13:8
[15] Matthew 10:2
[16] Luke 18:18
[17] 2 Corinthians 5:17

CHAPTER

3

God's Plan for a New Life

We are not told what Simon Peter felt when he was ushered into the presence of Jesus Christ the first time. Indeed we will only know when Peter tells it as it was. Perhaps it was like walking into deep sunshine after a dark, rainy day. Adam was coming back into the Garden of Eden to meet with God. Adam, who had so perversely walked out from the presence of God walked back in when Peter was brought to Christ. It was Peter's first impression of Christ, and it was a lasting one.

Things had been so different. A brother named Andrew could not bring you near to God, only a Priest, a bridge-builder, could do that. In parts of Japan only Priests were allowed to build natural bridges. That which represented the rainbow was built by men between men and God. For Israel, posts, pillars of brass with linen sheets attached by hooks around the Old Testament Tabernacle had been so relevant. Around the Temple there had been forbidding walls.[1] Yet, through God these were removed and reduced to a piece of wood seen in the shape of a Roman gibbet, a Cross. The many Priests became one in Jesus. The mere shadows of God, the things to come, became substance in Him. He was altar and sacrifice. Jesus tabernacled among us, tented among us as the Tabernacle did among the Children of Israel. Jesus made it possible and illustrated those possibilities when meeting with this disciple and as He allowed all to meet with Him as with a long lost

Friend. To meet with Him was falling rain meeting with flowing river as a flowing river is submerged into a swollen sea to be made part of it forever. Peter had heard the stories from the Old Testament and from patriarchal lips of the nature and accomplishments of the Messiah when He came. He had read such through the words of Isaiah, Moses, Malachi. He was about to be introduced to this complex figure on the perimeter of his own home town. Jesus had come to town! Messiah was coming to reign and Peter was one of those domains in which He would reign. Peter, along with all who came into the presence and felt the power of Jesus Christ was to be made part of the Kingdom of God.

What passed through the mind and heart of Peter as they met, recorded in John 1:40–42; Mark 3:16; Luke 6:14, we are not told. Did Peter feel like a boy meeting his hero? The stories of Israel that parents told their children before they went to sleep at night were woven around this Figure of the Coming One. To Peter it was the opening of the History Book with the written history presented before his eyes. As an Israelite felt when viewing the sword and shield of Goliath which David had used to chop off the head of the giant,[2] so this new convert, Peter, felt. Was it a feeling of meeting someone you had never met before, but you suspect they have met with you? Maybe you have seen them in some picture book or floating through one of your dreams? Was there a sense of a new start, of destiny as these two came together as joint to joint? It was the joy of finding that which had been lost.

Peter came as a soldier to stand in the ranks. The love of Christ had found a place for even a little rock. The lost Israelite had found his King. What was missing from the life in Galilee and in the life of Cephas was found in Jesus Christ. The introductory words in John 1:41 are 'We have found'—the missing piece, the missing link of love, the vital ingredient that completed the circle and squared the square were found in Jesus.

We are all special

Jesus does not deal with Peter as part of a flock or as one of many playing cards, numbered and marked only to be hidden in a hand or box. He deals with him as He deals with us, in an individual manner, as individual as the 'I' at the beginning of that word. At the commencement of any work of grace, as at the conclusion, it is Jesus and me. Zaccheus is called down from the tree which separates him from Jesus, so that the gap might be narrowed.[3] There is a special something about each one of us. If that is true of all who are born naturally, then it is doubly true of all who are Born Again, double born of the Spirit of God.[4] We are part of a pattern, the fitting together of a plan, and part of what was in Peter was in no-one else. You are so rare that the mould is broken as you are born. 'Never again' is written all over your life. There are things in you which do not appertain to anyone else. The tramp has things about him which a King never had. You can pass from the Book of Genesis right through to the Book of Revelation, from the Book of Beginnings to the Book of Endings and you will not find two people who are alike. All the disciples, all twelve of them, were different. Even the meanings of their names illustrate that. Andrew is represented by a Cross; Bartholomew is remembered by a knife; Peter's badge is a bunch of keys; Philip is represented by two loaves. Some have saws, others builder's tools to express their worth and work. There are no two fingerprints of God on any life which are the same.

Peter was very much his own man, very much an individual. That often comes to the fore even when among elite company. The way in which he is heard speaking with his broad Galilean accent, broader than his smile. The way he develops in witnessing, his approach, his youthful and boisterous spirit and his closeness to Christ, all belong solely to him. These are individual traits, never to be taken away. They are wrapped up in personality. You cannot take them and give them to another, not even to your best friend.

We all respond individually

Jesus never deals with any two disciples in the same way. They don't have to exchange garments or walk in one another's shoes. Every disciple came to Jesus in a different way. They came through many avenues. They were hand-picked men and it was the Son of God who was choosing sons of men. Jesus approached some, abruptly saying, 'Follow Me!' (Matthew 4:19,20) and they did just that! Others were more slow in their response to Christ. They were of the tortoise and turtle nature. When the animals entered the Ark some came much slower than others but they all arrived before one raindrop parachuted from the sky. The door was small enough for the tic, and large enough for the elephant, tall enough for the giraffe and low enough for the beetle. Some came as gently as the flower turning its head towards the sun, or as a leaf being blown by a soft wind. Others came as the Charge of the Light Brigade, the roar of the lion or the braying of the ass. With the son of Jonas it had to be contact or nothing. He must stand where Jesus stood. He must be where Christ was. It had to be more than a mere touch. He had to come a number of times to see, until Christ filled his whole vision. He came to listen and to learn. He had to be convinced of the charisma and the centrality of Christ before he committed himself.

Andrew, his brother, had come to Christ when hearing John Baptist say, 'Behold the Lamb of God who takes away the sins of the world' (John 1:29). He lived in the echo of what he heard. Philip was simply told, 'Follow Me' (John 1:43). Matthew is caught away from the tax desk.[5] We are never enlightened as to how or when Judas became a follower. The approach of Jesus is different. The manifold wisdom of Jesus is seen in how He deals with each person. The reason why Jesus draws anyone is not simply for service as a soldier, it is that they 'might be with Him' (Mark 3:14). That source of influence is as leaven going through the whole lump. Living in His shadow and enjoying His presence, knowing His ways, watching the way He walks, talks and responds. It is being with Him which makes all the difference. Peter's brightest and best, his most treasured moments, are with Jesus Christ.

Jesus seeing us, deals with us

What did Jesus think as He gazed on this weather-beaten fisherman? 'This is the one I have come to redeem.' The finding is worth it all! The searching has stopped where Peter's feet cease to move. Peter is there as a straying sheep returning to the shepherd. Here is the Shepherd, the door, the pasture. With Cephas, it wasn't clay coming into the hands of the Potter when he came to Jesus, it was the placing of hard granite rock into the area of influence of the Stonemason. Rock needs more working on than clay. There has to be more pressure, more dedication, more patience and much more grace. Jesus had to take it and shape it, and those different shapes appear in the Gospel stories. Some of them were repeated to John Mark by Peter. Mary told him some of the happenings. Peter told Luke and Luke penned them on parchment. Every happening is an influence, sometimes strong, other times gentle enough to blow the dust off the workings on the rock. The miracles, the words of advice and rebuke, the silent look, the falling tear, the prayers, the time spent on the Mount and in the home—all of these were to influence the rock-like nature of Cephas. The way in which Jesus deals with the religious, with the Sadducees and Pharisees are all lessons at the Master's feet. The man whose designation is a key must take a key from every situation and be prepared to use it. How diverse are God's dealings with us! Rainbow quality and star rating! He knows where to talk to us, He knows the words which break the bone even as the straw which breaks the camel's back. The measure of darkness or of light is allowed by God. The lesser and the greater are with Him. Some things we are not ready to receive. He has many more things to say to us but we are not ready to receive His message. He holds us back from the very things we desire until our desire is white hot. There was not an avalanche of ministry immediately from Jesus to Peter. As in John 1:38,39, we have a little glimpse of Heaven—going to stay with Jesus for a day! It was Saint Andrew's Day! He was the final link in the chain and Jesus became the lock at both ends of that chain. Peter was brought to Jesus, not Jesus to Peter. It was the final wave which cast the boat onto the shore after drifting so long without captain or compass. Peter, so far, had only known God in ships, shoals, winds and waves. The God of nature and the God in the Jewish Temple, the God seen only in the Jewish interpretation of Him now became much more real and personal. There must be a release of God out of that which surrounds a life, God who acts, stirs and inspires, God with the Face of Jesus Christ; God who reaches out in love.

Like all of us Peter needed something more than a shadow. He needed substance. He needed a substance bigger than himself. He needed something and some Person larger than the sea, something that would not be blown off course. He wanted success that was not based on the ability of the fisherman and the full net of fish. The sea can evaporate and be changed into a cloud formation, a watering can in the sky! Boats can sink or be lost in a storm, nets can break and fish can swim away. There was a need for permanence and fulness. Peter needed something to anchor to, something to hold during a storm. Peter discovered all these things in Jesus. It became his consuming passion for life. Everything that Peter discovered in Jesus during the three and a half years he spent with Him is written in his Epistles. The character of Peter is coloured by Jesus Christ and the constant companionship of the Master. Christianity will always be bigger than Peter or Paul or Philip, or Mary, Martha or Lazarus. It is bigger than any of us, yet it is not too big for us to enter into. The Post Office Tower in London is big, but not too big to enter. No matter how vast the sea there is room for the tiddler, and for me on my raft!

Someone had to introduce him to Jesus

It is a tremendous thing when a brother loves you enough to tell you of Jesus Christ. Each time Peter mentions a brother or brethren in his writings, think of Andrew who brought him into the presence of the essence of Eternity, the Bread of Heaven who brought him to the influence which was never forgotten. Peter owed a great debt to a man not normally recognised as an Evangelist—Andrew. He led him to where the path of Eternity commenced. Andrew caused him to walk the way of God and in the ways of God, brought him to reconciliation and to destiny. He left him with Christ, for Christ to deal with him. What a wise brother!

It was no profound message which turned the head and the heart of Peter. It was not a notable miracle or a sermon of the Mount in Matthew 5. It was a quiet simple act by his brother. Simple knots can join ropes together. Andrew said, 'We have found'—from that Greek word 'found' 'eurika', we have the thought of making a great discovery—the winning of a soul. Archimedes used the word 'eurika' when he discovered that a solid object displaced just as much capacity as its own weight. He leaped out of hot water when he made the discovery! California, in the U.S.A. has this word 'eurika' as its motto, because gold was found there!

A donkey, water, fish, rock, all are found in the ministry of Jesus. His whole life was consumed by reaching and finding. The Son of Man is come to seek and to save that which was lost, those things that were not in their rightful place, Zaccheus in the tree, Peter sinking beneath the waves, or Nicodemus in the night. He has to find that which needs to be transformed. A whole new creation was to arise in every convert, God was at work doing a work of creation again, not in natural elements but in spiritual dimensions, in the hearts of men. The influence of evangelism was growing. Andrew brought Peter, not to the natural source of life at the home, but to the Source of heavenly, spiritual and everlasting life. That was the greatest act of the ministry of Andrew. Whenever you find a Peter, search for an Andrew. Andrew always seems to take second place. It takes a second to support a first. Peter's brother always seems to be introducing others.[6] He brought them in and Jesus took them on. The Messiahship of Christ was turned loose into the life of Peter. Whatever designation was in the word Messiah was more than enough to win the war in Peter's heart. This Galilean whose nature had been pieced and patched through gripe and growth was brought to Jesus as he was. There was more to Peter than the outward skin, more than eye could see, lips could tell or hand reach. Peter would outshine Andrew by a thousand suns, yet it took a brother with a spark to ignite a fire in his relative. It fulfils the New Testament advice, 'Let brotherly love continue' (Hebrews 13:1).

As Peter came to Jesus it was the beginning of a life, for where He is the journey stops and restarts, old ways are turned into new ways, everyday routine is broken by the tread of Jesus Christ. The groping, guessing ceases and all becomes clear. He is indeed the One whom the Prophets saw afar off and told about in fragments. That which was a million miles away is now in the next step. Peter did not stop, as Moses did, at the burning bush to simply gaze at a miracle.[7] Salvation is coming to Christ constantly. It is the out-working of what is committed to the Son of God, living under His gaze feeling the breathing of His breaths, seeing the commands of Christ becoming the obedience of men, the call of Christ becoming the challenge of the heart. For Simon, it was another form of life going on forever and ever and reaching out after God. When he came into the presence of Jesus it was into the atmosphere of Eternity. The mysteries of God standing with open face. The clouded mystery with the curtains drawn back.

Peter was brought to where those eyes could penetrate like fire going through metal. It was where the voice of Jesus could be clearly and crisply heard and understood. Peter heard his first message from the lips of Jesus. His doctrines were formed as he himself was being formed. He caught glimpses of the sounds and sights of Heaven in that presence. His light came from the Light of the World. It was here that family boats, seas, fish and friends were put into the right perspective. Light from Christ helps us to see where things should be placed... everything in its rightful order. As there are natural laws which govern, so there are spiritual laws. It was Jesus and me with not a wind or boat or even a wave in between, just Jesus. Prayer and needs meet; Heaven, blessing, direction are the fruits and results of being planted in Jesus, of being brought not only to the side but placed in the hand of Jesus, made into His possession. That is peace and security which storms cannot sink. Christ makes us precious. He has personal responsibility for us. That is why He followed Peter all the days of his life. Where Peter went, so did his Lord. He carried baggage for one but had lodgings for two. Andrew's brother had to live in the echo of that voice as Master and servant, Teacher and scholar, question and Answer.

Jesus takes us through it all

Peter did not sink out of sight at sea, he did not come within sight of land yet not make it into port. He came to where Jesus was, where the School of Christ was. He came into the circle of influence, where things were made for Eternity. Whatever is found weighed in the balances and found wanting is not wanting in Jesus. Need is met in the Messiah. The heart is cleansed, the feet are turned back into the way. The sheep is brought out of the wolf's clothing; Seated and in his right mind.[8] May all your Peters be brought to Jesus.

Tradition tells us that, whenever anyone living near to the house where Jesus was raised became angry or frustrated they simply took a look at the Child's face and all their troubles melted away. His calmness and His composure became theirs. Even today His influence prevents all other influences tearing us apart.

There is a finality about coming to Jesus because one day that will be Heaven in all the fulness and presence of the Lamb. We feel we have returned, as Peter did, to where he always belonged. He didn't have far to travel either. Unlike heathen gods, our Jesus never goes on long journeys, He can always be found.[9] The words 'we have found',[10] brought Peter to Him. We have 'found' is finding treasure—the lost son—the lost coin—the lost sheep. The word 'Messiah' was like the raising of a flag. It stirred the Galilean blood. It excited the spirit. Fathers had talked to sons, sons to children about the Coming One Who would bring freedom from bondage and Peter was now standing face to face with Him. The Captain, the Leader had returned. Here was the standard they should gather around. The Cause was presented again, and already troops were mustering in the soul of Peter, the cavalry charging up from the hillside of his thoughts. David would ascend the Throne again in the Person of Messiah. Young Galileans would do any-thing to rid the nation of the Roman yoke. They hated Rome as much as they loved a leader. They wanted to replace the bondage of Rome with the sceptre of David and He was here! The glorious could begin to shine again. The Roman garrison would be quickly exchanged for the Throne! Peter was looking for excitement. He wanted to see the exploits of David with Goliath as Rome was overthrown. His imprisoned desires were now channelled into new things through this fellow Galilean. He had a zeal, for He was a companion of the Sons of Thunder.[11]

Jesus is Peter's canopy of love, the love which had followed him and Jesus had now finally caught up with him. To that which is in Christ and also in Peter must Cephas surrender. From the moment of his birth, in walking, feeling, thinking, doing, Jesus had in some way been involved. All was now to be revealed. Jesus had always been there in the shadows, now He steps out and into the light to claim His prize, the person of Peter. He requires the heart and not just the head.

Attitudes must be right

There is real difficulty with a thinking machine if it takes the place of a throbbing heart. When some came into the presence of Jesus Christ they fell as stones from the sky and He built with them and on them. Others knelt as if they would be knighted. One wanted to take Him by the feet and worship Him. The woman with an issue of blood reached out of the crowd to touch Him. This was not so with Peter. They met on solid, sacred ground. How did Jesus know all about him, even as He knew about the others who came into His gentle presence, those who were astounded by what they saw and heard? He sent for a donkey to ride triumphantly into Jerusalem and He knew its age, where it would be found, who the owner was.[12] By a word of knowledge and an unction which led the Holy Spirit into action there was a deep interest and insight into the life of Peter. 'You are, and you will become' (John 1:42). Jesus Christ the same yesterday, today and forever (Hebrews 13:8). He sees our tomorrows as if they were our yesterdays and He sees our todays before our yesterdays!

Jesus has all knowledge of you

Jesus saw deeply into the background of Peter. There are organisa-tions today who will, for a fee, trace your family tree right through the history of England. Peter's history started and finished in His story, the Gospel story. History can be re-written with the hand of Jesus on the pen. Peter was brought from backstage into the forefront, into the limelight. The old pebble from the beach became a rare jewel. Jesus was going to make Peter part of new operations in new dimensions. There were things in this one's life which were hidden and which had never been developed. He had never met anyone with a hand strong enough or an arm long enough to reach in and grasp what was really there. 'The well is deep and you have nothing to draw with' (John 4:11), might have been applied to Peter's life. You are the son of John and I know your father, mother, friends. Everyone you have come into contact with has been in contact with Me first. Nathaniel found this to be true, and when he heard what Jesus had to say he replied, 'How do you know these things?' (John 1:48), 'who gave You my autobiography to read?' How well do I remember Leslie Welch, the memory man who could remember so much about sport!

In the Book of Revelation 2:2,9,13,19; and 3:1,8,15,17, the key word is 'know'. Just to know that Jesus knows is a sure foundation indeed. He knows not as others with head and eyes, He knows with His heart. He has feelings which found Peter. Peter is not just found out, he is known and loved. He has become a book which has been read and is now to be turned into a history of Jesus, part of the Acts of the Apostles. He is an epistle written by Jesus Christ. Jesus wrote into the life of Simon just as He wrote in the dust on the floor when the woman was taken in the act of adultery.[13] With a pen dipped in love He comes again and again to this son of Adam. We find in the unwritten sayings of Jesus, 'Cleave the wood and lift the stone and I am there'. Tell me where He is? Tell me where He is not! It is only as we are brought into His nearness as Peter was that we realise that what was unseen, unsaid, unheard and unknown has always been with Him.

Queen Victoria would appear incognito at times and, neither recognised or known, she saw and heard things never previously heard by a queen. Jesus appears as He did to the disciples on the Emmaus Road, in disguise. He meets with many in the history of their family. Jesus knew His way around the life of Peter long before Peter was born, like Jeremiah, known before he was conceived.[14] There is a book in which all our members are written, our tears are in a bottle. The hairs of our head are numbered.[15] He knows our thoughts afar off.[16] That which contains knowledge is part of the knowledge of God. That which wisdom has been a part of His wisdom. The same can be recorded of love. We may live afar off, in Prodigal country, but Jesus will make us part of Himself. He will triumph. When the Israelite was cleansed from his leprosy he had to show himself to the priest who then pronounced him clean. Every dish had to be scoured, walls had to be broken down. The important thing in it all was the presence of the priest. The Revised Version says in John 1:42, 'Jesus looked on Peter'. What did He see? What did He witness that no other was able to witness? On another occasion when God's Son looked on this same servant He made him cry. When Jesus looked on Peter on every occasion it must have been as the gaze of a creative eye looking for the potential. Some only see branches, leaves or a bird's nest, others of a more creative nature would see wheelbarrows made from the tree, or boats sailing from the roots, oars from the branches. The Carpenter looks to see what beautiful furniture can be produced from one piece of wood, goes to the tree whilst it is still standing and dreams as He feels its rough bark. Michaelangelo looked on the piece of marble from which he created his statue of David and was heard to mutter: 'If you only knew what beauties are in you'. It is one thing to look and quite another to look with intention. God looked on Adam and saw it was not good for him to be alone. He created Eve to be alongside him.

Simon, son of Jonah, Jonah means 'dove' that which is timid and ready to fly away, frightened by fear, worried by the blowing of the wind and the moving of the grass. The dove is ready to fly before any storm. It is gentle and sensitive. 'You will be called Cephas'. The dove was to receive some of the stone, the flinty disposition of Jesus Christ. There would enter into Simon the dove some of the nature of the Rock of Ages. There is that within each of us which is like the dove and the waves of the sea still only for a moment to be swept away for days, months or years. We see with the dove's eyes the very Rock that we should be perched on and build on, but how to get there is a different matter indeed. In spiritual experience we resemble a washing line. There are two stops, one at each end with the clothes line in between. There is a great sag—we know where we started from and we know where we want to get to, but Oh, it is the inbetween which is the trouble!

The impulsive needs instruction

Peter was a man of impulse rather than of calculated decisions. His fuse was a very short one. If Peter had created the world he would never have arrived at the seventh day for a rest! He might have forgotten half of what was supposed to be created and many a thing would have been left half finished. Half a sun or trees without branches! There was a nature within Peter as there is within you, dear reader, which is rather like a babe in arms. The Bible, which is a commentary on life, speaks of the silly dove.[17] The word used for 'silly' is 'roomy'. It will take anything in and anything on board. It has a capacity for all things, it is as open as a mirror so that everything which passes by is reflected in it. Surely that is a reflection of Peter's character, and of all of us. It seeks to fly before the coming storm, wanting to hide out of the way even as Elijah flew into the cave.[18] It wanted to fly to its favourite place of safety if threatened by foot or flood. We all need a place of refuge under the shadow of the Almighty. That refuge should not be away from God where the old Peter or dove nature will take us, but nearer to God as the Rock nature suggests. There has to be that dove within all of us which will fly out of the ashes as a phoenix (Psalm 68:13) with wings of silver. Peter was given a new name, a name which had meaning and interpretation to it. In the Old Testament names were changed from Abram to Abraham; Sarai to Sarah; Oshea to Joshua. It happened when the 'J' from the covenant Name of Jehovah was added in Numbers 13:16. As believers we have a new name, we have new expectations, new things to live up to. Someone has written, 'Jesus means God to the rescue'.

We all possess potential

One of the strengths of Napoleon was that he recognised generals and officers as he looked at the drummer boys and raw recruits. He observed how they obtained objectives and he promoted them. The drummers were never taught to sound the Retreat, only the Attack. When one Corporal chased and caught Napoleon's runaway horse, Napoleon thanked him by saying, 'Thank you Captain'. The man immediately replied, 'Of which Regiment, sir?'

'You are Simon, son of Jonah, but you will be called Cephas' (Aramaic); Peter (Greek). That which Jesus saw He signed with His blessing. Jesus is the bridge and door from the old nature into the new. He will lessen the earthly aspect and heighten the heavenly part of nature. For Peter, as with all of us, there was a decrease and an increase. Messiah is saying, 'In the establishing of My Kingdom I will not leave you as I found you. You will never be the same again. You will never fall as some untimely fig, left to rot, never to be gathered and used'.

In Luke 15:15,16, the wayward son is found feeding among the pigs, but he is not left there. After returning to the father, after 'coming to himself', he is left as one who has been in some fainting fit, in music, dancing and the festivities. God never leaves us where He found us and He never leads us back to where He found us. We must go on in the knowledge of the presence of the Lord.

The things God allows

The Jesus who has known the past also recognises the present as a step into the future. Jesus is the future of Peter. Simon must become Peter. Jesus will allow tornado, typhoon, fever, shoals of fish, healings and opposition to bring this to pass. Jesus fulfils His own prophesy in every life. What He says He Himself will fulfil, He does not expect Simon to do. There is a favourite phrase of mine in the

Bible: 'And it came to pass'. The problem for Peter, as with other believers, is that he kept trying to step into the shoes of the past. Those shoes could only take him into the present, and there was no future in them. The name 'Simon' and 'Simon son of Jonas' is used some seventeen times and each time it is as if Jesus is sending a fresh call into the life of Peter. It is the call of the tide to the moored boat.[19] The chapter which contains the name the most is John 21:2,3,7,11,15,16,17; as if Jesus is making a final appeal before He returns to the Father—a sort of tying of the baggage more firmly so that the ensuing journey will not cause losses. The emphasis is in John 21 because Peter has taken a backward step, back to the fishing, back to the boats, back to the sea. There is no Jesus in those things. Jesus is on the shore. Peter has exchanged pulpit for ship. The teachings of Christ appear to have slipped overboard. The Bible of his heart needs a new translation. Be assured that no one meeting, not even many meetings or much ministry changed a Simon, a simple Simon, into a Peter, rocklike and Christlike, an apostle. Foundation stones and pillars take far more erecting, making and shaping than ordinary stones.

Jesus will never leave you

Jesus had to keep visiting as faithfully as anyone overseeing a business, as a gardener caring for the landscape, watching, pruning, strengthening, planting, arranging and guarding. He who has begun a good work must perform it until the day of Jesus Christ. He has begun a good work in you and will carry it on to completion until the day of Jesus Christ. When the word 'perform' is used it is describing the boiling of liquids...keeping on the boil until it is ready to serve. It suggests the carrying out of a command, completing a task. What a task Jesus had in bringing Peter through it all. God in Christ has to reveal many wonders to make us a wonder unto many. It is the life of Christ in us, working through us that accomplishes this. Peter is only reporting for duty when they meet for the first time. There must always be a performance of things spoken unto us by the Lord. God's arm is not short, neither is His hand shut. There shall be no lack of any good thing to them that love the Lord. Life can be an empty glass or shell until Jesus fills it, for He filleth all things.[20]

Jesus never gave up on Peter. He never came to any place which became the stopping-off or dropping-off place. This life and companionship goes on and on. When Peter went out and wept— when, after the Resurrection Jesus still has Peter on His heart, 'Let him know I have arisen from the dead' (Mark 16:7), means, in a fuller way, 'I can carry on My ministry in Peter's life. What has been from below will now be from above and below, from right and left, into the centre and working outward. Each way and every way.' When Peter wept, Jesus was there to catch the tear and interpret the silent sob of the hurting heart. 'Jesus wept' (John 11:35). Peter is the only Apostle recorded as having wept.

The deepening of understanding

It is this same Peter who asked for a difficult parable to be interpreted. He asked, 'How many times shall I forgive?' (Matthew 18:21). He asked what reward will be given to those who follow Jesus. The withered fig tree does not escape comment from Cephas.[21] Peter not only asked questions, he was a question, and Jesus was the Answer!

The ultimate maturity

If you visit one of the Galleries in Europe you will find some of the earliest paintings by Rembrandt. Hanging by the side of the obvious masterpieces you will see little dull sketches, rough, imperfect, faulty. Compare these earlier works with some of the later ones of this great painter and you will realise just how much he has learned and how he has matured. It is a little like comparing the Peter of the Gospels with the Peter as found in the Acts of the Apostles. Every writer began life as a scribbler! The greatest architect began with building bricks, and even the most astute lawyer began with classroom debate! The Peter who stands before Christ on the sea shore is not the same Peter who will stand in Heaven before the Beemer Seat. Then he will be a refined son of God. There will be the quality of love, depth and enrichment in the one standing before the Throne. He will be included in the promise, presented 'Without spot, wrinkle or blemish' (1 Peter 1:19; Ephesians 5:27), as penned by his own hand and found in his own writings. If

Jesus can do so much with Peter, so that even his shadow becomes a source of comfort and healing, this same Jesus can do it for you. Can any good thing come out of Nazareth? Yes! Jesus, Peter, Nathaniel, James, John, and on into the Book of Revelation (Chapter 7:9) to be part of the number which no man can number!

We all have photograph albums filled with precious memories and we can see by looking at photographs taken at different times and in various places how a person has altered. Humanly speaking there is a continual degeneration, a constant wearing away as nature draws lines on the face and forehead. Spiritually speaking there is a renewal day by day. There is a stretching and reaching out of the spiritual man which is within each of us. The New Testament gives another photograph of Peter. Each time we see him in different situations he is like the modern photograph, fully developed in the dark. Through the modern science of photography we can see a flower literally go from bulb to stalk, growth, petal opening after petal in a matter of seconds as we move from frame to frame. It takes longer with human nature. The latest innovation of funeral directors' achievements is to have a photograph of your lost loved one placed in an embossed frame in a sealed unit at the foot of the grave, placed so that, as you look at the altar of marble in the memorial stone you can see who lies beneath the earth. There is more than mere words.

Peter, when writing, wanted to stir up pure minds by way of remembrance.[22] Let us remember Peter and act bravely! Rise above the waves! Be brought to Christ as you are and go on to be what He desires. Your wisdom will be of another world. Such memorabilia is left with us of Peter, through the Holy Spirit's inspiration. Nothing is hidden. It is told as it was. It is spoken as it was said. We can learn through the mind of the Holy Spirit.

Notes

[1] 2 Chronicles 32:18
[2] 1 Samuel 17:51
[3] Luke 19:5
[4] John 3:7
[5] Matthew 9:9

6 John 6:8
7 Exodus 3:3
8 Luke 8:35
9 1 Kings 18:27
10 John 1:40
11 Mark 3:17
12 Matthew 21:2
13 John 8:6
14 Jeremiah 1:5
15 Matthew 10:30
16 Psalm 94:11
17 Hosea 7:11
18 1 Kings 19:13
19 Matthew 16:16
20 Ephesians 1:23
21 Mark 11:21
22 2 Peter 1:13

4

Listening To Jesus

There is more than one calling on a life and many happenings are but echoes of the Master's voice. Many times the things that are said are difficult to interpret. Sometimes they are as muted mutterings from the mouth of the Mighty, whispered so as not to frighten, yet strong enough to claim and to call. Peter discovered this.

In the life of Cephas the promptings, the voice of Jesus came in many ways and as frequently as the ships which sailed the waves of the sea. Jesus had called Peter earlier, in John 1:41,42, but his response was as a ship which lacks water, steerage or anchorage and is swept off course by strong winds. Whether Jesus thought Peter would return to his fishing after that first contact we do not really know. His nature is so like our human nature, it takes a lot more to get onto the hook than any fish! Peter was not willing to trust his all until he was sure. We very easily become part of every day things. We settle back into what we were. That is why we need to hear His voice often. The appeal of that voice needs to be stronger than those things around us which beg, plead and coerce us into following them. It seems difficult for God to make us part of the Eternal things, we cling to the things of the world, we want to substitute the unreal for the real, making the work of God in us far more difficult. The making, shaking, creating process is denied. We have to be brought to a place where we rest a while and, during that pause, God fills in the missing parts. We think, as Peter did, that the purposes of God are made redundant by our actions. The deepest sea cannot stop a ship—neither can we fully stop the workings of God. Delay does not mean destruction. It didn't for Peter. Jesus returned to the place where He knew Peter would be. He knew those things that influenced him the most. Some things have to hesitate to receive their second wind, to gather more strength, before trying again and bringing new success. Even in the times when there seems to be nothing happening, God is arranging that which surrounds us. What is circular to us is a Potter's wheel to God. What is sometimes paining or crucial to us is the crucible to the Almighty.

The challenge continues

There are parts of the history of Simon which appear to be missing, yet nothing is. In the intervening hours God is still at work, although He does not reveal everything as it happens. There are times when He works from behind the curtain. All the work of God is there, just as the miracles were there. Even in a miracle you may witness what has outwardly happened but there is much more unseen working by God. That which is hidden away as a seed waiting to be watered is still there. Nature is at work under the sod as well as on the branch. God has given us eloquent testimony to the fact that He works whether it is seen or unseen, known or unknown, heard or silent. Jesus is still at work when we are asleep even as He was when the disciples, Peter included, fell asleep whilst He was praying, sweating drops of blood on their behalf.[1] The missing days in Scripture, the full account of events, are never missing from God's diary or calendar. You may have seen calendars where the opening date of the month has a picture drawn around it. God draws sketches like those around every day of our lives. To see the aura around the moon you need to wait for the blackness of the night. God's days of working in a life are full days, not only full of pleasure but full of measure from the Divine appreciation. After coming to Christ every day is full of Divine deposits, asleep or awake. Each day is a Red Letter Day when we walk in the light as He is in the light and the blood of God's Son Jesus Christ cleanses us, in Greek tense He 'keeps cleansing us' 'from all sin' (1 John 1:7), even when we are found wandering as

Peter was along the beach, gazing on the sea. There is a sense in which every day is an offspring of our birthday. All our days in God are related to our meeting with Jesus Christ and being born again of the Spirit of God.[2] They are days of light. They are days not only of us seeking God but of God seeking us maybe a second, a third or a fourth time as He sought Peter, the wandering sheep or the floating boat.

We all have loose ends. There are uncertainties about the way in which we follow Jesus. We commence with a rush and a run and develop into a rut. We find ourselves, alongside Peter, between the waves of the sea and the pebbles on the beach.

Some will only follow Christ whilst they can see, hear and know with their physical senses. The problems commence when they are called into the arena of trust. We need to be as sure and as active in His absence as we are in His presence. One boat is as good as another on the beach. 'Absence makes the heart grow fonder', so the saying goes, but in the life of this disciple absence made the fond heart wander.

On the first occasion Andrew brought Peter to the Master. The second time Andrew and Peter were walking, talking, working together. James and John are on the same stretch of sand and they are challenged afresh. Two can be together and be brothers yet not be with Christ. It is a relationship based on brotherhood rather than the Fatherhood of God. Cain killed Abel. It is important that Andrew and Peter have a right relationship, but that must include Jesus Christ. Jesus comes again to them to place Himself in their little circle of two and to cause it to grow into something more. It is important for them to have a right relationship with Jesus and then to love one another. We can only live in peace with our fellow man when we love the Lord our God. It is then that we love our neighbour as ourselves. If we build in blessing, working, witnessing, the good and the beautiful without Christ, it will all lack, as a flower does without scent. A service without Jesus becomes a meeting. An offering becomes a collection.

God does not give up easily. He has been coming to people ever since He came to Adam and Eve in the Garden of Eden. He is still behind every hill, descending from every mountain. There are as many opportunities as there are needs to bring us to that place where we walk in the presence, power and purposes of Jesus. God has to move and walk as Jesus did until Peter's footsteps fall into the ones freshly made by Him. Disappointments can be appointments. We have toiled all night and taken nothing except a cold and it is into that situation that Jesus steps. There is a deeper work taking place, a rarer happening in the dark than we could ever know. Unless a corn of wheat falls into the ground, into the darkness and be covered, trodden underfoot, it will not bring forth a harvest. It abides alone until it dies. The diamond, opal, amethyst, the gold, the valuable things in the material world are all formed in the darkness of the earth. They are buried in rock. The carat value of so many valuable things is received in the distant and unnoticed places of the earth.

The second opportunity

This was Peter's second opportunity. The Romans had a god named Janus, a god with two heads, facing both ways, the god of the golden opportunity. Our month of January comes from his name, January which leads to April, meaning the 'open door'. Every scientific and medical discovery is a second opportunity. When men have sailed the world on voyages of discovery they have provided mankind with second opportunities. Many of the Classics are stories of second opportunities such as Anna Sewell's *Black Beauty*; Daniel Defoe's *Robinson Crusoe*; Charles Dickens' *Oliver Twist*, all are books of the second opportunity.

In Charlotte Bronte's *Jane Eyre*, Jane was to marry Edward Fairfax Rochester. Then she discovered that he was already married and to a mad woman, and she left. She returned to find the old house burned to the ground and Edward blind, having been struck by a falling beam. He had also lost a hand during the fire. He could hardly believe that Jane had returned but by her doing so he is offered a second opportunity.

When R. L. Stevenson wrote *Treasure Island* he was really giving a wily old fellow who was a patient at the hospital where he worked a second opportunity. Long John Silver, the man with one leg and a crutch was really the hospital patient and somehow Silver never dies. Stevenson let him live on. He did not want to see him hang for his crime, so he lets him slip out of the story, on to another opportunity. We never really discover what happens to him. He had a second opportunity. We are all granted second opportunities by God.

When the late Donald Gee, an early Pentecostal leader, was to face an operation, the surgeon told him that, if he underwent the operation, he would have another springtime. A second opportunity.

The Greeks always presented opportunity as a man with a bald head and with just a little tuft of hair at the front. This was his forelock and his only lock! The rest of his head was greased. If you missed him at the front as he came by you stood no chance of taking hold of him from the back! Others presented opportunity as a ship with full sails blowing in the wind, sailing out of the harbour. In fact, many of the artists' impressions of opportunity were seen in pictures of an open harbour. The very word opportunity is from that suggesting an open harbour.

Jesus was presenting opportunities in the sea as Peter and his companions were walking on the beach. If you want to catch fish, big fish, then you must go to the depths. Go to where the storm breaks over the head, where the prow of the ship is buffeted and baptised with every breaking wave, where the storms have their playground and where Neptune reigns supreme. The walls of the waves are as high as any Jericho wall. It is there that people are in difficulties. Jesus went there to find Peter. He came to his workplace and playground. Lions go to waterholes to catch animals, it is there that they are the most vulnerable. Jesus knew where Peter was and He knew what Peter was, but He also knew that He would make Peter into a real living saint of God in the forefront of the battle.

Jesus threw another lifeline to Peter. He came just as the net was being cast into the sea. Peter had tried and tried again to catch fish and despite toiling all night he was willing to have another go. God in Christ uses the same tactics. The Master of the oceans who spreads them out as a chart on a desk knows all about trying again. The patience of Christ brings us all to our destiny. The final port is into Jesus Christ. The story of Robert Bruce and the spider is first written here—try, try, try again and, if you do, you will win. Find out how many times the word 'again' is used in the New Testament.

Many, many times we read 'Jesus came' (Matthew 9:23;

16:13; Mark 9:14). There are as many opportunities as there are meshes in the net. Every time the Master comes to the servant He has some new things to say. Some new and larger aspect of the work is presented through His word. There are as many paths as waves of the sea along which He longs to take us. He cannot present them all at once, we could never take them in. God knows the depths. God knows where you are, that little beach on which you have been marooned. You may have your Island of Patmos, yet not be there for the Gospel's sake. God knows what to give to Peter, order follows order. Our word chaos originally meant a yawning chasm. Jesus fills such a chasm with choice selections. Every happening in life can be a footprint, the footfall of God along the sands of time. Those markings become our markings, the ready reflection of our Maker. Jesus knocks on the door not once but many times. 'Behold I stand at the door and knock' (Revelation 3:20). The Greek tense is 'I keep on knocking'. The tide comes in and goes out governed by the moon and opportunities will come to Simon, with God controlling events. They will be stage managed but it will be God Who is the Stage Manager, He who arranges the rising of the curtain and the falling of it at death, and He who will also arrange the applause, if there be any. Remember God is not waiting for the stars to shine—He makes them shine! He is not waiting for the fish to feel hungry before they take the bait, He causes it to be. God causes them to come even as He brought the animals to Noah's Ark.

Obedience and surrender

The steps leading to surrender are sometimes many and they steepen with every step. Every one is a challenge. We agree with the Greeks that mountain is piled on top of mountain and that is the way we ascend to Heaven. Yet these slopes were never meant to be hurdles and, inspired by God, we can take a youthful run at them. Arriving at the top it is only then that we realise that God has been pushing us all the way! We need, in such circumstances, to pray that God will make our feet like Hind's feet.

To obey God is as having the sea made calm, as if the Jonah rebellion has been cast into the boiling cauldron. To disobey God is to toil all night and take nothing. There are times when we have been sinking and have taken more water than fish. The only thing we have added to our lives has been the day itself as it has been marked off our life-span making its notch and reminding us of death, adding yet another wrinkle to the face or furrow to the brow. We have sailed to the bottom. We have been as the man who entered the boat one dark night and began to row, fully believing that he was going somewhere. In the light of dawn he discovered that he was stationary and realised that he had forgotten to remove the anchor! We have been guilty of the one-oar obedience, using the one-oar system and have simply gone round in circles, all splash, noise and effort but no real progress. We mistook the circle for the circumference of the sea. Peter tried, on occasion, to place the whole sea within a shell or pool. In his folly he was like land-trapped sea drying out under the blaze of the midday sun. The burden of the day has caused it to grow smaller and smaller until the sea has been transformed into the land. Christ longs to catch our capacity. Our nets have been broken by the sheer capacity of what we have involved ourselves in, seeking to handle things far too big for us, things which were meant to be placed in the Hand of Jesus Christ. There have been times when the nets have broken and we have dragged them through the waters wondering why we have not caught anything. The fisherman knows, in a measure, that the sea must get hold of him before he gets hold of what is in it. The same applies to our lives in Jesus Christ. It is only when God has brought other partners along that we have reached the shore and found Jesus standing there (Luke 5:6). It is not a net He requires, but nets.

Commencing all over again

When we come to Christ then Peter's God will be our God and his people will be our people. We shall be made ready to sail again. Paul wrote to Timothy, 'the man of God must be fully furnished' (2 Timothy 3:17), furnished as a ship with all its provisions and full complement of sailors. Without Christ it is a lonely single-handed voyage around the world. The famous prayer is heard 'The sea is so large and my boat is so small'. You are the lonely yachtsman, a member of an exclusive sailing club, so exclusive that you are the only member! Payment for membership is boredom.

We can only conjecture how long the time stretched between the initial call and Peter's second contact. We do know that it is possible to make a commitment to Christ and, years later, find that through discouragements and other wrenching episodes devotion lies shattered. There are wrecks which are not found on the sea bed. Jesus was here to rectify all that. He was here in bodily presence to tighten what had become loose. That which did not matter was made to matter by His presence and in His presence. There is many a wind willing to sweep us off our feet so that we never arrive at our destination and that which should have filled our lives has simply gone with the wind. Sometimes the natural is far more appealing than the spiritual. The known, the seen, that which we feel and taste is better than the unknown. Jesus wants to bring Peter to that place. Not as a mule or a horse which needs bit and bridle before it will obey. When we have arrived at the place of response then we can be given responsibility. A Peter who loves Jesus dearly can be trusted with a whole armada of ships, an ocean of sea, as many fish and friends as you can find! Without that deep love there are many claims laid on the life and yet nothing to restrain them. Jesus can go to sleep in the boat once we have been brought close, so very close to Him in prayer, in worship, in daily living. God can then sing over His people with joy in that situation. When Peter could surrender the fisherman's pillow to Christ, the pillow reserved for special guests, then there is progress (Mark 4:38).

Prompted to follow by repetition

John Baptist in John 1:29–36, had to repeat the words twice before the disciples followed. His preaching shook people...'Behold the Lamb of God who takes away the sins of the world.' There are second opportunities for everyone. What does not take place the first time can take place the second time as we respond to the challenge. The first time Peter and the other disciples probably listened without hearing, looked without seeing. The second time they looked, they lived, they learned. We all know that Peter's namesake, the Jonah of the Old Testament had to be called upon twice to fulfil his ministry, 'the word of the Lord came unto Jonah a second time' (Jonah 3:1). God's grace is multiplied many times and is multicoloured, multipurposed. It is multiplied twice, three times, seven times until it develops into the seventy times seven which Peter had declared unto him.[3] That can be the amount of grace required before we are moved to God and for God. What was whale to Jonah will be whale to us. When Jonah goes where God is going then the word 'up' (see King James Version, 'arise') (Jonah 3:1) comes into the narrative. Previously the word 'down' has been the operative one.

Second blessings enlarge us

Genesis 1:6–8 tells us much was created and happened on the second day. We can thank the second day for Heaven. The sky appeared. There was a place now for the upward look, the downward look, the outward look. There was light to see everything. The Second Adam was so helpful to us and in that sense Peter was in the same mould as Christ. Sometimes that which is best of all comes last of all. Last of all 'He sent unto them His Son' (Matthew 21:37). Last of all, like the wine at the Wedding in Cana of Galilee.[4] The son of Jonah, this son of Jonah, became the man of the second opportunity, and what God accomplished through Him! He is there as the shepherd of a flock and we are part of that flock. It does not mean that God closes the gate after the second attempt. He loves us so much that He takes the gate off its hinges so that we might be led to our destination by His side. Time and time again God brings everything before us. We need to read books and to listen to preachers so that influence can come to us from every quarter until we are made into one whole man in Christ.

It is quite amazing how Jesus Christ takes this one of the twelve and conquers. Jesus, my friend, is re-writing the history of Peter, and it is this 'same' Jesus who is the Author. There is something very beautiful in the word 'again'. It is a word of grace. 'This woman has done a beautiful thing to me' (Matthew 26:10). What Jesus was doing in lives such as Peter's was returned to Him. When Jesus came to Peter again it was as if He was playing a game with him. He came with outstretched heart saying 'In this game of life it is now your turn'. The modern equivalent would be 'the ball is in your court'. Many battles can be fought and lost on the same stretch of land where, eventually, we conquer. David conquered

Goliath at a place where the whole army of Israel had been defeated, the conquered returns to conquer! That which in seed form falls from a tree rises up and grows as a tree. The place where Jesus gives us a second opportunity becomes a sacred place, a place of promise and rescue, a shrine and altar of all that is held dear. On that altar Peter offered his dedication. In the absence of light we all learn how things can run to the ground, how the brightest and best can be blighted, we learn what happens when we go our own way. God bends all those ways until they converge into His Way, as streams and rivers run into the sea. Peter's travels and escapades were all leading to this central point, to this stretch of beach where Jesus would meet with him. Many ways lead to Christ but one way leads from Him, the Heavenly way, the way to Heaven. That call and claim of Christ had not diminished. It was not made weaker or less, it was still the same because this was the same Jesus. As a fisherman Peter knew how to catch fish. Jehovah's Son knew how to catch men!

The faithful Christ

There is a unique faithfulness about Jesus coming again to Cephas. In another way Jesus will come to us again.[5] He always comes. The cows will come home and your ship will come in. We sometimes hear the same message from the same quarter and it loses impact, then along comes another with a little more zeal, more of a cutting edge, the same message, but we gladly respond.

From the context of Matthew 4:18 we understand that Jesus was walking along, setting the pace and forming the direction when Peter came and walked alongside Him. It was a matter of Peter getting in step once he realised that he had walked everywhere without Jesus and had arrived nowhere. There was and is nothing static about Jesus. He is going forward. He is not a statue meeting a need but a living, walking, talking Christ. There had to be communication and impartation. A moving Christ moves the nature of Peter. He leaves footprints for all to follow. The word 'destined' means that which causes to stand. Having a vision, a mission, a hope set before us in a walking progressing Christ, causes us to stand.

The first call was simply a voice and meeting with Jesus.

'Come and see' (John 1:39). Nothing else. To contemplate, like Mary at the feet of Jesus. It must develop into something more than meditation. This is why Jesus returned. He must develop hearts and lives into something more than a religious fetish or emotional thought. 'Come and follow Me' (Matthew 4:19). One was to be static, to look and to see. The second call was to move on into something new, something larger. On each occasion there is the promise of a change of nature, just as the sea by its constant battering wears away the rock into sand, so the ministry of Jesus comes to shape and to sharpen all who call on His Name. 'I will make you a fisher of men' (Matthew 4:19). One call referring to character, the other to evangelism and charter.

That second can lead to the first

The word 'second' does not mean reject with God. The second visit and the second letters of Paul and Peter hold great wisdom and much content for our admonition and learning. The second opinion is sometimes that which gives hope and we cling readily to it. Like Dresden China it has to be fired again and again until the glaze is beautiful, enabling it to withstand the knocks of life so that rain will not wash away the pattern.

A second visit means interest maintained, suggesting love stretched, shown and deepened. Jesus came to see what had happened to that which He had left behind the first time. What did He expect to find? The same landscape, the normal happenings on this sea? A different man, as changed within as he was without because the sun had looked down upon him? It was when the cock crew a second time that Peter remembered the word of the Lord. Every second counts with Christ. Every hour is one of healing. Every day is one of display.

Did Matthew 4:18 come flooding into Peter's mind as he betrayed the Lord? The things that Jesus and all the miracles failed to do a simple creature of God's creation did by its crowing. The herald of the dawn awakened remorse and repentance in Peter.

A Minister was concerned about the love his people had for Christ so, after realising that their love blew the way the wind blew, he had a weathercock placed on the Church to remind them of Peter. Whichever way the wind blows, so the love of God is the same, it faces your direction. Peter wrote his Second Epistle to help those who might be coming in a second time.

Called to follow Christ

Cephas is called to follow. He, with us, must be in Christ. Some were called to be healed, others to be helped. All the Apostles were called to be with Christ. When and where the finger of God points so the hand of God will make a way. When we hear the voice of God it is an urging and encouraging voice. If it is a stony path we are being called to walk on this second time, God will provide strong shoes. Your feet will be shod with the Gospel of Peace.[6] Like the two on the Emmaus Road another presence will draw nigh and go with you.[7] It drew near to Peter and he went with it. The old proverb says, 'There are never two dawns to a day.' That is true, but there can be new ways in every dawning. Jesus wanted to make Peter as large as the sea and as full as a fishing net. God wants your depth to be as your height, and your breadth to be as your depth so that you might know His fulness. To the human mind it might seem as if God is wanting to place the Pacific Ocean into a tear. We often need to remind ourselves that the pool of water can contain the image of the tree on its banks or the sun and moon way up in the sky. A reflection of Heaven found on the earth.

The only thing at this second time that Peter is asked to do is to follow. He wasn't called to be a better fisherman. He wasn't called to be clever. 'Follow Me' (John 21:21,22). Having all the choices in the world, but making Christ his choice. Following as thread follows the needle. There are certain things that Peter knows, but there are things clustered around his life that he is not fully cognizant with. He only really knew and understood some of these things as he followed Jesus. This servant of the Leader discovered that when we are crucified, Jesus is on that cross. Wherever we are led, whatever place we arrive at, Jesus is always there first. To follow is to flow with Christ. It is to be part of Him. It is to be an instrument in the whole melody and orchestra.

The children's game of 'follow my leader' was made far more difficult by the things which the leader did and which had to be copied. Everything that the leader did had to be attempted by those following. Paul, in 1 Corinthians 4:16; 11:1, 'Be ye followers of me, as

I am of Christ.' Be imitators and mimics. Do as I do and say as I say. Be as I am in the world. Be that other side of me. Be an ambassador, meaning a hinge. The hinge allows the door to open and shut. Those who pursue the Lord, Peter realises, must do as He does. When we come alongside it is a well worn path. All the saints since Peter, right through the Ages, have travelled this same stony pathway with every step they took.

Every disciple travels without rigid demands. We can never be as the train on the lines or tracks. We are flesh and blood, we do right and wrong, we make decisions and those decisions become easier if we feel the warmth of His presence melting our icy hearts. We are not as a computer having discs fed into us which, at the push of a button responds. We are all, with Simon, flesh and feeling, human beings, some better shaped than others. We operate and walk forward according to feelings, facts and emotions.

The Greeks believed and taught that every life is represented as a chariot with horses pulling it, some good and some bad. We have the edge on this belief because we have given the reigns into the hands of Jesus. In Acts 8:38, the chariot of the Ethiopian Eunuch was commanded to stand still whilst Philip did what he had to do. Philip the Evangelist was that man's second chance, one that was not brought or bought by riches or by travel.

When Peter was challenged afresh there had to be determination and commitment to Christ. It was this same Peter who later spoke about following the Messiah to prison and death, but only went as far as the palace. There must have been something in those deep eyes, in that look on the face, words spoken which must have been very musical in Peter's mind and heart. This call of Christ is so real. Missionaries have travelled the world because they heard such a call. They have faced tremendous odds but have rarely been regarded as being 'odd' or old hat. They have worked until men, nations and governments have respected them.

Responding to His voice

It is when the voice of Jesus becomes the important constituent that we truly begin to follow as if we had no choice, yet we have all the choice in the world. That voice in the Book of Revelation is as the sound of many waters. How must that have sounded to a thirsty person or one, like Peter, who was a man of the water? The New International Version gives the wording as 'rushing waters'. On another occasion in that same Book it is defined as a trumpet blown for war, appealing to the soldier in most of us. William Branham described how, as a small child, God would speak to him through the wind blowing among the trees. There are situations which are the voices of God speaking to us even as the empty nets spoke to Christ or as a mother-in-law with fever spoke to Him. Now Jesus comes and calls Peter afresh and the loose things are made tight and strong, the feet which were turning towards the sea and the boats were turned in another direction. Peter, fall in love and you can do what you wish to do, love God and do what you want to do, submit to Jesus. Anyone with a light can come to any darkness without fear or torment, because that light will create avenues through the darkness.

It wasn't the call to be an Apostle or a great Evangelist—that came later, in John 21. This was a simple call to be faithful to first principles, love and desire, as the writer to the Hebrews had to be (Hebrews 6:1). Jesus was calling the fisherman to be with the Creator of the fish! He was calling Peter to be His friend, companion, journeyman, fellow worker and helper, esteeming Him so highly and taking no other to himself. If Jesus had been calling the future Apostle to brave a storm, sail uncharted waters or go on some long journey the response might have been immediate. Some calls are to stick with it, to remain faithful in the situation you are in, that is what produces quality.

The great problem with Christianity is that it is a day by day, hour by hour, moment by moment way of life. You can never take it off as an outer garment and place it in a wardrobe. The problem of the cross is that it is daily.[8] Just prefaced the call to take up the Cross for all believers with the words 'If any *man* will take up his cross'. Jesus was to discover if there was any man-reserve in Peter, anything not used up. There is enough in the voice of Jesus to command the storm to be calm, to heal the sick, to open the eyes of the blind, and that voice must find a ready response in Cephas. It was that voice which made Peter. It foretold His death and denial. It was not only rich in words and phrases, but there were words of wisdom, peace and grace uttered as waters from a fresh spring, as the flight of the gentle dove. It was the same voice which echoed the end of the world, it bowed womanhood into worship as Mary worshipped Him in the Garden. The woman who had listened to another voice in the Garden of Eden now came to listen to the Lord.

Jesus has said 'I will never leave you nor forsake you' (Hebrews 13:5). I will never be out of touch, out of grasp. I will never be where I cannot hear your voice in prayer. I will never stand where you are not. There will never be even the thickness of a skin between us. His voice is in the thunder and in the gentle murmur of the stream. Psalm 29 is the Psalm of the voice of the Lord, verses 3–9, the many references to that voice as revealed through nature. May all our hearts be touched by a Psalm of the voice of God, rich with what the Word of God has to say, rich in the accent of the Word, that we might find ourselves following in the wake of Peter, Paul, John and Mark. There are shadows of compelling things which flit across our lives everyday and when we catch their meaning then shadow becomes substance and shade on our right hand and on our left. Sometimes we only hear a muffled voice, a muffled call. We are shouting so loud that we cannot hear what God is saying. 'He that hath ears to hear, let him hear' (Matthew 13:9). J. B. Phillips: *He that has ears should use them.* Sometimes the very word believe contains the thought of hearing and obeying. We can, with Peter, only obey what we hear. We can only follow what we discern to be the leading of the Lord and the voice of God.

Jesus did not just say to Peter, 'Follow Me'. In Mark 1:17, King James Version, He said, 'Come after Me'. 'Where He leads me I will follow, where He leads me not, I will falter'. Some will lead and their footprints are but in the sand. I am not inclined to follow prints that disappear. The wind sweeps them away or they are lost as the sea sweeps over them. Not the footprints of Jesus! It is a living Saviour Who leads. Some have wondered why feet do not wear out as shoes do. The answer is that shoes are dead leather, and feet are made up of living skin with blood flowing around the bones. We must follow that which has Life, that will last forever, such life is in Jesus Christ.

I walked with knowledge and it talked all the way,
I walked with reason and it bade me stay,
I walked with ambition which rushed me off my feet,

I walked with peace, and calmness was brought to the fray,
I walked with Jesus—and found all four in that day.

The Greeks in their Academies would teach as they strolled
through the gardens. Questions were asked and answers given as
they walked along. Many times the text book was their minds and
the master wrote on the very air they breathed.

Peter, who had wandered away from Christ, needed to be
brought right back to a new beginning. Sometimes the word new
means the reorganising of that which is already in existence, or it
can mean that which is for the first time. Both can be applied to the
second opportunity for Peter. He took it and in doing so he entered
into a deeper relationship with Jesus.

Notes

1 Matthew 26:40
2 John 3:7
3 Matthew 18:22
4 John 2:10
5 1 Thessalonians 4:17
6 Ephesians 6:15
7 Luke 24:15
8 Luke 9:23

CHAPTER

5

Receiving a Miracle

The teaching of Jesus Christ from the boat in Luke 5:1–3, was not enough. It might meet the needs of the crowd but it had to be more than that, it had to be the power of God revealed to Peter as an individual. It had to be ministry to the one disciple. It is in our natural environment that we feel the best and respond the most and Jesus wanted Peter to launch out into the deep, into home territory. Peter lived, breathed, ate and slept the sea. From the boat Jesus taught the crowd, from the sea He taught His servant. Peter, after toiling all night and taking nothing was ready to receive teaching and direction. The teachings of Christ were sealed in salt to preserve them. That is why they move from the shallow waters of the coastline into something so deep that great things could be taught, away from the shoreline and the crowds. There must be a movement, under the direction of Jesus, away from that which offered no challenge. They must go on to the place where sea and salt whip as a lash across the face, where storm and tempest hold court. Will Peter sink, swim or walk on water? How will he be affected? What of his future? Before any discovery there must be enterprise. The prow of the ship must do its cutting work amongst the waves. Hidden in the sea were all the treasures of wisdom and knowledge waiting to be released by the presence of Jesus Christ.

Jesus knows that to catch fish successfully takes time and practice. It demands that the same waters are fished time and time

again, throwing the nets over the side of the boat at every opportunity. Human nature is as slippery and as scaly as any fish!

The appeal of Jesus

So many things appeal to Peter's nature. The miracles of Jesus
became as steps to Heaven and Peter is prepared in such an
ordinary way, through everyday happenings. It is just another
fishing trip, but in it, through it and over it Jesus Christ is ready to
make another appeal to the human side of this son of Adam. As
humans, many times we request the miracles without letting down
the nets. We want to see the power of God without being moved.
There must be no stirring on our part, we want the bread without
the fish, it must be without a Cross, without a launching out into
the deep. Not so, says the Sovereign Lord. There are nails and
splinters in the Cross of Christ. We desire water to be turned into
wine as in John 2. We want the wine but are not prepared to carry
the water, let alone the cumbersome clay water jars which need
bringing to the place where Jesus can perform a miracle. It was not
going to be easy for Peter. It never is when God is working on our
characters.

The whole context of the complex dealings of Jesus with this
little rock is the unfolding of the power of Jesus Christ being poured
into Peter's life. What fullness! What shapes and designs! There are
difficulties to be brought through. He takes us into them and He
brings us through them. He went in with empty nets, empty boats,
but he came out with full boats, full nets and in fellowship with
others.[1] We are empty and discouraged as we face many a salty sea,
yet how full when we obey the Son of God. Peter, through Christ,
had conquered the shallow waters and the salty sea. His mission
had been an inglorious failure, but it was turned into glorious
success. He had fish, an abundance of fish, to prove that success.
There are experiences to be found in the profound waters which
God allows to come in. The power of Jesus Christ had been set free
into the sea and every wave had become conscripted into the
King's Army, every fish had made up the ranks, obeying His
command. The empty part of the sea is suddenly teeming with fish,
active, ready to obey their Master even to death in a net. The deep,

the unknown, the dark had provided an exciting prospect. This was no splash, no throwing up of the water, it was the real thing!

Peter is so like all of us. When the Old Testament sacrifices were being led to the alter to be slaughtered it heard the sounds, saw the sights, could smell the blood and it would begin to take backward steps, slipping and sliding on the blood-stained floor around the altar. Hence the term in the Bible 'as a backsliding heifer' (Hosea 4:16). We are happy, even as Peter was, when there is no great demand placed on us. The quiet waters, the gentle teaching, greatly appeal to us, until we see the shape of the things to come. The demands are placed around us as nets around the bodies of the fish and it is then that we would retract. When we get into the deep waters we start digging with our oars to get back to the safety of the shore. There is a challenge in going into new areas, staying there until shadow is turned into substance and our fears are drowned in tears. We have a clearer vision of the purposes of Jesus Christ. We find it is hard to kick against the pricks.

Frustration and emptiness dealt with

This miraculous transaction in the life of a disciple tells us that when we do not go to God with our frustrations, emptiness, weariness and toil, He will come to us. Then the fish will begin to swim into the nets, then the song will be put back into life. When Peter did not go to Christ with his emptiness, Christ came to him with fullness. Peter could not fully control the emptiness. He had toiled all night and taken nothing. Nor could he control the fullness, because the nets broke. The breaking of the nets can be the tearing apart of the old life. It was the end of natural prospects for Peter. He wasn't ever going to mend those nets after this miracle! The power which saw them destroyed would be allowed to operate without question in his own life. God has to give us something so big that we cannot handle it and in it is a message of surrender of the old haunts, the old ways, the old life. Jesus was really saying to Peter, 'Now I have torn them, leave them!'. In the Old Testament the tearing of a garment meant that a kingdom was finished, it was concluded. Notice 'their' nets began to break. Not God's nets or purposes, not God's ability or power. It was not power reduced but power increased because of a miracle. The power was there all the time just waiting for the nets to be lowered into the sea. The net touching the water was the signal for the fish to swim.

In Luke 5:1–11, the scene is set for Peter to look and learn from the activities of Jesus Christ. New truths are taught, truths that were to be long lasting for they were written into the rocklike nature of Peter. Jesus did not need an oak pulpit or a Church to preach a sermon. He used the birds of the air, the trees of the field, the sheep in the fold and the fish in the sea. He had pulpits galore! He preached sermons as they happened. Everything we meet with in Jesus can be an open mouth to speak to us and an open hand to give to us. We need the open heart and the listening ear. Everything can spill out the word of God, can contain the Will of God, even as the oyster contains the pearl or the fish the coin in its mouth.[2] There is no amazement that the fish became the emblem of the early Christian Church. The Psalmist, years before, had recorded 'If you would see the works of the Lord you must go to the deep sea' (Psalm 107:23). We hear sermons and the ligh˙ of them is extinguished before we reach the Church vestibule! Not so with Jesus. When we toil alone we catch nothing, but with Jesus we have boats full of cargo from the King's Treasury. Jesus speaks in our native tongue, we understand and interpret. He spoke to Peter through this miracle in his native sphere, just as He spoke to Mary in the Garden. When Paul spoke to the crowd in the Hebrew tongue they were silent and listened, as if listening to the voice of their fathers (Acts 21:40). Jesus talked to fishermen about fishing. He took the very things they understood and performed a miracle of net-breaking proportions. He used it to catch Peter. To the ploughman God will come to the field; to the butcher, baker, candlestick maker, God will come to where they are, saying and doing what they will understand. God has no need to go to the world at large to teach things. He comes to our own back garden and doorstep as He did with Peter. Our own door can be the door into the classroom. Our own garden gate can be the gate into the University of Christ. Within our own boats, our own life and character there are so many lessons to be learned. All the equipment Peter needed for catching fish, plus the power of God, was in the boat with him. There is a usefulness and a fruitfulness we can hardly manage when Kingdom principles and authority are acted upon. Partnership ministries are needed to help contain and utilise the blessing.[3] You have enough bread and fish to spare. You are able to fill other boats with the overflow.

Jesus places His influence into a whole sea of personality and character, seeking to bring from the depths within us all the things that will astound us. Those things that are long buried, sunk by piracy, those things which years ago struck rock and reef.

Answers to prayer put extra pressure on the believer but those answers are meant to create questions, to develop and to bring ministries into operation. How often in life we have been where the waters are stagnant, where nothing stirs or floats. Then Jesus steps into the arena and suddenly there is activity. As with Jonah, the counterpart of Peter, it was easier for God to catch whales and prepare winds, for Jesus to catch shoals of fish, than to persuade Peter, to bring him into the folds of the Shepherd's heart, to multiply the grace of God in his life! There is a suggestion here of the depths to which Jesus is prepared to go to reach, bless, teach and see that our nets are so full that we become useful in the Kingdom. Peter has to be more useful than an empty net.

I was meditating the other day, wondering how many people come to God in middle life. Throughout the teens, twenties, thirties, God is pleading with them, visiting them again and again, and each time He leaves a marvellous deposit of His presence. Acts 4:22 — the man healed at the Gate Beautiful was over forty years of age. That was a miracle. Some seem to be ever swimming towards the net or leaping on the line, but they never finish up in the boat. There is a constant flapping, kicking, wriggling, jerking, but never a keep-net security. Jesus has to deal with Peter as large fish are dealt with, given a little line, going back and forth until they tire themselves in the struggle. The battle is won when the fisherman's hand is placed around the fish to release it. It must be allowed to struggle until all resistance is removed. Peter was restless in his resistance. He was like the waves of the sea, rising as if free from the rest of the water only to plunge back and become part of that which it sought to leave. Even the whale of Jonah fame had to be made to vomit before it released its little parcel of evangelism! It housed a Prophet of God.

God will not send fish until the nets are ready. Jesus must get the craft sailing first into the depths before any miracle can take place for Peter. When Christ commands us to lower the nets we must lower our defences. Our own ideas of what might or should happen must be baptised into death and the depth of the sea. God wants to salt old lines with new ideas. There are fish right there. When we do lower the nets we allow the shoals to come in.

Jesus Christ has power in every realm

This power of Jesus Christ had to take many shapes and shades in the life of Peter. Wind, water, electricity and light can appear in so many different forms and the power of Christ had to be seen and known in every realm. As Peter knew every inch of the sea in which he fished and sailed, so he must know the power of Jesus Christ in all realms, from the sea to his escape from prison. The sea was large, wide, deep, and so was the power of God. The hurt and the illness, those things which need rectifying, are not the measure of the power of God, Jesus Christ is. All that happens is but another opportunity for God to step in bringing all things into the captivity of the power of Jesus. As He denounced the works of the devil, so He announced new hope in the Gospel. The largest and most difficult area for Jesus to operate in is not the sea with its tides, currents or hidden reefs, but the human heart which is far more complex than any seven seas! All the doings of Jesus resulted in extending the heart of Peter until its fringes touched the hem of His garment. His love was poured into the heart of the big-hearted fisherman. Jesus was going to make him too big for his boats! The knowledge of Jesus, infinite and thorough, capable and complete was being tide-borne into the finite knowledge of Peter. He finds missing footstep in the step of Jesus, missing light in the Light of Christ, missing love in the Love of Jesus. A swelling heart assisted by a sure knowledge, that makes for a prophet, a disciple and results in an apostle, one who is sent.

Peter, after toiling all night and taking nothing but sea water bordered on boring until Jesus stepped in and reconstructed the whole scene. It was almost like a stage play where the scene movers, under the direction of the Stage Manager, move the scenery ready for another part of the action. Jesus moves the pieces into play, almost as if He is making moves on a chess board. Sometimes what Cephas requires comes in healing forms, other times in a multitude of fish. It may not seem remarkable that so many fish should find their way into a net if you take into consideration that a weather-beaten hardened Salt has just toiled all night and taken nothing. Now, when the shadows are cast upon the waters, he is instructed to let down his nets. He can actually catch that which was missed the previous night and add the morning's catch to it. The result is that the nets were ready to break. In that same sea, at that same place, it was the same man with the same boat—the only difference was the amount of fish! That does something to you! It did something to Simon, it made him want to worship. As Elijah's servant did we must keep looking until the cloud as small as a man's hand becomes a thunderstorm and rain, plentiful rain, falls from the skies and the moisture replenish's the dry earth.[4] Jesus could not only appear and say He had all power on earth, He proved it. Jesus must be as Christopher Columbus and discover new worlds in Peter. It takes as much to conquer a human being as it did for Edmund Hilary to conquer Everest. Jesus has to deal with as many Peters as there are fish. That is what Christianity and Christ in a life is all about, being on a sea in an open boat with Jesus Christ. When we are sick, weary and tired God is at work on our behalf. To every burden there is another shoulder and for everything we need to lift there is another hand. We learn the largest lessons, as Mary did, at the feet of Jesus. Peter learned at the side of Jesus. Each disciple learns the lessons of life as he takes up his Cross and follows after Christ. Christ in a crisis with you is worth following, worth knowing, worth having.

The real lessons are learned in your local Church. It is there that we get to know the salty waters, the brackish, sometimes stagnant waters of everyday living. Fields of buttercups and daisies have thorns and thistles in them. There is always a place for the nettle and the sting.

Friendship deepens into fellowship

Once a year we would gather around a community bonfire. The whole street would turn out, yet the real depth of friendship and fellowship was not around that bonfire. It was around the smaller fires in the grate. With Peter, as with us, it is not with the big evangelist, the large gathering or the firework display, it is in the situation and locality where Jesus meets us. We deal in ones and twos, but Jesus deals in winds and waves, shoals and full nets. He can break all nets. He can tear down our defences, but He loves to see us willingly surrender to Him those things that He asks of us.

Simon Peter had been in home waters as a child and as a youth. It was here he had learned his craft. He had grown to know and interpret wind and tide and every movement on the surface of the lake. The thing that Jesus did had never happened to him before. When we know it all we have only just started! God always has some new thing for us. Just when we think He has finished with us He starts again! Many times it is in the flow of everyday things that Jesus performs His mightiest miracles. We often say, as Naaman did, 'Are not other rivers or waters better than these?' (2 Kings 5:12). I am quite sure that when Jesus added spittle to dust and mixed it as a remedy for blindness there would be those hygiene experts who would have preferred a bath of holy anointing oil! There are always those who think that clear crystal water would be better, anywhere would be better for a miracle than where they are. God can work anywhere, but not here! Jesus proved that thinking and thankless theology to be a nonsense. The juice of the apple or the orange would have tasted sweeter than these sea waters, but there would have been no miracle performed there for Peter, because it would have been man's choice and not the choice of God. Where God chooses, there He places His choicest.

In a measure, Jesus failed. He was successful with wind, tide, storm and He could even walk on water, but within Peter there was something more which needed to be caught. Jesus would try with many boats, nets and rods until, at the end, Peter would be fully persuaded to burn his old boats and send them to the pews and pulpit of Davy Jones. Let them be soldiers of Neptune! Human nature is such. It is larger than the world around us. Put all the world into it and it is still quite empty. It is capable of so much and yet it is incapable of responding to smaller things. That nature in Peter always wants the crown, without the throne. The responsibility is shunned, shied away from.

Peter, in Luke 5:8, according to the King James Version, was only brought to the knees of Jesus, yet that is a start. At least at the knees you can see the feet more easily. In one Church there is a statue of Christ and, in order to see His face, you have to bow at

His feet! If we can be brought as little children, soft, pliable, ready to learn, then there is a whole classroom of teaching. We should listen and learn from the knees up, of Jesus Christ, and then, from the head down to the feet. You will find that all things meet at His feet. We should learn from the knees of Jesus the lessons learned from Eternal Ages. Jesus is the pages of Eternal Ages. The Book of Learning is constantly resting on His knees.

How will he respond?

The response of Cephas was rather unexpected. He had just seen the greatest miracle since Creation, since God said, 'Let there be fish,' and fish teemed into the waters. God fishing with His power in Peter's pool, yet in Peter's heart what would He catch? Jesus wants heart-fish. Things like love, devotion, kindness, reality, faith and commitment are all swimming around inside us, looking for bait on which to rest their lips. Verse 8—the mission of Jesus was to bring Peter nearer to Him to make further discoveries, even as we put out the tongue for the physician to examine the health of the body more closely. Here the opposite is the result, 'Depart from Me'. The Holiness of God and His working of miracles was too much for Peter. He feels threatened when he should have felt helped. This new power, this new vision, the claims of Christ coming at us is too much. All those fish in the net, yes, pressed down, shaken together and wriggling over! This is why Jesus must work little by little. The light must not dawn all at once. There must be little outshinings as miracles. The new comes little by little and the old goes bit by bit. It is always the intention of Jesus to bring fresh fish swimming into the old stale nets. He puts new things into old disappointments. Into those things which are quite dead He brings beams of resurrection life. These are happenings which will bring to the fore the very Holiness of God and which will make us uncomfortable. Why couldn't I catch fish like that? Peter is asking himself. The answer is because Peter is not God. Let Peter be better and let Christ be Christ. Many modern miracles have decreased the Holiness of God. He has been turned into a *Jim'll Fix It*.

All some have ever been is a tied up boat, no sailing, no challenge, just messing about on the river. The early disciples in

Acts 2:1 were like that, all gathered together, so much potential, and suddenly there came the sound of a blowing wind. 'The Spirit came as a gale' says one translation. The result was that they went everywhere preaching the Word and many fish were taken. This was so on the first voyage of the Pilgrim Fathers. What a blessing it must have been as they sailed from Plymouth reading that Promise of God to Abraham... 'I will make of thee a great nation and I will bless thee and make thy name great and thou shalt be a blessing' (Genesis 12:2, King James Version).

Investment with interest

Notice the exchange rate Jesus offers! One boat for so many fish, one life for so many blessings, one act of surrender and there are as many miracles surrounding it as a flower chain around the neck. Give one mite and there is more in that than all the others have given, because all has been given.[5] One life with so much to offer. 'Give Me to drink', and in exchange she receives an offer of the Water of Life which wastes not away.[6] Five loaves and two fishes are surrendered and a whole multitude is filled, with baskets to spare. There is a super-abundance about the miracles of Jesus. If something from those miracles can trickle into the poor heart of Peter it can be made so much richer, wiser, deeper, fuller. Jesus Christ never created one lonely tree or flower. That is why we have forests and fields of flowers. Not even Wordsworth's 'Lonely Cloud' is on its own when God is at work! Everything is in abundance. Spring and Summer are other terms for abundance and variety. Blessing is another word for profusion. Love is so munificent that it takes a whole chapter (cf. 1 Corinthians 13) to describe its nature and activity and then it is illustrated throughout the sixty-six books of the Bible. All these things are at work in the story unfolding before us. How this must have spoken to Peter. Everything, the tiredness, the waters, the waves, the worry, the emptiness and the toiling all night and taking nothing were left behind. You need a Jesus big enough to fill a boat as well as the horizon. It is then that emptiness, human emptiness is met in Divine fullness. It is of little use granting Him a net, an oar, or just a part of your equipment. Jesus operated alongside the fisherman, not from some distant ivory palace. Sink or swim they were in it together! This was not a rod going forth from Zion as an edict from abroad. It was mouth to mouth and ear to ear, face to face and heart to heart. It was service and action. Jesus must rule and storms and worry are conquered by Him. He wants to get that which has lost its usefulness floating again. When there is only salty sea and a taste left in the mouth, then Jesus can fill all we have with something wonderful. When He steps in it can be so big that we cannot fully manage, develop or control it. That is why, in Christian fellowship, we need each other standing by our ships ready to become a Fellowship, to help others to keep and to use the blessing. It must not be allowed to swim away, be wrecked or lost in the unfathomable depths which surround us in the world we live in.

This happening reminds us of the story of Ruth, where handfuls of purpose—handfuls on purpose—were left for her! Corn was let fall and left where she would find it, deliberately placed. If God has given an answer as a result of obedience and request, as He did with Peter, then get others to help with it. Those who call on Christ for help will call on others to help them disperse the help given. A lot of fish, a great catch soon makes others appear as partners. Peter had a lot of friends but they only appeared when the blessing was multiplied. The boat that has Jesus in it catches fish! It becomes a miracle heart and through it, He operates His ministry. It was first converted to preaching, in verse 2 of Luke 5, then it went out to do some fishing. That is the spiritual order of things. It witnesses miracles, it fulfils its potential and its purpose in life, touching new depths. It witnesses a fullness. As boat to water, so the believer in God. The purpose of catching fish had gone until Jesus stepped into the boat. He does not want us to be just floating around. There was teaching in that boat—verse 2. Such truths came over its sides as were never heard at the feet of Gamaliel or in the Academy of Seneca. Boat was converted into pulpit. The boat was converted, but what about Peter? Fish and nets, sea and boat were conscripted. They fell within the heart of the power of God, the God who steers stars and clouds, sun and moon was steering this small craft. These things created an opening, a door for Peter. That teaching the claiming of Christ must go further and deeper than across the face of the lake. It must not be a swallow skimming the surface of the water, it must go deep down and touch the shoals which are under the surface. That is more difficult than it sounds.

There are old ropes which bind us to certain havens. There are lusts as anchors and bays of pleasure we all love. There are chains which charm and claim, binding us. The most difficult thing for a weatherbeaten fisherman to do was to allow Jesus Christ to take over in familiar territory. Going back to where you have been, your intellect telling you that nothing is different, nothing is unusual, being willing to go to the very place of disappointment and, at the Word of Christ, see victory. Finding that life in that area, the same area of disappointment is not as empty as you thought. This is when ceremony glows and ritual releases new things into a life. God can send fish into a net and that same God can send them away. God had been arranging all this, so that Peter might learn from Jesus. Peter had to realise that with God in control there is great activity and even greater capacity. A dead experience, a dead sea, becomes alive with activity. There was more under the boat than was in the boat! We cling to the known rather than the unknown. We constantly put up with empty nets rather than face fresh depths with Jesus.

There is a favourite strip of land which seems to us who are in this Peter-School to be far safer than going where the nets might break and the storms might come. The breaking of the oar could take place here. We have to face past disappointments, face up to them in Jesus and see a whole shoal of fish come from those disappointments. Human nature would rather sow in the land than fish in the sea. The boat with Jesus in it must move into deeper waters, the waters of trust and discipline. We need to walk in the water, to let it touch the feet, then the ankles, the knees, the loins until it becomes so deep that a boat is necessary.

Step by step, little by little

Have you noticed how Jesus took Peter one step at a time? One fish with a coin in its mouth, two fishes with five loaves, then a shoal. Jesus stood by the side of the lake.[7] He wanted them to thrust out just a little from the land (v 3). The word 'thrust' is the same word used to describe the 'bringing' of Peter up the stairs, showing him all the good things that Dorcas had made.[8] There are a variety of things awaiting men of action, those who act on the teachings of Christ and take the plunge, step by step until we are in the deep

with Him. Jesus is always seeking to get Peter out of the shallows of
uncertainty into the depths of reality. The seeds of a revival and
revival principles are set out in this story. We must move with Peter
away from the shallow and carnal, into depths where we have to
trust Him, to move where the fish are found, to the place where the
shoals are and the nets are tested—the area of activity. Thrust out
a little from the land and you will discover Jesus afresh. The only
difference between the first occasion of fishing when he caught
nothing was the inclusion of the Words of Jesus.[9] Let Him baptise
your life afresh with salty waters and your vision of Him will be
clearer. Discover His Lordship and power over all flesh, all fish.
Jesus has conquered on the land. He has conquered sickness and
death. Will He be the same when the waters of the sea cover His
zeal? Will they lessen His fire? These questions must be answered
for Peter. A Christ who is only powerful on the land is limited, a
one-sided Jesus, a sort of God of the mountains but not of the
valleys. We need, as Peter did, to discover an all-round Christ who
has a ministry for the high and the low points of life... 'on land or
sea, what matters where, where Jesus is, tis Heaven there' (taken
from an old hymn).

Nothing is hidden from Christ

Peter realises that Jesus can see beneath the waves. By the anointing of the Spirit a Word of Knowledge is granted to Jesus. His all
illuminated Mind and seeing Eye discerns fish before we know
where they are. His eyes light up the path of the deep. Water does
not stop the works of Christ, it only increases them. Jesus did not
need periscope, microscope or telescope—He could cope! Shall not
the God of the Universe know where His creatures play and make
sport? When we let the land go then the spiritual supercedes the
physical and mental. The man ceases to be earthbound. Abraham,
from the Ur of the Chaldees, Paul on the Damascus Road, Jacob,
Isaiah, Isaac—were all called from their strips of land into Something deeper and wider. They were called to discover what God
owned. Isaac had to dig wells in the earth.[10] We are all timid when
it comes to severing the umbilical cord. Here was a challenge to
leave the beaten pathway of the safe shore where seeds fall and
birds land, the place where boats come and go. Here was a chal-

lenge to something new in God. Make God your goal. You may not have excellent eyesight but you will certainly have a large target. It needs a word from Jesus to bring certain areas into life, to be made part of our activity.

We, like Cephas, can manage teaching that will not rock the boat, that will act as a zephyr against the sail. Yet it never really changes or challenges. Here was a challenge to go for deeper things, the unlocked vision, the covered challenge, that which is hidden under a curtain of water, to go further where you must trust God. Here is the essence of pastoral and apostolic teaching. Going where you have been many times, doing it again in the Name of Jesus and expecting to see results! It is being and going for what you were really created for. Better than a rod is a nod from the Saviour! Better than a net is His knowledge. One is reminded of how fishermen of old used to go to the high cliffs overlooking the sea waiting for the sun to break through the clouds and, scanning the sea, see the shadows which revealed a shoal of fish. They then would direct crew and ship to that very place. Before the days of the modern freezer, if they wanted to preserve anything, they would salt it. Jesus is doing this with Peter. He wants this to be everlasting and to remain fresh in his memory. There must be nothing shallow. There must be no lukewarm sheltered waters, nothing half and half. Peter's trophies and evidences of miracles were in fish caught. As one fish swam from the hand of Jesus into the net of Peter, Jesus was not really wanting the fish, He wanted Peter to swim into this new life and stay there forever. He wanted Cephas to be as some fish let loose after captivity in a jar, to swim into the depths of the sea. Jesus was in the boat and on the water which meant that He laid claim to all around Him. Where He establishes His Throne then and there every knee must bow. You can only find depth with Jesus in the boat. The weight of what He is will take that boat to the Plimsol Line. The cry of the Church and the need of the hour is for more depth. Some are soon lost because they are soon caught, being too close to the surface. They make crab pools their destination, small ponds and pools on the beach which are soon dried up, replaced by sand. You will never see the real miracles in shallow waters, nor will you see them without challenge. Those things around us, mountains, trees, unknown Continents, the moon and the stars were placed there to be a challenge, to meet the sense of adventure in all those who refuse to accept the title of Earthling. There are many who want the old landmarks. They feel better if they can see the contours of the land and count the pebbles, crabs, shells on the beach.

Launching out into the deep

Greater depths of water await Peter. Depth can suggest many things. There are the great waters of the Deep. Peter had to learn that water, fish, depth are all ministries in the hands of Jesus. Every wave is blown along in the breath of God. All our beliefs, ceremonies, all our fundamentals mean nothing if they are not baptised regularly in water. They need to have salt poured through them. They must hold fish, they must do and be something.

Let down your nets! Nets in a boat with the fish swimming around are of little use. Put what you have into the waters which surround you. That sounds easy but if you are a fisherman and you have tried it all without success then you are reluctant. You must be as Peter who, without ceremony or question was willing to drop the net over the right side of the boat. Learn to fish in the beam of the eye of Jesus and you will have good success. The fish that go to Him for shelter will come to you.

We always pay for partial obedience, even as Peter did. We pay with broken nets and lost fish. The King James Version says, 'Jesus said, Let down the nets'—plural. Verse 5, Peter let down the net—singular. Sometimes we think we know better than God. The capacity which Peter expected meant one net. If nothing goes into it that doesn't matter, there isn't too much embarrassment. The results which Jesus awaited demands NETS, not simply a net. The measure of the surrender is sometimes the measure of the blessing, but not always. To our meagre surrender God sends a whole army. Partial obedience must always result in breakage and strain. The boat will tend to sink instead of sail. Its best journey will be to the bottom! This is the lesson learned by the Galilean. There was an overflowing capacity which needed an overflowing surrender. It should have been nets without measure to catch fish without number. When Jesus expects to give such an abundance He expects us to surrender to Him that which can handle the same. 'Give and it shall be given unto you', does not say how much to give or how much shall be given.

Partial obedience invites frustration

The largest fish caught that day was Obedience. The net which needed breaking was Mistrust. Doubt and gloom needed to be sunk as a torpedoed ship. The piracy of self needs to be made to walk the plank. That which is standing in the way of God, old attitudes, the knowledge of the human mind, and endless genealogies must sink as stone to the bottom. There were a whole shoal of spiritual attitudes to be caught. I believe the more nets, the more fish. God doesn't answer our prayers fully because of the lack of obedience. Verse 7—They both began to sink. Jesus will never be brought down to our level of faith. This is what partial obedience always does. It sends you to the bottom. It allows the very blessing you are seeking to escape. It brings us low. The load is too much because the obedience is too little. Verse 4, Twentieth Century New Testament—'Push off into deep water and throw all your nets for a haul'. Peter said, 'At Your word I will let down the net'. The Word which created the Universe was about to operate in the world below. It was the same Word which calmed the troubled sea. The same Word healed the sick, cleansed the leper, allowed nose and fingers to grow again, illuminated the blind, steering them into the light. It was a Word of authority. Fish come to the net when the Word is in the heart. It was a Word which, once spoken could not be withdrawn or questioned, but sped on its journey in order to accomplish. The Medes or the Persians never had such a word as this which could break but could not be broken. It was Heaven's Word to meet the needs of the earth in Peter. Cephas had heard good and bad words, words of advice from his father, words of wisdom, guidance, even encouragement when the fish had become but sprats. He had never heard a word before which had guided him to the exact place where fish freely surrendered! Fish are swimming for the nets as a runner towards the finishing line.

At the word of Jesus the fisherman responded. That word was good enough to heal and teach. It was about to teach Peter the lesson of a lifetime. If it was good enough to teach, it was good enough to act upon.

The result of the miracle in Luke 5:10 is don't be afraid. Learn to trust. Learn to lean. Learn to do what Jesus says even when you cannot fully understand.

Life for Peter had become just an empty net, a fishing trip where he caught nothing and then, maybe, had to invent stories of the ones which got away. Reality and fullness was brought in the Divine Christ. He put a stop to one thing in order to introduce another. The closing of the door on perplexity opened the door on to expectancy. Jesus leaves Peter with the lessons taught and learned. God's capacity is greater than our fullness. God does not measure as we measure. Carnal reasoning based on past happenings can never grasp the immensity of the Divine Mind.

This one of the twelve had been on many fishing excursions but never one like this. Storms, rough seas, mist had perhaps stopped them entering the bay and coming to land, but never before or since had they had such an abundance of fish in the net. This is one day at sea which will live on in Peter. He is brought out of his own little sea of weakness and failure and he has acquired knowledge that familiar things can be false things lacking depth. Verse 11, the final testimony. Everything was lifted out of the sea, not just the fish. The boats were being placed on one side and Peter was following Jesus Christ into a new area of enrichment and fulfilment.

Notes

1 Luke 5:7
2 Matthew 17:27
3 Luke 5:7
4 1 Kings 18:44
5 Mark 12:42
6 John 4:14
7 Luke 5:1
8 Acts 9:39
9 Luke 5:5
10 Genesis 26:18

CHAPTER

6

Christ In the Home

When Andrew and Peter first came to the Master they lived in
Bethesda and later, in Capernaum, apparently with Peter's
mother-in-law,[1] a family of at least four people. There is no mention
of Peter's father-in-law. Tradition speaks of Peter's mother-in-law
being named Joanna. His wife, according to Clemens of Alexandre,
was named Perpetua. The fact that Peter was a married man is not
in dispute.[2] Married life brings problems of its own and many are
home made, yet the Son of God takes every thread and unites those
things of importance in Peter's heart. The ugly, the arguments, the
misunderstandings are all used by Jesus Christ as His presence
brings harmony into such situations.

The house in which they lived must have been quite spacious,
because crowds came to hear the Prince of preachers and teachers
expound the Word and heal the sick. Richard Glover, the Puritan
Commentator, says, 'They had a house in the south in the home of
Mary, Martha and Lazarus, and they had this home in the north
belonging to Peter, where his relative was taken ill with a great
fever' (Mark 2:1).

Peter had been a firsthand witness of Jesus performing miracles in the synagogue among the crowds and on the streets. Would
this same Jesus have the same power in the home? Would His
influence wane in the presence of the familiar friend? Could the
power of this Leader extend and move among the furnishings of the

house? Could it work as much in the bed as it did in the open air? Questions needing an answer, and were answered by Him who was the Answer. Should Jesus be placed only among the candlesticks and upon the High Altar in the ceremonies to be sung about from a hymn book? Never! A Christ of truth needs to be transported and translated into the happenings of everyday life. The Christ in *The Growing Pains of Peter* is not a Christ only of the Church. He is essentially the people's Christ. Was He simply to be left among the relics of religion, or even among the learned as He was left years earlier by Mary and Joseph?[3] They had sought Him sorrowing. They had looked anxiously around every corner, seeking Him amongst their own kinsfolk. Here Jesus is put where He belongs, not in a Garden, not in a nation, not in any tribe or tongue, Church or denomination but in the home. If Jesus rules in Peter's home He will rule in every other part of his life. Any follower of Jesus must discover for himself a Christ who is relevant on the street, in the Church and in the home. Jesus is everywhere. Every day He is to be found in every thing. The happenings in the home can be interpreted by His presence. The home can be His Palace, the place from where edicts are uttered and knees are bowed. The basic thought in the word 'home' is 'to rest'. 'Come unto Me all ye who are weary and heavy laden and I will give you rest' (Matthew 11:28). Rest in His rest and sleep in His sleep. It is a Jesus in the home with us who eats, sleeps, thinks, wakes with us until not one moment is free from sacredness. He must be the permanent Guest, never the lodger. He must be light, door, atmosphere, passageway, decor and view. Jesus is the Room with a View. Heavenly things are brought to earth's hamlets and villages in Jesus Christ. Here was Someone who could do something, and He did. How sweet and lovely when Peter turns to Jesus and tells Him, as we can in prayer, of trouble in the home. He is not only a Church Christ but a Christ of the home and the most intimate of relatives. It is the presence of God which sanctifies. Christ must be seen in Peter's home to be as strong and as helpful as He is within any other society. You can take Jesus home with you!

A Man for all Seasons

Simon is still at the discovery stage. He is discovering a Man for all Seasons, a Jesus just as much at home when touching fever as when testifying to faith. 'I am with you always' (Matthew 28:20). I am with you in every season, season of age or of nature. The Evergreen of a fading world. He is the nations' Christ, the national, the international Christ and the next-of-kin Christ. Whatever the weather you will weather the weather if Jesus is with you!

Jesus touches everything and anything and makes it Holy. That which is carried out in the home, conscious of the fact that Jesus is there, can be and will be an act of worship. It is all related to the spiritual. The Person of Jesus seen, known and recognised alters attitudes. The hands which can be raised in worship are the same hands which reach for things in common surroundings. Those lips are the same lips which talk to God. Jesus lifts us from the secular and into the sacred by recognition.

The married man, the family man must, of necessity, be the Godly man. He becomes such a man when Jesus is recognised as the Head under which that man operates, when authority in the home rests in Jesus. Enoch walked with God after the birth of his children (Genesis 5:22). Jesus becomes the centre of conversation, more talked about than the fever as He is brought to the sick bed. If we are sick and bring that sickness to Jesus, or Jesus to it, He won't simply mend it, but rebuke, cleanse and cause it to be as if it never existed. He is not only brought to the sick bed but also to the laughter and the tears, the room of joy and peace. He walks, talks, stays and stands with us. Even though we are surrounded by bricks and mortar we really live in Christ. Jesus is an atmosphere of healing in this home. The leader of the Apostles learned more about Jesus and His healing, raising, quickening power in his own home. It was a home-bred Theology, not something received from the hands of others but received directly from Jesus Himself. He had the experience in the home that he never knew in the synagogue. You can be a silent witness to many miracles but you are still only a bystander, an observer unless it takes place in your own home. I love conversions which result in Jesus being in the home! What He is in the home can be a reflection of what He is in the heart. It happened with Jesus and Zaccheus.[4] I must stay in your home today. Zaccheus received Him joyfully. The Church is a good place to see the power of God but the home is a better place! It should commence in the home. If it is worth anything it is worth having in the home, as well as in the Church. You can hide in the pew and be lost in the crowd, but you cannot hide under the pillows of the home. There you are known.

Being in the synagogue must have been rather like being on the Mount of Transfiguration, good for them to be there because He who is all good was there, and they were in His shadow. The greater challenge was to be found when they stepped outside. The home should be a reflection of the Church and the Church a reflection of the home. Jesus was interested in Peter but also in all the disciples. He was and is totally committed to nation, people, tongue and tribe. He was interested in the family, the spiritual, the natural, and Peter was part of it all. God operates in every realm and it should be just as real in the Church, in the synagogue and in the home. When we close the door of the Church we do not leave Jesus out in the cold, marooned in Christmas or Easter. He is Alpha and Omega of the whole year. In our humanity we build compartments and make distinctions, but there are no distinctions with Jesus. To Him the bathroom is as good a place as the dining room. In the home Peter is learning that every man can be a preacher. You can live Christ. Every chair becomes a pulpit from where Christ can be expounded. It is here that the songs of Zion burst forth from the sons of Zion. When Mary said, 'My soul doth magnify the Lord' (Luke 1:46), she was in her own family house.

In sickness He is there

When the home becomes a hospital, and it only takes one sick bed to make the change, then Jesus is able to operate in that home. The shadow of His presence gives shade and comfort to torment of the mind. There are messages here to be heard and understood. Peter does not have to go to some special school. Wherever Jesus is, there the teaching is ultimate. The book, pencil, the equipment of teaching and learning are all resting in Peter's mother-in-law. Into that sick room came the smell of health as Jesus entered. He was the prescription and the chemist. Health and healing were in His fingers when He touched this woman fettered with fever.[5] Moffat:

'She was down with fever'. Things cannot remain the same if Jesus is in the house. There is only room for one throne and He must fully occupy it. When He comes in, sickness goes out. Cephas is watching wide-eyed, as inquisitive as a child. The Physician lives up to His Name.

There are many synagogues, many Churches, but only one home to which you belong. Jesus is needed for that home. It was in the home that Peter received depth of teaching. You can go to the synagogue, hear the Scriptures, read from the Roll, but the difference is made when Jesus is taken home as a Friend. Boy takes girl home only when they are serious about each other. The house where Peter's mother-in-law lived had to be a reflection of Heaven but sickness was there. Where fever burns freely, where the burdens of the home crush into the ground, from the footmarks of Jesus new hope and strength spring. That raging temper, that awful fever, is used for the glory of God. Jesus lessened the burden for Peter and his wife by raising up his wife's mother. With one touch, one word of command the worry, the nausea, the inability were denounced. Jesus placed something into her in order that she could place something before others. Delivered to do, and Blessed to be. There are people in the home who are sick but are not in a bed, they may have a hidden sickness. The symptoms are there but are unseen. It takes Jesus walking with Peter to make the full discovery that is the commencement of the full recovery. We have to believe in an administration of the glory of Jesus in the home. It is as much needed as the switching on of the light as darkness falls or as the closing of the door as the wind and rain blows. It wasn't time for worship or fellowship, it was the time for healing, not fine words but deeds, dynamic and relevant. As Joanna had served others she too is now served. Jesus was more than the man or woman from next door, more than a kind thought, more than a person in a book, even the Bible, placed on a shelf. 'I am among you as He who serves' (Luke 22:27). Service which, no doubt, was rewarded with a good meal. That service of Jesus stands her on her feet. Jesus became again a servant to the server. He comes to what we are to make us what He is. There is a message for all who gathered in that home. The light of the home is switched on again. That cheery disposition is seen in all its radiancy. The dusk is turned into dawn, sunset into sunrise. Previously the woman's work had been around the house, now it was around Jesus Christ and the disciples. She had found her true Centre. She steps out of the dust as if Eve was created afresh from the side of Adam. Every act, deed and word sprang from her healing. Everything she did was a tribute to the power of Jesus. Eve stepped out of the shade and back into the sunshine taking those things that had been learned in the fever through into the fellowship. These are deep teachings to the heart of Peter. How the emotions of Peter and his wife must have been stirred. The fact that Jesus was in the house could not be hid.

Making room for Jesus Christ

They were an affluent family, yet poor until Jesus came. They were near to Him, but it did not exempt them from sickness. 'The wind blows where it will'. Sickness will come, until it meets with a greater Will. They entertained Jesus Christ who stayed with them and brought a little bit of Heaven with Him. Heaven, where there is no sickness, no night, no fear or torment. It was customary for Wise Men to bring gifts for a king, but who had heard of a King bringing the gift of health to a woman? Jesus came to where the sickness was. They could only tell him of her but He acted on that information and did what He knew best to do, He healed.

Peter would not be the only one returning from the synagogue or Church to find fever tucked up in bed, but he was the one who saw deliverance because he was prepared to take Jesus all the way into the heart of things. We can come down the steps of a Church after a marvellous exposition of the Word of God and those same steps can lead into hell. Stand back! Give her air! Let the breathings of God come to her. Make room for Jesus! Like this apostle in the making we are not alone when facing such things. Those whom sickness has thrown to the floor we must meet in the Name of Jesus. Let us meet health and sickness with the same spirit. We are overshadowed by the Almighty. What we meet does not matter, it is what we meet it with! The place is not important but the power is. It was a battle, with Peter as a bystander. If we meet oppositions with Jesus at our side then we are victors in every battle. Like many of the plays of William Shakespeare, they take place behind closed doors. We are allowed by Scripture to take a peep into the sick room. What we see and hear we come to know.

The happenings and the dispensations of grace act as a Urim and Thumim of the Old Testament, through them God spoke to the people.[6] Jesus turns the bed into a throne and from it He not only conquers the fever but enters the heart of Peter to influence him for ever. In future days Peter would put into operation all he had seen and heard. In any sick bay mission the Master's formula would be repeated time and time again. From that throne room went forth edicts throughout time and eternity, sent out as messages of consolation to every needy family and servant of Christ.

The anointing sets us free

Jesus healed because of the anointing upon Him as we can see in Luke 4:18. This anointing was part of the recovery process. Fever was a flame and that flame was met with the fire flaming through the eyes of Christ. It was an eruption of thirst, met in the fountain of love and the thirsting experienced by Jesus on the Cross.[7] When health comes in through the door sickness must leave by the cellar and as it sinks low it touches the very source of the hell from whence it came.

Peter evidenced Jesus in powerful action and that power was all power. It spoke to the disciple who was being shaped into apostleship, 'This is what I am able to do and greater works shall you do because I go to the Father.' These actions and statements became proof texts for Peter's future sermons. There is nothing like seeing a miracle, having first hand information, to help you to believe! Peter could say, 'Come, see a man who told me all things' (John 4:39). Part of the Majesty of Messiah was to heal the sick, cleanse the leper, raise the dead.

Power over all sickness

Jesus 'rebuked' the fever, in Luke 4:39. The same verb is used of rebuking the wind and waves when calming the sea in Matthew 8:26. Peace, be still. Be muzzled. As if it had been a mad dog with rabies. When Jesus entered the room the fever was flaming, but, when He left this fever was settled and surrounded by the power of Christ. The body was released from its grip as from a straight jacket or handcuffs. Peter is being fed on miracle ministry. This miracle, along with other miracles, is making way for the Master. Mark 1:29 tells us they had just returned from the synagogue when it was reported that there was a sick person in the home. The devotion in the synagogue and outside of the house was brought to the house. The devotion to the cloth must be the same as to the couch. The greeting smile, the open door, the cheery face, even the smell of cooking was missing. The initial evidence of love and activity in a woman was not there. The lamp of the Lord was burning low. There would be no woman to see that the water bowls were placed for the washing of the feet. The perfume phials which were handed out to kill the stench of sweaty flesh would not be provided, unless other servants saw to it. She who had been on her feet when they left was on her back as they returned. Who or what had caused this? That which had bowled her over must, in turn, be bowled over. Stand still, Peter, and see the salvation of the Lord. Pious prayers do not boil kettles, but the prayers of Jesus do!

The Christianity that we preach, practise and are must last from the Church to the home, it must be as brightly lit in that home as in the Church, overspilling into all the corners. The Jesus who is with you in the Church is still 'this same Jesus' in the home. Peter realised that the Jesus who heals the sick does not have to be in a Church. Prayers need not be said in a sanctimonious way, true inspiration will take Jesus home. The light received in one place must shine in another. If it will not give light in the home then it is no real light at all. It was but a flash from a passing shooting star. We have to receive enough from the personal presence of the Son of God to be of use when ministering in the home. The peace which flows into the heart must flow out in the home. The presence of the Saviour must go from altar to attic. The epistle written and read must not become a different translation in the short journey from pulpit to pantry. There are rewards and compensations for Peter. Jesus puts things right in the home.

Deepening relationships

The Christ and Peter relationship has to be taken outside of the Church to the light of day. It has to be taken into the community for it to do any good. It might be good but it is a goodness which is covered until it is taken to where the need is the greatest. The woman took the measures of meal, placed leaven into them and, from that point, it grew and influenced.[8] Christ in the life of Peter must run in through the front door. If His influence is not there we cannot call ourselves apostles, disciples, servants, followers or believers. The Christ simply hanging on a wooden Cross outside a Church or crafted into a stained glass window is of no relevance at all if He doesn't come into my heart and into all my decisions. I must be able to draw this Christ in the dust of the busy street and see Him in the carpet in the home. The crucifix must not be a symbol of power. It is not a Jesus set in gold or silver worn around the neck or etched onto a badge, He must be a relevant Christ for today and everyday in my home, Peter's home, John's home, Paul's home, and your home.

Near to where I live a couple have purchased an old Church building and converted it into a house. It was sad to see a stone Cross on the fascia being chiselled off and the Church being turned into a building without any suggestion of what it had once been.

Jesus cannot just be a thought, the Bible or picture book. Christ must step out of the pages and into the home. Do not shut Him up in a book. He must be a Christ of action. From one musical note you can tune an instrument and in Jesus all lives can find their proper place in God.

A family purchased stone from the old Church building which was in the process of being demolished and had a fireplace built from it. That fireplace became a sort of altar in their home. 'What mean ye by these stones' often echoed from them.

After being equipped in the Church,[9] we return home, as Israel came out of Egypt, fully armed. The armour they really required was within themselves making them into a fighting force. The King James Version uses, in Ephesians 4:12, 'for the perfecting of the saints'. The word 'perfecting' means putting back into joint that which has been dislocated. It is relocated in its former place. Peter saw Jesus putting order into disorder.

We need the spirit of Jesus as it was in Peter and the spirit of Francis of Assisi who said, 'Grant that I may not so much seek to be consoled as to console, to be understood as to understand, to be loved as to love; for it is in the giving that we receive, it is in pardoning that we are pardoned.' These are some of the lessons learned as Jesus deals with fever. He wanted Peter to know that

Christianity was more than buildings, it was meant to touch people.

Christ is more than a hymn or a song. Songs are part of the war cause but they must never be substituted for that war. Even weapons are not the war. After the singalong, after the weapon practise we must face the real thing. After the singalong must come the walk-along with Christ. The path of your spirituality may have twists and turns, it may reach up hill and down dale, but it must not stop short of your own front door. The Christ who goes to the synagogue with Peter returns with him! He must be set free in the home. No closed door must be allowed to shut out His power or presence. Some of God's greatest miracles took place in the home. When He performs great outdoor miracles it is so that the world might watch and understand, that angels and seraphims might pause with open mouth. What is received in Father's house from Father's Son must be divided among Father's children. It will heal Father's family if it is from the Father. If your house belongs to God then 'in My Father's house there must be bread enough and to spare'.

The nature of the need

At this time it was not a matter of seeing the walls of Jericho fall down. It wasn't to see a belching Sinai turned into a mountain of snow, or to witness Jonah struggling in the belly of the whale, it was to see Jesus in full Manhood and measure of His ministry raising one up to serve at the table. That is what salvation is all about. As she was touched by the heart of the Servant Son, as He controlled the raging torment within, she too received a servant's heart. She wanted to serve Him who had served her. That which is written on the scroll and read to the congregation must be let loose in the home. Peter took his Friend home and all the types, shadows and ceremonies did not remain as symbols but became living truths in that habitation. Spurgeon, in his Commentary on Matthew, makes mention of these verses 'You have some one-worded miracles,— Speak—See—Hear—Come—Know.' An army of one-worded sermons. You may have a thousand shining guns unloaded but they are at the mercy of one loaded weapon of war. The smaller the word the greater the power—'but I say unto you'.

Jesus brought it all down to two Commandments: Love the Lord your God, and love your neighbour as yourself (Matthew 19:19). Peter loved his mother-in-law enough to bring Jesus to her side. The best thing to ever come home from the synagogue! Healing is not a multiplicity of words. Peter realised that every word of Christ freshly spoken is ready to heal. Jesus is not only effective on the mountain or in the manger but in this home and among this family. Charity begins at home but it doesn't remain there. Go home and tell them what great things God has done for you.[10] The home of Cephas became the centre of God's power. It is needed in the home. There was a need for an open window where one could see new sights to excite the spirit and Jesus was the window of Heaven. He was the oxygen of new life. Jesus at sea, drawing, catching, landing fish, and Peter looks on as Jesus does the same in the home, catching from sickness, taking a loved one from its watery waves. A miracle was performed. The word miracle is from the Latin 'Mirari' meaning 'to wonder How did it happen?' When Peter had been fishing for a living he took home with him the very essence of the sea—the fish. Jesus came in like a breath of fresh air. Peter is still impressionable. In the Gospel according to Mark 1:17 he had just been called to follow Jesus. Peter still had the noise of the waves ringing in his ears.

The essence of prayer

In 1 Kings 10:19, we have some interesting suggestions about Solomon's throne. There were steps and, on the end of each step, there was a lion. If the first one did not get you the second would! These steps and lions led to the throne and the armrests. You had to brave twelve lions before you were heard. If you were not seen it would be too late. How different in the New Testament when, with all our needs, we are told to come 'boldly' to the throne of grace.[11] The word 'boldly' is with freedom of speech. Joanna had met with the step and the lion but now she was on the armrest. Grace takes us straight to the armrest on the throne—His arm and my heart.

The fact that Peter was in fellowship with Jesus affected his whole family. This was not the Welfare State, it was a state of welfare with Jesus. Nothing puts fever out as the fountain of love does. It says, 'She was sick of...'

Luke 4:38, by doctor Luke is called 'a great fever'. The area was notorious for fevers and malaria. It was swampy, dark and oppressive, yet it was where fish of the human kind could be found and healed. God uses strange areas and circumstances as a base for a healing. He chooses some strange places to commence a healing ministry. Jesus was the fragrance after the rain. He came as crystal water flowing from the throne, finding its own level that He might put this fiery fever out forever. As those who were bitten by serpents in the wilderness and experienced this same torment had to look to the brazen serpent on the pole as a type of Jesus Christ so this one had to look to Jesus in the same manner, with Peter helping to turn the head. They tell Him of her, Luke records. They besought Him for her, says another.

Apostolic ministry

I believe in Apostolic succession, providing Christ is in that succession. I can believe in any man if he can bring Jesus to a situation and see it turned into that which no longer matters. I believe in Apostles who do what Peter did, walk in the Master's presence and open doors for Him to step through. A ministry that brings Christ from the outside to the inside. Those who present an opportunity for the touch of Jesus to reach relatives and relative things. Be an apostle in your own home! If you go to Christ He always sends you home first, there you discover if it is real, if it will last. If it works in the home among the known then it will work amongst the unknown also.

God was doing the sending, Peter was going. The term Missionary was taken from the Roman Games. The men in the theatre were in mortal combat, one man being defeated could raise his hand for clemency. Caesar from his raised platform, the judgement seat, Greek—Beemer Seat, would send a man on a mission of mercy, despatched to the aid of the suffering party. He intervened on behalf of the one in need. The journey was called a mission and he himself was a Missionary.

The rewards which Jesus had mentioned to Peter were brought into the home. The presence of Jesus enriches the home. His power brings peace and harmony. All cries are turned into smiles. He was there as a Living Christ. He is the one who stops, forever, the march of fever. He trips it up and bowls it over with His mighty foot of brass.[12] Halt, who goes there? Friend, fiend or foe? If it does not answer in the name of love then it is rejected.

The Name of Jesus

David Livingstone, marching through Africa, said...'I have thought much today about the Name of Jesus. It pleases me to hear it ringing in my ears as I walk through the wild. 'Not tongue or pen can tell the worth of Jesus' Name.' No voice can sing all the songs and melodies that are in it. It is filled with melodies which soothe at a time of fever.

> Nor voice can sing, nor heart can frame,
> Nor can the memory find,
> A sweeter sound than Thy blessed Name,
> Saviour of Mankind.

so wrote St Bernard of Clairvaux. Jesus is the perfumed breath.

The power of Christ, if it is to mean anything at all, means that Jesus comes into His glory in very natural ways. Peter's mother-in-law did not commence performing miracles, she began to do the things she had left doing when the illness struck. The woman did what she did the best, cooking. Sickness may have wrought a devastating work, but when Jesus leaves, things are so different. He leaves part of Himself in a body of health. His Kingdom is established where thieves had broken through seeking to kill and destroy. He has come that they might have life[13]—that they might have life in all its fullness. It needed Someone like Jesus to come to the rescue to defeat fever with the burnings of His Eternal love. It took Jesus to bring her back again, to help her to work again, to live again, to believe again.

The importance of the home

The home and the family are very important to God. Only God can turn a house into a home. Peter realised that, without Jesus, you have a home without a foundation, but with Him that home becomes more than bricks and mortar, it is where God dwells with

His people. The fire in the hearth is an emblem of devotion to God. The light typifies the Light of the World. Every meal is a token of the Last Supper. When Jesus has come with healing power to any home the conversation is hallowed and sweet. How many homes we have visited and have smelled the fragrance of the flowers in a vase sweeping across a room. It is Home, Sweet Home when Jesus comes home. That home, any home, becomes a Bethel, the House of God. What was for a time in the Tabernacle and then in the Temple is found in millions of homes, set as cities on hills letting their light shine before men.

Jesus commenced His earthly life in the home of Joseph and Mary. Each home where Jesus is Lord is an extension of that early home in Bethlehem. Peter begins to realise some of the potential as his mother-in-law is raised up. She was sick with fever. Fever, from the German, means 'a fire'. Peter is an eye witness not only of the glory of Jesus on the mountain, but also by a sick bed. The brush of the artist was flowing freely, a little stronger, more colours added. It is witnessed that the fingers of Jesus act as a guard against the fire, the fever. His little finger is stronger than the loins of sickness. Jesus didn't poke the fire, He quenched it. He didn't lessen its torment, He dealt with it altogether. Not even the smell of burning was left. There were no ashes!

This same Jesus deals with one and all. It is not a different Jesus for the Church, the sea, the healing, the home. He is the same yesterday, today and forever.[14] Not the sameness of boredom, staleness or dullness, He is of ample variety. No two things in Heaven are the same. The theology of Peter was being formed, from theory to fact, from fact to faith. That which was soft and clay-like was setting in the heart as Peter looked and listened. The look of 'Now I know' was forming on his face. Mystery was solved. He must be influenced not only by the waves of the sea but in the tranquility of the home. Note also that there are things to be rebuked in the home. Peter is learning how to pray for the sick. He is as the ship being refurbished, receiving its coat of paint. He is about to be loosed into the Acts of the Apostles and there, all the influences, great and small will be fully seen and understood. There are those who would listen to him preach, pray and serve the sick who would say, 'That is just how the Master did it'.

We hear much today of home therapy, home visits, home

accidents, home counselling, but what about home miracles such as this? There are many of them and, if called, they would rise up and speak out of the flames which have been extinguished by the tears from the eyes of Jesus. These are things which are seen in marriages helped by faith in Jesus Christ, marriages which have become founded upon the 'Rock'. Those who were sinking have found themselves rising above flood level because of a home visit from Jesus. There are misunderstandings in a home which can rage like fire. There are those behind closed doors, fraught and aflame with fears. The sleep of death can come too early. There is that which is dying within long before the body dies. Curtains are drawn that are not made of a material substance. Homes that should be bright are arrayed in black. They need Jesus. These miracles are filling the circle of Peter's eyes and the words are filling his ears, giving this man who sits with Jesus an all-round and rounded ministry. In every part of the battle he fears neither battle nor war. Peter is never the ready-made person, but he is always willing to be made into something more. The packaging can mean as much as the present within it. When the door to this home opened it was the door into the laboratory, the door to the classroom and the University of Life. It means something to Joanna, it means something to Peter, the man in the making.

Notes

1 Matthew 8:14; Mark 1:29; Luke 4:38
2 1 Corinthians 9:5
3 Luke 2:41–48
4 Luke 19:5
5 Matthew 8:14
6 Exodus 28:30
7 John 19:28
8 Luke 13:21
9 Ephesians 4:12
10 Mark 5:19
11 Hebrews 4:16
12 Revelation 1:15; 2:18
13 John 10:10, NEB
14 Hebrews 13:8

7

Training
For Leadership

There are moments when Jesus seeks to draw us away from the crowd. He becomes the God of quietness and seclusion. It is almost as if the materials for the Sculptor of Life to work on have to be taken from the hustle, bustle and rowdy rodeo of life to be brought to a place in His hands. Christ brings Peter a place where there are no distractions, nothing to snatch first one way, then another, the place where all voices are shut out and all that is heard is the echo of eternity.

It was to such a place in the Diary of the Lord, as in Mark 5:37–43, that the band of three, Peter, James and John, were brought. Each one represented a ministry, an angle of living, but the focus is on Peter.

We are not informed about how they felt when they were brought by the Light of Life into this house of death. They may well have entered somewhat forlorn and discouraged, but when they had formed the grand crown around the work of Christ as a circle, they left that house with a clearer vision and a greater conviction. They stepped out as those other noble three—faith, hope and charity. They had witnessed the conquering Christ with power to seize from the jaws of death. It was Jesus working through grace to a member of the human race. It was love and faith at its best. They saw all His power concentrated on a need, the revealer of truth, love and compassion. He had greater weapons than death. He had and was Life! They had seen Him with power and now He penetrates within and behind the veil of death itself, proving that all power is given unto Him in Heaven, on earth and under the earth. Power is His in all regions beyond.[1] He came to see what devastation death had wrought. The flower stem had bent and had been broken, crushed by a clumsy boot and driven into the ground forever. Yet no memorial stone will be erected here, there will be no funeral chant. Put the false mourners outside! There will be no funeral. It is a birth. Grave is replaced by Glory! Darkness must give way to Light.

Peter, coming to a family broken and disorientated by death could tell any family in the future that Jesus had been there. He had seen the Master at work! The heart of Jesus went out to the little bereaved family in love and compassion but where our feelings fail and dry up, His went on to take the child back from the cruel arms of death. What was broken and empty, the contents spilled as milk on the sandy floor, was pieced together and filled again, even as Peter watched.

Christ's power over death

Some died at different ages, corruption was more advanced in some than others, but Jesus brought them all back from the dead. One died in a house, yet another was already on the way to the cemetery, and Lazarus had been dead three days, by now he stinketh. This was not a whispering hope but a shouting, a trumpeting in Peter's ears. There is no place in life or death where the arm of Jesus cannot reach, His hand cannot grasp. There is nowhere, known or unknown, where His feet cannot walk. His eye sees behind the hills of death and beyond the grave. His voice sounds out in the deep and even in death can reach us, His smile still affords the sunshine of other dimensions than those found in this world. (See the Author's book *Dying is Living*.) The greatest lessons Peter ever learned were learned in sorrow, darkness and in loneliness. Every preacher, following in apostolic steps, can tell his congregation that there is life after death. Beyond the grave we rest in His bosom and we still feel His hand near, wiping away the fear and the worry.

This house of death was a house without door or windows, a

sealed tomb until Jesus came into it and fitted the windows and the doors. Where tragedy sat on the throne and contentment was in the dust, Jesus came and placed triumph in the heart of His message right where it belonged, here in this house at the very centre of a calamity. He sows His seeds and plants His flowers where the earth is the darkest. The best we can do is place flowers on a coffin—not so Jesus Christ, His sunshine spreads across the coldest and widest parts of the river of death. Jesus was teaching lessons where a bright smile and a laughing face had been turned into a cold mask. Youth had gone beyond old age. A young woman had died, would they just sympathise? No, Jesus would not accept the status quo. He had to act. His compassion must do something. That which had been taken must be given back. The bed must be slept in again, with life operating through the young body. The seat must be filled again by the same young girl, this time with the scent of glory on her and the light of a distant land in her eyes. Going into the house of death Peter, who had always accepted death as inevitable, is taught that it shall not be so—what seems to be shall not be if Jesus is in the midst. He takes the shroud and places it on Himself. He takes the covering cloth and turns it into something else, the death shroud becomes the Christening garment.

The power of death defeated

The girl dies. In Jesus that is not the end of a life. There are possibilities of further life and adventure. To Peter's mind this was rainbow indeed. As the Prodigal Son, so she is away from home. It is not a journey she had taken willingly, the choice had been snatched from her and the crown of youth knocked from her head. It is lying in the dust to crown what she is through corruption and the course of nature. Not so, says the Sovereign Lord. She may be away from home, even as Peter had been at sea in many a ship on dark nights, but she is never away from Christ, never beyond His grasp of love which is as wide and as long as death. There must have been the sowing of hope and expectancy in the former fisher-man's heart. Make room for more, Peter! There is so much more to come that will influence and control! Jesus knows all the back lanes, all the roads and, without signposts, He travels beyond death to claim a child as His own, throwing the strong arms of God around her. Death is not and never will be a cutting off from the presence of God, it is just a step and Jesus can take that step. These things had never been told to Peter as a child at school, he had to wait for the coming of Christ to discover that Messiah had a Kingdom not only in this life but in the life beyond. All find resurrection in Him who is the Resurrection and the Life.[2] It was to death that Peter was led in order to learn the lessons of life. He was taught just how big Jesus and the worlds He control are. It is from Scriptures alone that we have the real foundational truths about dying and living. It was to a seeming tragedy that Peter was taken in order to be taught, not to a sunlit landscape. The gold receives its glory in the crucible. It is in pain that great patterns are formed, almost as if the needle point is making the hole for the golden thread to follow and form a pattern of gold. When men want to impress they will show a sunrise, when God wants to do the same, He will take you to a sunset. The world takes you to a wedding, Jesus takes you to a death, for in it there are profound lessons to be learned. The palm leaves of victory are sometimes found on trees which are planted in volcanic ash.

How Jesus sees and describes death

That which is laid low cannot help itself. That which is torn apart is pieced together with one word from Jesus. 'She is not dead but asleep'. That which is really dead is made altogether living. Jesus is seeing death as a cradle—'I will go and rock her and in doing so she will awake'. 'Little girl, get up!' That same voice commanded the worlds into being,[3] and is creating a new life in the world for this little one. Cephas—learn! What person is this! What a message! The dead, the deaf, the dumb, the blind can still hear His voice. Peter, you will see greater things than these if you believe. Another will, a stronger will, is forced upon death. It cannot stand the challenge. For the moment death is not banished but its will is suspended by a greater will. If you close the curtains you suspend the sunlight, but only for a time. If you open them, light which has been suspended floods in. The flowers surrounding the body on the bier are even sweeter smelling than before they were picked as the maid opens her eyes. In this School of Christ the fees are high, the chairs sometimes uncomfortable and, just occasionally, your flesh is made to creep! The lessons are many and long. That which was at the centre of this miracle of the raising of Jairus' daughter must be centred in Peter. Right here is the Academy of Christ. He teaches not from dry and dusty books or a dead theology, He takes real happenings of everyday life as His textbooks. Peter doesn't know what to expect next. Life contains many masters ready to teach him many lessons, but none hold as many as the Life of Jesus Christ. The intention is that Peter will become a star pupil. There are those doubters who think it more likely that a donkey will win a thoroughbred race! It happens in God!

With God we can win

Red Rum, the horse which won the Grand National a number of times, was known as the 'Nag from the Slums'. Successive owners rejected him, and he was eventually found in a field being used as a plough horse. One or two believed in him, commenced training and finally he went on to win one of the most coveted prizes in horse racing, jumping fences to become a great success.

When the maid is loosed from the body, Jesus is there. When she returns to her parents, He is there. The faithfulness of God reaches to the clouds and down to the gates of hell itself. The student is being taught by the Master how to let faith loose. What tremendous possibilities there are in companionship with Jesus. Faith overcomes fear and becomes a reservoir used by God to stand people back on their feet. It was a common occurrence, an every-day thing for a child to die in these parts. To the discerning spirit there are valuable lessons in it all. There is gold in the hills of death for the prospector. There are no distractions when it is Jesus and you! There was nothing else, no other voice, shape or ghostly form to trouble this little one. 'You are with me', literally, you, me, nothing in between. (See Author's book, *Paths of Righteousness in Psalm 23.*)

When Paul wanted Timothy to influence others he asked him to pass on to faithful men,[4] men that could be trusted with the truth. Peter is taking in what he will give out in future days. Just to be in the presence of Christ is an influence. It is as a piece of fruit ripening in the sun.

A lady, hearing a noise at her door, opened it to find a dog with a thorn in its paw. She bathed it in milk, added a little antiseptic and off it went, wagging its tail in thankfulness. A few days later she heard a scratching sound and, opening the door, was amazed to find the same dog, its paw now healed, with a puppy by its side. It too had something wrong with its paw! That which had been received was passed on!

Releasing what He makes us

Mark 5:37 shows that He let no man follow Him, only Peter, James and John. Petrus (Latin) will be made into Peter...James will be made into James, and John will become John. A mould was prepared for them and they would fit it as glove to hand. There were sacred and secret lessons for each of them. As the stream trickles over stones who can tell which way each one is being shaped? The course of the river decides that. These three would not be intermixed or made into the likeness of each other. Jesus never intended to alter what we are in personality. He simply wanted to share His life with Peter and by doing so heighten and set free all that Peter was. Jesus becomes the potential for freeing all that we have and are. He enlarges what the disciples are. He doesn't change the shape of the face, but He does put a smile on that face. He doesn't change the shape of the foot, He simply makes it strong enough to walk further and bear more weight when carrying the messages of the Lord. Sitting at the feet of Jesus we become what we would never have been without Him. We, with Peter, would have remained in seed form forever, like seeds found locked and sealed in the vases from a Pharaoh's tomb, or locked in ice for hundreds of years. Jesus preached to the crowd and said what He had to say as if only one of the crowd mattered. He allowed them to follow, for He knew where He was going and what He was going to do. Much of what had happened earlier was a time of preparation for Simon. He was going to face calamity and death and the son of Jonas could face it all with the Son of God. Jesus did not turn His back on death or calamity and pretend it was not there. We know from Gospel records that, on another occasion during another teaching lesson, when Peter took his eyes off Jesus he lost his radar sense. When looking at other things he began to sink. We can face anything with Jesus Christ. We step in His steps, we go in His going, we follow step by step. Like the troops in the Army these were allowed to take a look at the face of their King before departing for battle.[5]

Receiving and obeying His teaching

There are vital lessons to be learned and principles to be put into practice. This is no mock exercise, it is the real thing. Cephas must look, listen and learn. In His presence in looking we see, in listening we hear, in being taught we learn. There would be people as dead in spirit as this child was in body in Ephesians 2:1. Peter would meet those whose little girl, whose dreams and ambitions, had died early. Their sun had set early in life. Without the intervention of Jesus this youngster would never have reached maturity, and in the world at large the same is true. Mankind without Christ will never grow up. We must, by His power, grow up in Him in all things.[6] Only the influence and the voice of Jesus can do that. His capabilities combine to make a success out of a disaster. Jesus restored a young girl, still greedy for life, yet it was a little more than that, it was the child with Jesus and there was an added quality. She was never where Jesus could not reach her. There is that in every disciple, that is never out of reach of Jesus.

Peter notes that Jesus did not follow the formal and normal custom. All the falsities of life are missing. The man-made and the man-paid were turned out in order for real and sweeter influences to work. The lesson was not in the crowd, the family, the parents, the dead body or even the house, it was in Jesus. It was in the house of loneliness, the house of calamity and disaster that He began His teaching work. Jesus will not only build a construction,[7] a house or a family, but a young life and through it all He will build the faith of Peter from grain of sand to solid rock, from mustard seed to tree. Give Him time! Watch His workings and the timing in this servant's life.

Jesus will often return to add to or take from until His transforming power has gone to every part. The little girl, like Peter, had to be made alive in every part. Jesus made her as she should be, and He wants to make Peter into an Apostle, fully formed.

The lessons of life

There are lessons in life when every other influence must be placed on one side. None of us can walk on water and cross bridges at the same time. One thing at a time and one realm at a time. It is amazing the number of believers who are going to be different— someday! It is Peter and Jesus, Jesus and Peter. The shadow of the one falls gently across the path of the other, metal to metal as friends who sharpen one another by the cut and thrust of their conversation. Sometimes the lesson is in a gentle zephyr, then it is in a howling wind. There are times when we need the Euroclydon in Acts 27:14. Peter is enlarged through a miracle. He must be bigger than his boat, bigger than the sea which has held him in its wet embrace for so long. There was not only a child who needed a resurrection. There were things in Peter which were quite dead, quite oblivious to the Master's voice and they needed bringing back to life. There is always something being bowled and blown over which needs to be stood back onto its feet. Everything rises in the presence of King Jesus. Broken ends need tying, the bruised and the hurt need ointments. We need the soothing of His rich resonant voice. There were moments when we feel like lying down and dying. Let us go and die with her! If presence of mind is needed then it is His presence and His mind!

Peter is being taken down a long road, obtaining strength for the valleys, the hills and the mountains. It is a long way that he treads, for it is called a lifetime. We need to go further in order to go deeper. Like the Cornish Tin Mines, the deeper they went, the richer they were found to be.

Death is devastated by Christ

The funeral party, with Christ, stayed to witness a birth! From a dead corpse a pretty little thing steps forth, as sweet and as neat as any Esther prepared ready for the King's presence. This was the essence of future endeavour. Seeing new forms arise from old shapes, finding rare flowers in the shadowy areas. It wasn't the time element procuring this, it was Jesus who stepped back in time to bring into the present. He updated a life with two words 'Talithi-cumi'. From that bed there stepped something greater than a

Cinderella. This is God's doing! It is the power of God. I am
training you, Peter, for such occasions as this. That which is broken
open and taken over by Jesus reveals some delightful qualities. If
this miracle had been the only one that had taken place it would
have been worth Jesus coming and dying. One Zaccheus, one Paul,
one Peter, yet there are many to follow.

We are never beyond His reach

The voice of Jesus went to the place and sounded where the
daughter was. It went beyond time, beyond season, beyond reason,
travelling through history as the carrier of a message. Tell all who
have died that there is hope! It by passed all known civilisations,
commanding the sentry of death at the door or the dungeon. It
went back, back, back, to bring the maid forward. 'The Master had
come and He calls for you.' A human voice of comfort, setting
everything in tune. Here was the Gospel of Christ before the
Cross…Jesus calling lost sheep from the hills of God. Jesus will go
to the heights of Heaven and to the depths of hell to rescue one. All
had to be sealed and settled by His blood.

In Luke 15:8 where did the silver drachma roll? Where it
went, however far it rolled, it never rolled out of the owner's house.
God owns it all and we never roll out of what belongs to Him. It
rolled to the feet of Jesus. Where she went at death she never went
too far away from Him. Wherever we go, He has gone. Wherever
we land, we land where He is. Whatever our destiny, He is there.
She was called home. She was called by her name. Word went
around Heaven 'Loose her' even as the donkey was loosed outside
of the door.[8] We are always just outside God's door, within His
hearing, reaching, touching, calling.

The Apostle had seen the dead body for himself. All the hard
facts of death were there, pain, misery, tears, grief. Yet Jesus acted
as if these facts were not present at all. He was oblivious as to how
things were! He was like a man coming to a swollen river, knowing
that a boat had been secreted earlier to carry him across. Jesus
didn't say the Last Rites. He did not pray from the devil's manual.
'If it be Thy Will.' Here was one who knew the will of God, who
was that will, lengthened by a rope into death to lift and secure.
There was no reading of the will. What death had pronounced,

Jesus pronounced louder! The greater authority was with the Son of God and not the son of death. The scythe was snatched from the grim reaper. Jesus saw death as a sleep, as a repose, a taking a nap. 'I will go and wake her up.' What an interposition this was for Peter, going and waking people up! That is the definition of the Christian ministry. The morning had dawned, the deep sleep of the night was over, the Light of the World was here. Death had switched the light of life out, but Jesus has light within Himself to lighten every dark corner. We see the new message regarding death springing up with hope eternal. Death may be night, but where Jesus is there is no night. These things became relevant to Peter. There is a house, a room, a corner, that Jesus turns into a stage for one of His greatest productions. There is a space in life where God brings us to reveal special miracles. Peter has to learn how to bring up spiritual children in this way, getting them to hear the voice of Jesus, learning how to see the young raised up and going on into womanhood. Jesus didn't immediately raise the child up into a woman, that took time. Her life was a miracle. He raised her as she was to grow into what she should be. It is a matter of growing into what we should be, not jumping into it.

There are many things entering into Peter's heart. There must be no corner where a part of immaturity lurks or sleeps on a bit of sacking of the old life. Jesus is putting jems into the soul of clay, working, prising death open as an oyster to discover the pearl therein. Peter knows that the voice of Jesus can call, command and touch even departed spirits. They still belong to the One who died for them, proving that He has power over life now and power over life to come. Nothing had destroyed the child's right to be a child. Absent from Heaven Jesus is still the Lord of Heaven, of the Universe. He is the Universal Lord. Here is the answer to 'Thy Kingdom come on earth as it is in Heaven.' That Kingdom takes so many different shapes, multiplications of bread, recovery of sight to the blind and here, life back from the dead. This side of Heaven and the grave as on the other side, Jesus has unlimited power. There are two sides to us, there is only one side to Him—He is it! The battle between life and death had been witnessed and there was only one winner!

Submitting to teaching

God's vessels take a lot of making and launching, particularly when those same vessels are going to be much used, shaken, knocked over and chipped! He makes them little by little, adding this and that from the seasons and scenes of life, taking from the strife and the peace, combining the two. The time will come when Jesus will have departed and schoolroom talk will become the language of the highways and byways. What is learned in the classroom will come out in the playground. That which is told in secret will be shouted from the rooftops, even at Joppa, when Peter went to the top of the house to rest before a meal and received a revelation of the Divine intent.[9] Not all lessons come from a computer or appear on a print-out, they are not all written with a pen dipped in ink. These lessons of life will never be found in a textbook or written on paper. To have knowledge of death and life you have to be one and remain one with Christ in a crisis.

It would have been marvellous if Jesus had gone to some Terracotta Army and raised them to life, or even if he had made every tree blossom in winter, yet it would never have been as marvellous as what He did do. There was a reason for every miracle. He did more than all the natural things He ever accomplished when raising life from the dead. He brought a lifeless form, a little parcel of humanity from which the string had broken, back to the place where it belonged. This child represented the whole of humanity brought back to the side of Jesus Christ, in fellowship in the same house with Him. Jesus deposited life in this chunk of love. Loveliness and happiness were blended together. Peter gazes admiringly at so great a happening, a masterpiece. That little house, the small congregation, became a Bible School, seated around the heart of Love.

The privileged scholar

There are privileged experiences that God will not give to everyone. Peter was pondering these things, turning them over and over in his heart, a sort of churning the milk into butter. Sometimes there is the death of a loved one, or one is called to minister to a malformed child. Bad news is received. That which we thought should never be, is, yet we rarely think of it as God trusting us with something that others cannot be trusted with. Where were the other disciples? Why weren't they trusted with these miraculous happenings? The answer is that they were not yet ready for such teachings, they had not been brought to the yieldedness that was necessary in order to witness such rarities. They were not all ready to receive. There are different stages of grace. When everything is ready, Jesus begins to work. Jesus was able to successfully take Peter through the music and the mourning, the darkness of death, and show him a Light.

I must confess my admiration for those who raise children who are deformed. The grace of God flows through such families.

One man in despair cried out, 'I wish I had never been made!' A gentle voice came back through the anguish saying, 'You aren't, yet!'

The disciples needed an incentive. That word is from the Latin 'incetivus' meaning 'setting the tune'. We can all be in tune if Jesus sets it. Through Him we have an incentive here, now and in the future. When Jesus sets the tune we can praise the Lord at all times, His praise is continually in my mouth. Peter is learning the songs of sorrow, seeing them turned into joy. The lament becomes the lilt of life. Jesus plays, we dance and we sing. The baton, the plucking of the strings and the beating of the drum is for our blessing.

The journey to where Jairus lived was a long one. Miracles happened on the way. Jesus was delayed a number of times yet He came at the right time. The fire and the iron are never cold when God strikes. Peter stayed with Him all the way. Think of what he would have missed if he had fallen by the way. That proved his faithfulness. In this story, Jesus proved His faithfulness to a family. Jesus wanted Peter to understand that there is no need to lack miracles in faithfulness. Faith and faithfulness can go together. There is power and resurrection. The unexpected, the unarranged, does take place. A light does surprise the Christian as he travels along the way. That which has been dropped and broken can be brought together again by Jesus. Into the vacant lot there are things to sow. Even before her parents had had time to fold away her clothes she reappeared! Before the next scene was prepared she was ready, dressed for it by the hand of God. Death may seem to blow the candle out in a wild wind, but it is the hand of Jesus which holds that candle. Where does the flame go when it is blown out? Jesus knows! Jesus is able to keep it burning whilst it is away from its source of light.

There is another side to every problem and difficulty. Jesus is on every side! He is at every side!

The Sovereign Lord

The sovereign coin used long ago was minted in the realm of King Henry VIII. As the Royal Monarch he appeared on it in full Kingly dress. It became known as the Sovereign. Jesus in every realm must appear as He is—the Lord of all glory, the Master of every matter. He must appear as Sovereign in the fullness of His power in the midst of the diversities of life and as in life, so in death.

We must learn with this small throng that nothing stops the march of the triumph of the Son of God. The family did not understand why this had happened to the maiden. Peter was to witness what Christ did and does in every cliff-edge drama. He was as cool as the proverbial cucumber, even in the face of death itself. It is seen how He restores smiles and joy. We can only discover a Christ for the crisis when we are in a crisis. The presence of Jesus must be unfolded before us, His likeness seen in everything, even as this child's likeness was seen in the face of her mother. Let what and who He is unfold before us like the telling of a good story. There are things which even tremendous miracles never taught Peter. The Children of Israel saw all the miracles of God and yet many of them perished through unbelief in the Wilderness.[10] It is to the discerning eye that appearances are made of the presence of Christ and are interpreted in love. Bread multiplied might fill hungry stomachs but there are longings lodged in the cavities of the heart, yearnings within that are only met in Jesus. What this girl required was in Jesus. We learn at His feet that the common people need a common Christ. Peter was not being taught miracles. You can believe for them but you cannot teach them. They are a sovereign act of a Sovereign Lord. Miracles cannot be taught, but they can be witnessed! There are times when we do not write down what God is teaching us. We are like the lizard and the jurors in *Alice in Wonderland*, writing down their names with squeaky pencils. Alice removed the lizard's pencil and he continued to write with his fingers, yet left 'no mark on the slate'. The only time he did make a mark was when the queen threw an inkpot at him and he used that ink, trickling down his face, to write with for as long as the ink lasted.[11] We can have squeaky pencils, when what we need is real ink and real pens to mark down in our lives all the wonders of His work. There is part of us, as ink from our own inkpot, that we need to write with. Like Petrus, taking from the situation and writing in our own hearts. The black charcoal of death may glow again with Jesus blowing on it. There are potential fiery things in all situations.

Learning obedience in surrender

We have to learn to surrender to Christ, to let Him be in the situation with us, recognising it, recording it, and rejoicing in it. Peter is seeing everything through the eyes of the Master, as if looking through the window of Heaven and seeing it established in this home. It is the turning of a house into a home. Every time he looks, it is to see the handiwork of Jesus, not in a blazing sphere, but in a darling heart. Jesus, larger than time, bigger, stronger, larger than death. He doesn't place flowers on gravestones or coffins, He places His memorials in the hearts of those in the most need. Nothing can fully sleep when He is awake. Nothing wilts, dies or is lost in the presence of Jesus.

We must join Petrus' Parade, his School of Theology, learned over a death bed. When that happens we are listening and hearing. People listen more intently when the stench of death is ready to be released. It tells how to make ordinary folk happy with the Resurrection and the Life. As God brought Eve to Adam, so Jesus brought this maid to Peter to be cared for and helped. That new life needed helping and developing. Blessed is the Christ who raises from the dead and leaves us clothed and in our right minds sitting between Jesus and the potential Apostle.

In modern teaching methods there are remedial classes. A small number, sometimes just one, is taken out and is given special teaching to help with their learning difficulties. Weak points are made strong, and strong points even stronger. Jesus is doing this with Peter. The little bits of grit have to be removed from the clay to give it a smooth texture. As it happens, he must not let life run him ragged. Don't let your life become the rag doll in the dog's mouth, chewed furiously and thrown from side to side. There is a better way, a new way, a more sure way in Jesus.

What God is seeking in teaching

When, like these three, we come to a crisis, stop and ask, What is God trying to teach me? What is the essence of this unfavourable happening? Is this God, trying to reach out and touch me as He did this little lamb and as He did with Cephas?

They went to where the child was.[12] Through a door, along a passageway, to see a little mound on the floor which had been a living child. If Peter could have raised the child, if James or John could have, they would have done. Shall we attribute less love, grace and mercy to Jesus Christ? He did what He could and that meant resurrection and reinstatement.

What happened is illustrated in the story of the life cycle of the Dragon Fly. It commences its life as larvae in the mud. It is so umpromising as the filthy waters sweep along, passing over it again and again. Yet, as time passes, through the nature it has received, it commences its journey from that house of mud, that black prison, up through the waters as if lifted by a fluid hand towards the sunshine and ultimately appears as the Dragon Fly, filled with a multiplicity of colour, developed and received whilst in the mud! It commences life like a coal miner and emerges as the Coal Queen among the fly family! Beggar, dunghill, prince.[13]

The new life illustrated

The girl was set on a new walk which commenced with Jesus. She began to walk around Jesus, taking steps she had never taken before. She walked all around Him, this fashion model of Heaven. Here was teaching. How to live and display your new God-granted life in the home! The little one may have worn many dresses before, but none like this new life given by her Saviour. Had she ever had a change of dress like this one!

Was Peter asleep again, as he was wont to be when Jesus was doing exciting things? Was this but a dream? If it was, it had come true before his eyes. He had a vivid imagination, but not this vivid!

Was the child sleep-walking? Was it another dream or vision as at Joppa?[14] It was worth being there to see the smile return, the voice heard, the movement activated. As they cried—for I am sure these hardy fishermen would have cried—each tear would hold the image of that little girl walking.

Training for reigning

What God did with Moses, and Moses did with Joshua; what Elijah did with Elisha in training, so Jesus was doing with Peter, preparing him so that when He had returned to His Father, Peter might stand as a rock and that these miracles might continue. Jesus is building a man, and a Kingdom of which that man is a part. The warriors of God are not the worriers of the way. Peter must never be half finished business. Jesus is building not in bricks but in people. He wants to get the soul moving even as this little maid moved. He is not training Simon in the works of this world but in the wonders of my God and King. The artist will take the pupil along day after day for training but he longs for the day when the pupil can go it alone and do it alone!

There are so many times when we let the mountain speak to us instead of us speaking to the mountain.[15] We must learn to command situations and not let situations command us. We can say to this mountain, Be cast into the sea. Have we enough faith to say to this sea, Be you cast into the mountain? Let the sea go to the mountain and appear on it as some giant tear on the cheek. Learn to make mountains cry. Hurt them! If we haven't the faith to move mountains, let us at least have the strength to climb them!

In all the happenings of life, look for the evidence of His smiling face. His smiling face is Heaven. Listen beyond normal listening, hear beyond normal hearing, see beyond normal seeing. Jesus Christ re-arranging everything as it should be, bringing all things back from the dead, back to original colour and contour, tokens of Resurrection life, that which makes Peter's spirit, and ours, dance in the joy of the Lord.

That voice of His will come as a hind over the mountains, skipping. At other times it will sound as a trumpet. There will be a crispness about it as a musical mountain brook. When you see youth and zeal restored, when lifeless forms arise in new shape, fit and ready to enter the race of life, then you have heard, learned and understood as the son of Jonah did.

What will the next happening bring? Who will be the next to call out to Jesus for help? Help may be needed in many areas and it will arrive from many quarters, all centred in this Man with a Mission. One day with lepers and sinners, a night with Nicodemus, the tax gatherer another day. There is a multiplicity of needs and they are all met in this Source as if plunged into a stream for cleansing.

A Missionary was moved when a native wrote a poem consisting of two words and he asked him to read it. He knew that the Missionary had been discouraged, the work was difficult with few rewards. The native wrote the poem as an encouragement. It read, 'Go on, go on, go on, go on, go on, go on, go on, go on...' and so it continued.

The teaching opens wider as we progress. If Peter had stopped at the Beatitudes, in Matthew Chapter 5, then what wondrous things he would have missed! There need not be anything missing, all will be there as we stay with Jesus.

Notes

1 Matthew 28:18
2 John 11:25
3 Colossians 1:16
4 2 Timothy 2:2
5 2 Samuel 18:4
6 Ephesians 4:15; 1 Peter 2:2; 2 Peter 3:18
7 Matthew 16:18
8 Mark 11:2–4
9 Acts 10:9
10 Hebrews 3:19; 4:6,11
11 Carrol, L., *Alice in Wonderland*, pp 91, 92 (Wordworth)
12 Mark 5:40
13 1 Samuel 2:8
14 Acts 11:5
15 Mark 11:23

8

Who Is Jesus Christ?

No one is able to walk for any length of time in the shadow of Jesus Christ without discovering new depths, without a realisation as to His purposes. The revelations of God are as gold. They do not come in a crowd or immediately, but little by little, and are like the path of the just which is as a light, shining brighter and brighter until the perfect day. As we go on with God, and in Peter's shoes, it seems as if He is switching off the earthly lights in order that Heavenly lights might shine the more brightly so that we may see Heavenly things more clearly, not the lights of sense and knowledge but the convictions and revelations of new life. That which is discerned with the natural eye is superceded by the spiritual. To Peter, the knowledge received from God as to whom Jesus Christ really is, was profound. There had been a silence. There had been no open vision between the Old and the New Testaments for nearly 400 years, now here is God stepping into the darkness as a Flaming Light. What God reveals is beyond all depth, all reach. It is deeper and wider than any sea on which Cephas may have sailed. This is the measurement of Heaven, as long as it is broad, as wide as it is deep.

Jesus rarely appears in full glory. He comes like nature itself, little by little, season by season, year in, year out, a little here, a little there, sometimes at a snail's pace, until we, in our finite minds are able to understand what the Divine Scribe is bringing from His

Treasury. Such revelation becomes larger until it grows from a spark into a dazzle until, as Philip, we know who He is and that is sufficient, it satisfies the longing soul. There is initial enlightenment for Peter, a blinding flash, in a moment, like Paul on the Damascus Road, then a constant adding to what has been revealed.

Revelation is by degrees

When Jesus takes hold of any life He becomes the door and all other dimensions are built around him. Windows, walls, rooms, stairs and floors are all added. Jesus is the Man who went to build a tower and was able to finish it.[1] What Jesus is can be revealed, almost like saving pennies in the piggy bank until the box is full, like Moses who died full of years. Anything in nature worth having is given and received little by little. One burst of the sun from behind the clouds is not the total sun, and the revelation that Peter had of Jesus in Matthew 16:16 was not all that Jesus was, it was but the flash which shows for a moment where we are. When using a camera just enough of the light is admitted to take the image and plant it on film.

When the Romans were about to attack a village they would send flaming arrows into the centre house of that village which, as it became illuminated, would cast a great light, sufficient for them to see where to send other arrows and enough light for troops to see clearly what was happening.

The title of this chapter could well have been 'Orientation'. The Old Mariner is at sea. He has sailed long and it is a cloudy night. He looks anxiously at the Heavens. Then the clouds part for a moment, the moon shines and the star he is looking for is glimpsed. He takes a reading, adds it to his chart and knows where he is! He is re-orientated, back on course! Peter so far has seen through a glass darkly but now that 'darkly' is taken away and he sees clearly who Jesus Christ is. There are flickers of light before the dawn, a comparative fullness when Peter says, 'You are the Christ, the Son of the Living God'. God is found! The Son is found! Messiah is reigning!

The first glimpse can be as some blinding light (Acts 26:13), the question still asked, 'Who are You, Lord?' It can come as a quiet light as it came to Peter. Ever after this his prayer was the same, 'Don't teach me to remember, but teach me not to forget.' May our prayers be but an echo of Peter's. He wanted to live in the glow of that light, the memory of it needed to live on throughout life.

Christ's charter is character building

Jesus must always be the Carpenter with His bag of tools. There were times when He made something from wood which could operate in the way and in the realm for which it was created. The same happened to Peter. The wheel received its essential spokes, the shaft fitted perfectly into the joint and it is now ready to plough and to pull.

A man was in prison because he loved Jesus Christ. The prison was small, without window or means of light, so small that it seemed to be like a metal waistcoat to the prisoner. He had with him his Bible and the only time he could read was when the meagre supply of food was passed to him through a little hole in the door. The light came in for a moment. His Bible was open and, as the food was unceremoniously pushed through the hole in the door, he read the words which kept him sane.

Jesus had begun to catechize the disciples. The rigours of discipleship were being placed upon them.[2] He did it with a question, a question that provided the answer. Many times the questions of God contain the answers for Peter. Whom do men say that I am? found a ready response in Peter. He is already becoming the spokesman. Questions can be answered, correct answers given and wrong answers rectified. The cover is taken off the masterpiece, the spotlight centres on the heart of Jesus.

When Sir Christopher Wren began his renovation of Saint Paul's Cathedral for much of the time it was kept under wraps. From the outside no-one could see the magnificent building under the coverings. Yet the day came when the workings of men were revealed in that Cathedral.

All questions are answered in Christ's knowledge

Anyone who answers questions must be prepared, as Peter was, for further comment and enlightenment. Jesus must fill that flash of light with something more. A dawn must have a whole earth and sea with valleys and rivers. The substance of Peter's revelation did not come from history or geography, there was no 'what meaneth this?' In clarity of eloquence Peter makes his profound statement. Peter was challenged by Jesus in the depths of his heart and this statement surfaced. Christ was leading Peter to a place of fresh insight all the time. Caesarea Philippi, which was so rich in historical happenings was as good a place to commence as any. Twenty-five miles or so from the Sea of Galilee it was filled with idols and idol-worship. Here Pan, the god of nature, was supposed to have been born. The legends of the gods of Greece were woven around this area. The Historian, Josephus, tells us it was purported to be the source of the Jordan. Here was Caesar's white marble Temple of worship. As the sun cast its reflection it cast a thousand spears into the air. It was appropriate that God's shining should be revealed to Peter at this place—known as Caesar's town.

The Son of God has a way of placing things in the heart. A Rabbi was asked by a pupil who had read Deuteronomy 6:6...'And these words which I command thee this day shall be upon thy heart' the question, 'Why aren't we told to place them in our hearts?' The answer was, 'It is not within our power to place Divine teachings directly into our hearts. All we can do is place them on the surface, so that when the heart is broken then they can fall into that heart.'

From this time on Peter would be under attack and if the candle could be blown out it would be. Some winds can blow out a candle and the next wind can blow into the eye of the little amber glow and it springs back to life and to light. There is a picture 'Watching Unto' among the pictures of St Gudule. Hope is seen carrying a lantern through a dark wood and the trees are hiding evil spirits which blow the light out. When this happens she prays 'Lord, help.' Straight away a warm breath from above rekindles the flame and she can safely see her way through the wood and the trees.

A personal revelation

Jesus was always trying to brighten that initial light. When the lightning struck the fire fell, there was the opening up of a life to the sacrifice of discipleship. The dark areas, the unknown and the doubtful flooded with light. To know who Jesus is is worth a lot of light. The Celestial Choirs broke into song in Peter's soul as the light penetrated on that day. Line upon line of angels sang the Hallelujah Chorus! This was better than a calm sea and a full boat of fish! What the shepherds heard at the Nativity of Christ, Peter hears at this moment. The light of Heaven had come down to earth, an arrow of light had penetrated a soul, uniting it to light forever, as if a child born deaf and mute had suddenly uttered its first words. 'You are the Christ'. The infant of grace utters gracious words. The child of light utters illumined words. The Son of God recognises the Source of Peter's light and Jesus would interpret what that light meant. It is only the beginning for this brother of Andrew. He must accept the challenge. The light of Heaven turns his gaze, as any real unveiling will, to look and to speak out for Jesus Christ. That light is a Holy glow in his soul. In which direction will it take him? Where will it lead? What situations will it bring him through? It was enough at that moment to discover the presence of Jesus Christ. The future must stay with the future, even as the past must stay with the past. The light was not put into Peter's soul to illuminate the past or the future, it was for the present. It was not a continual speculation but a forthright declaration. What had been Greek and an enigma, was expressed in an Aramaic way by Peter.

The Source of all revelation

This revelation, which came from the same Source as the revelation received by Moses, the writer of the Pentateuch, contained the creation of the world. Later that same inspiration revealed the design of the Tabernacle with all its furnishings and outer court.[3] Job was able to recount the creation of the world without having been there. He describes the circuit of the earth,[4] the fact that the world hangs on nothing, suspended.[5] John received the whole Book of Revelation through the Spirit of God. The many-sided God has many ways of revealing His nature to us. At Caesarea Philippi this was a new creation, a new world, a fresh start for mankind. Here was the gap in the forest of trees for Peter. There was light at the end of the tunnel.

What made this statement of Peter's important was the fact that nobody believed in Jesus, but he did. It was commitment in words, the placing of the soldier's hand on the Bible swearing to be true to God and country; the hand on the Word of God as in a witness box swearing to tell the truth, the whole truth, and nothing but the truth, so help me God. In turn, when Peter counted for little in the eyes of the people then Jesus remembered and believed in him.[6] It was as if a very private person, a peasant in many ways, had recognised royalty. When a woman realised that Queen Victoria had visited her incognito, she swore no-one would ever again sit in the chair that the Queen had used during that clandestine visit. The same is to be said of Peter's heart, bathed in Heaven's light, helping to heal earth's hurts. He was saluting his Master. The Coronation of Christ was for this disciple and the throne was his heart. It was the crowning of Christ with human adoration, an act of worship.

Jesus is more than just a teacher

There will always be those who see Jesus as just a teacher sitting on the edge of a well. They will only ever see Him in the pages of the New Testament or among a crowd. They never see Him or know Him as He really is, seated by God in the Holy hill of Zion and therefore they never worship Him as they should.

Peter was not John Baptist: 'Are you Him or do we look for another?' One look at Jesus as the Lamb of God and we forget what others look like. 'Since my eyes were fixed on Jesus, I've lost sight of all besides. So enchained my spirit's vision, looking at the crucified.' The heart has to be broken into small pieces, placed in the hand of Christ for Him to piece it together again. The best way for you to receive Divine Light is to put out your own light. Peter had to. Simon is as the child counting pebbles which turn suddenly into diamonds. The number of them has been the same all along but suddenly they add up and make sense. Formed as a pattern in the heart, lodging in the soul as honey in the honeycomb, what Prophet, Priest and Potentate have longed for, diligently 'searched' for. In 1 Peter 1:10 searched diligently means to trace by minute investigation, a gentle diligence which leads to a satisfactory result and confirmation. The word searched suggests dogs as they track game, spies surveying a country, a cold trail rediscovered. It can also describe a lion tracking its quarry. It is the addition to the 'We have found', of John 1:41. It is now Cephas discovering for himself.

It was a like experience in John 21:7 'It is the Lord!' The Emmaus Road is here. Eyes were opened, recognition came. There are certain Churches where, at a particular time and if the window is so placed, that the sun shines through and rests on the altar forming a Cross of light for all to see.

Jesus is more than just a man

There are always those who will see Jesus Christ as another man, another form, different to that revealed in the Scriptures, one who is forged in feeling and produced by mere speculation. The blurred became focussed as Peter made his willing declaration of faith. It was faith with trumpets blowing, faith with the sound of the mighty rushing wind. There had to be a moving on for Cephas, as for all who follow Christ, from one sphere and one realisation to another. Jesus must not simply remain in a boat, out of touch, only reached by strong swimmers, He must be the Christ, the Son of God. The word 'Son' makes Him very human, the humanity of a servant.

Notice the contrast between the revelation received and the religious person.

Paul: Who are you?

Nicodemus: How can these things be?

Nathaniel: How do you know me?

Peter: You are the Christ, the Son of the Living God.

There is no doubt in these words of Peter's. If only there was less doubt about the meaning of the latter part of the statement: 'Upon this rock I will build My Church'. The religious zealots have doubts whilst Peter has the whole of Heaven gathering around him. The words Peter uttered would be severely tested, that mouth from whence they came would be dry and parched in tremendous suffering. They are words of conviction, as real as the sparks flying from steel being moulded. They were not just spoken, they were born out of an actual observation entering into the heart, and were a power which turns the wheel, moves the heart, makes the tongue speak, the lips quiver. The light received will be used to brighten the way, to reveal the nature of every happening and become the bench mark. It will be the acid test of every other statement for time and eternity. Once a man is convinced, then he has convictions, a cutting edge, there is no stopping him. As Elijah receives the meal and is touched by the angel, he goes on in the strength of it for many days.[7]

Jesus is more than a prophet

Jesus is compared with men with a mission (exciting men)— Elijah, Jeremiah, John the Baptist—yet none of these men had illuminated other men. They had a message, but Jesus was THE Message. He was not part of the truth, He was the whole Truth. The writer to the Hebrews uses this argument in Chapter 2:2–5. Moses helped to build the house, Jesus was over the house. He builds all things. He is not part of the revelation to Peter, He is the revelation itself, nothing more, nothing less and nothing in between. These other men were glorious but their glory faded. Peter realised that they lived and died and their work died with them. Jesus lives after the power of an endless life.

Jesus is more than John Baptist

Some saw Him as John Baptist, as a warning to flee from the wrath to come. They had seen His ministry as the axe to the tree roots. What about the transplanting, the new growth, the shoots, fruit and leaves? A ministry of a different order than that of John is needed when the old trees have been chopped.

Jesus is more than Elijah

There were those who saw Elijah in Jesus, bringing Israel back to repentance, a rescuer of a nation. Yet, after being brought to repentance, there has to be another ministry to take even further. That ministry was found in Jesus Christ. He is something more than all these, as Peter witnessed. You can always relegate Jesus by taking His crown from Him, making Him like other men, other prophets, but He is the God of the prophet.[8] The outshining of the splendour of God. The express 'image' of His person. It is from the Greek word 'image' that we obtain our English word 'character', the character of God's Being, the stamp which made the image and the image itself.

Jesus is more than Jeremiah

Jeremiah was a prophet of pain, a man who swam in his own tears, a gentle, sensitive man who was hurt by the people around him. Crying, complaining about the sins of the people, but unable to deal with them effectually in forgiveness. Jesus must be more than the suffering servant, He must be as He is sketched in Philippians 2, the glorified servant exalted far above all. Jesus is more than the historical prophet. The words of Peter are 'You are the Christ', standing right before his eyes. History has become News in Jesus! He is the Almighty who 'is, was, and is to come'. 'I am He that lives. I was dead but I am alive for evermore' (Revelation 1:18; 2:8). The question like a circling bird or a fluttering leaf in the wind must come to nest or rest... 'What do you say of Christ? What do you say of yourself?'

Jesus must be heard and declared

It can bring glory to God when other lips tell what He has always known and declared His Son to be. This statement sorted out the stones from the rocks. Leadership was witnessed. Blessed are you Simon Peter. Peter said, 'You are the Christ'. Jesus said, 'You are Simon and you will become Peter.' What we know of Him makes what we say of Him important. Relationship with Jesus will always be revealed in declaration. What we say, born of experience, makes us worth listening to. That revelation is full of revival, full of new and interesting things. As Peter speaks, all Heaven is hushed. He must be the Christ beyond all reasonable doubt. Only Peter seemed to sparkle when asked this question. Demons and devils could answer it better than men,[9] they knew He wasn't a prophet. To Peter, Jesus means God to the rescue. Of all the things which ever entered Peter's mind this sticks fast until it affects his heart. The crowning of Christ meant the crushing of other influences. It meant the sinking of ships, the swimming away of fish, the casting of nets never to be taken up again.

The source of inspiration and revelation

There was a source from which the insight sprang. It wasn't the light of taper, candlestick, lantern or modern bulb. The New English Bible translation states: 'Man, flesh and blood has not revealed this unto you.' It hasn't simply got to be 'unto' Peter, but 'into' him. A man who has light within is better equipped than the person who has light outside. Great sayings and statements of faith begin with Christ and end with God. If that is so, it means they are open ended. Much of His life and enrichment can be added from all directions. It placed Jesus at the side and in the same sentence as God. God, the source of all knowledge gives knowledge of His Son to whom He chooses. A God of light creates light and stands His Son in it for all to see. There was no communication from Jerusalem. Pharisee and Saduccee had nothing to say. The Sanhedrin never made such pronouncements, they were as camels trying to get through the eye of the needle. As Physicians they were too busy healing themselves. Not being prophets they did receive honour from their own people.

The lamp of revelation had been extinguished for so many years, and year added to year had multiplied the darkness and dimmed the wick of hope until there was not even a flicker. Suddenly there is a burst of light! No man can call Jesus Lord but by the Holy Ghost. What was lit in Peter's heart was lit by God. There was no dark corner, no word which did not cover the Mission of Christ. Many times in the future Peter's mind would be stirred by memory. He would think back to this time. When in darkness or doubt he would take light from this and illuminate that darkness with such a light that nothing could put it out. When he fell flat on his face this memory would stand him on his feet again. When he fell backwards this would throw him forwards and onwards. Weak knees and hands which hung down would be strengthened. There was no place for defeat in what was said and recorded. It was such a depth of conviction that temptation could not wash it out or off, or overboard. It is written in the rock with a pen of iron. It was not a lesson received and soon forgotten. These sorts of deep longings are met with deep responses from God. Jesus stands as the Lightning Conductor. The unveilings from the heart of God lead us nearer to His heart. He that is sent from the heart of God will offer a full explanation. Like Peter you must get to know whom Jesus is for yourself, then on that rock you can build. Noah's Ark had a first plank of wood, and there must have been a primary in the making and creating of the Tabernacle. I wonder what the fundamental piece of rope looked like in David's sling? When you think like this and speak like this you have a whole reservoir of truth at your disposal. In a changing world you need a world-changing Apostle, ready and clad for war. There were stirrings, the same movings that Samson felt when the Spirit of God began to move him in the camp at Dan when echoes of Heaven bounced onto the earth.

Obtaining a revelation

Some have never been to the Source of the manifestation. They have never had it placed in its rightful place in their lives. They are the proverbial man who lights the light and puts it under a bushel. It does not give light to all in the house. When Peter made his statement then everything else made sense. The expectancy of truth was raised to a new height. He had often heard the debate as to whom Jesus was. The man who made this discovery had no need to read or write it. He said it! It is the Father's insight to a son about a Son. It is the inner circle increased to include those outside. His head and heart were turned in the right direction, the direction of the Lord. Anything which heightens Jesus Christ in the life and living is from God. We must receive light to walk in the light. We must have light to produce the fruits of light. He has come from a burning bush, from Sinai, to the final act on the Cross. This is a step towards that. The days were short.

Blessed, happy, spiritually prosperous and enlarged are you, Simon, son of Jonah. It is a new and a real discovery of the person sent by God. The man stepping out becomes as blessed as the man in Psalm 1... 'Blessed is the man who walks...'

When Jesus pronounced the Beatitudes, Luke says, He sat on the mountainside and the disciples came to Him. True blessings come as we come to Christ, beating a path to His heart along which the light shines. The conviction runs so deep. He never formed His own denomination, although there were those who would have done so in His Name.[10] This revelation did not cause a splinter.

The very essence of it was union with God and then with one another. It is full of the kisses of God.

The enormity of Jesus

One man painted a picture of the Messiah and the great painter Raphael visited his studio. He took one look at the painting and simply wrote one word underneath—BIGGER!

The unveiling of the Messiah must be done in such a way that Jesus walks before all the world every day in every believer. Yet Peter could never receive or see Jesus bigger than He was. He might grow in us but He inhabits all things. He inhabits eternity. We must give our time and let Him fill it with His eternity. Jesus never came to cramp a style or a personality. He came to give it wings that it might fly into other areas. The boat would have remained moored forever in some little inlet or some far off island, yet Jesus set Peter free to become Peter in every way and dimension. He came to give new goals. It was but a statement that Peter made, but it became a way of life. It took one close to Jesus to interpret Jesus Himself. There were many more things to be added to this doctrine. Do not be happy with one revelation, there are more on the way! The man sees things differently from the child. There is a blessedness in naming Christ within the scope of your living. That which is granted by God as some precious gift is rather like those which are opened to find another gift inside each one. There are many gifts. Only one is received at any one time and that one has to be enlarged before another is revealed. Joshua must blow the trumpet before the sword is placed in his hand, even as Moses must use the rod before the sea parts and its waters roll up as a blanket. Burning bush is added to the burning Mount Sinai, and even that is lost in the presence of God as revealed to Moses in the cleft of the rock. It says in 2 Kings 9:13, 'They crowned the King on the bare steps.' This is what was happening here. His weapons, officers, soldiers would be different from the world's concept of the military. His Kingdom was not of this world, it was from above. Expect then its demands to be higher. He is different, His hallmark will be Holiness.

God revealed in a moment, in the twinkling of an eye, what others searched for. 'Searched intently with great care' (1 Peter

1:10).[11] As somebody uncovering a vessel to see what it contains. Searching begins with the Wise Men who searched for the young Child, but it ends with the same Man Child, Christ Jesus.

What the Rabbinical Schools, the Doctors of Law, the Interpreters of the Law with their 300 explanations of some words, what the Professors and Schools of Wisdom of this world failed to grasp, Peter received. The world in its wisdom knew not God's Christ, but the unschooled knew Him. One caters for the head, while the other meets the needs of the heart. Men may know of Jesus Christ through doctrinal theories set down in books, but God's way is the best way. It has no second-hand thing bouncing off the clouds as it came to Peter. Fresh from Heaven it was fresh to his heart and it freshened his heart.

Peter does not say it all or know it all. There is nothing full or final in what he has to say. It is but a starting point. A new dispensation of revelation has come. Peter is opening the door and the space beyond is large enough to receive the world.

Notes

[1] Luke 14:28
[2] Matthew 16:16–18; Mark 8:27–30
[3] Exodus 25:9
[4] Job 22:14
[5] Job 26:7
[6] Mark 16:7
[7] 1 Kings 19:8
[8] Hebrews 1:1–3
[9] Mark 1:24
[10] 1 Corinthians 1:12
[11] NIV

9

How To Build
a Growing Church

The simple words of Jesus in Matthew 16:18 and more importantly what He meant by them, have become a battlefield from which many have staggered wounded, bleeding and dying, separated from friends, thrust through and hurt by misinterpretation of the Scriptures. The Church has certainly scored a home goal, has shot itself in the foot right here among these words! Jesus brought a sword which has cut and pierced many a believer into submission. It was not meant to be a cutting weapon of war at all, simply a measuring rod. The debate has raged over the years as to what He really meant, on whom was He to build the Church? Was Peter the first Pope? These verses have become a very stormy sea for Theologians and Christians of all denominations. Catholic and Protestant, East and West diverge at this point.

To Peter, the imitator of Christ, these words were a challenge, a comfort and a voice for change. It was the new order of another dispensation of Church building. The called out of God were to be called in. Jesus was making statements and men would live and die for them. These were the words of the Master builder before He commenced His project. Do we know what Jesus really meant? We can only offer the Scriptures and our ideas on how we think Peter would have understood what was said. Ours can only be an echo of his, catching faintly what was said, let alone known and understood. We do know that this Church Building Programme came out of a manifestation from the Father as to whom Jesus Christ was. Jesus said, 'I must be about My Father's business' (Luke 2:49).

In the days of yore a gold claim was sometimes made on the basis of one speck of gold dust. That dust, that one small glittering piece was enough to convince that there was more, and the land on which it was found, be it desolate and barren, was worth registering. A Certificate of Registration granted mining rights.

In the mind and eyes of Jesus, Peter was as that gold. In an area notorious for idolatry and false worship, Jesus saw something in Peter which sparkled, and He registered His claim to the life of Cephas. 'Can any good thing come out of Nazareth?' was asked, and the answer was provided in people like this one following the Lord. The twelve came from those parts, and so did Jesus. Jesus had to build them together and make a Church. He began with Simon, a fisherman, a sea-driven man of the open waters who was to become part of the Eternal plan now being executed by the Lord of Eternity. That foundation before the world was and is now being brought into time and a Church was to be established.

Interpretations are many, truth is one

There are a number of suggestions as to what Jesus meant by the words 'Upon this rock I will build My Church' (Matthew 16:18). One thing is sure, Jesus was going to build His Church and Peter was going to be part of it. He was, he moves on in Acts 12, then reappears as a pillar in the New Jerusalem, and a foundation stone.[1]

The Roman Catholic Church will tell you that Peter was being installed as the first Pope. All Popes from that day follow an apostolic line of succession. The foundation had been laid for the Roman Catholic Church.

The Protestant Church takes a completely different line of argument. They stand in a different light and see a different meaning to the words. It was not only upon Peter but upon the twelve and upon all who believe and have a revelation of Jesus Christ that Jesus will build. It is Jesus Who is the Rock and not Peter. Peter died. Jesus the Rock, the Foundation, lives on, a solid rock foundation of His Church.

There are those who state that when Christ said, 'Upon this rock' He was referring to Himself. The Greek word Petrus means a mass, a large rock. 'You are Peter', the Greek Peter, means a small rock, a small piece of rock. Upon the mass rock, the larger rock, I will build My Church. It is only Jesus who is able to sustain the Church and hold it together by the might of His power. Only Jesus is large enough and powerful enough to hold it at the four corners, from above and below and from the inside. You, Peter, along with all who have a manifestation in their hearts, as in John 3:8 I will use as part of that Church. Whether something small or large, significant or insignificant, I will use it in building. This will be no Babel. You will be built on the foundation of the Lamb, finding your place alongside others in Christ. Upon Jesus the large Rock and the solid Foundation the Church was to be built. Every believer becomes a stone which is built in and on Jesus Christ, the Chief Corner Stone. Peter in his Epistle lays the foundation stone as he sees and understands it.

There is a definite play on words in Matthew 16:18. Peter is called the little rock and Jesus is called the larger Rock. To be identified as the same rock nature as Jesus! The one who was all sand and sea is suddenly defined as a rock. Greek, Peter, little rock; Aramaic, Cephas, little rock.

When an Israelite wanted to claim his Lot in the Promised Land he took a stone from that land to the Authorities, registered the fact that he had been there, and laid claim to it. This was happening with Jesus and Peter. Abraham and Moses were referred to as rocks by those writing of them.

Peter's place in the Church

There is another thought that Peter would be the first rock and others would follow. Jesus had to start somewhere and what better place than right where He was? The words weren't 'I will build My Church on any old rock'. There was a need for Peter, as with any believer, to have rock-like devotion and rock-like dedication to the cause of Christ. He was to be part of that builded together for an habitation of God, through the Holy Spirit.[2]

We must never go to the extreme of denigrating Peter because of what others have said and done. Peter and Mary both have their rightful place in the Church, blessed among men but not above them. Mark, who received many of his facts from Mary, hardly mentions her at all. No one else could take the place of these two, even as no one else could take your place in the Church of Jesus Christ. You are what you are, to be what you must be. No other can take your place in the Church.

Peter was not given the headship of the Church. If anything he was allocated the bottom rung of the ladder. The foundation stone is at the bottom, not the top! The Corner Stone may be at the top, but the foundations are buried. Indeed, with Master Wesley, we say, 'God buries His workmen whilst His work carries on.' All have come and gone but Jesus remains the same, yesterday, today, tomorrow. Peter was the first stone, laid flat, cut, shaped and settled into position. *The Growing Pains of Peter* is all about that formation of the foundation stone. Some have stated that we need another revelation from the Throne to know what Jesus really meant. Jesus adds building to being and being to blessing. It starts with a blessing, 'Blessed are you Simon Bar Jonah' (John 1:42). He declares what Peter is and what he shall be.

The nature of the Church

What this foundation stone received was more than a stream of light on a sunny day, it was a throb from the heart of God, a gleam from His eye. It was a new environment where all men would be equal. It was new dimensions, not as the Jewish Church simply for Jew, but for Jew and Gentile together as stones in a building. It was that from God which comes to us all and makes us worth something. Something of Heaven is put into us to make us part of the Church, not stuck on, but added to, internal, not external.

Some are made great by association. Peter is worth something because of Jesus Christ. William Shakespeare's pen was auctioned for many thousands of pounds. The diaries of Scott of the Antarctic are precious because of his association. Time and age, history and circumstance do not mean a thing, but association with that which is counted as great means everything and value is sometimes interpreted on that basis. It is Jesus who gives virtue and validity to Peter. Jesus pronounces something to be of eternal value and it is added to the life of this loved one. Jesus always adds more than He takes, pressed down, shaken together and running over! How much it runs over we are not told. In the Parable of the Sower and the

Seed (Matthew 13), it was one seed that had fallen into the ground alone bringing forth thirtyfold, or sixtyfold or a hundredfold. God gave one Son that He might be returned with interest. There will be millions in Heaven because Jesus has brought forth a hundredfold!

The new birth

Some think that this was the moment of Peter's new birth (1 Peter 1:23) when his name was written in the Lamb's Book of Life, when the spirit of adoption entered into him and he was able to cry, Abba Father, Daddy, Daddy.[3] If that is so then his spirit recognised Jesus for Whom He was. There was that deeper insight than flesh and blood could grant. In turn Jesus recognises the voice and the source of the outcry. The words must be positive, 'You are the Christ'. There is no stammering tongue or quivering lip, no concealment. Jesus did not deny what Peter was saying. The candle, which is the spirit of man, was lit never to go out.[4] It would face many storms and high winds, be blown upon by the bad breath of religious tyrants, but such a light was lit, as Ridley and Latimer said, as should never go out. Flesh is outward, this was inward. Blood is inward but only to a point. There is that in us which is deeper than blood coursing through veins and arteries like rivers going to the sea. Blood makes up family, type and group, has connections with Heaven's family of the Bloodwashed, with God at the Head. Not born of flesh as the will of men and the desires of men but born of God.

The Rock on which to build

I think that the revelation which Peter received would become the rock on which Jesus would build, not Peter as a person. The words Peter spoke were a prophecy, a shorter catechism. This was the fundamental of his faith, recognising Jesus is the Rock. God can build on that. The moment we believe, repent and receive, the Building Project is pronounced. Having a right relationship and a right concept of Jesus is the very Rock most lives need. They build on sand without Him, but with Him they build on Rock.[5] If we see Jesus as He really is everything else will fit into place. The Spirit is spirit and on that the Holy One will build. As oil to oil, flour to flour, God will come and make His abode. Once our life is surrendered to God He will make it part of His collection. Everyone who receives such a message from God and insight as to the Church of God, becomes part of Ephesians 2:20. Here as a building we are built together as living lively stones to be lived in by God through the Holy Spirit. Our revelations and insights become like the stones of Jacob.[6] They become our stones and we build on them. We conquer with them as David did with the stone from his sling. Like the nation of Israel we carry them with us from the Red Sea and from the Jordan, and having collected the stones we need to eat of the corn of the land the same day. Everytime someone believes in the death and resurrection of Jesus, a stone is erected as part of the Church. Great discoveries are but one step for any man but giant leaps for mankind. Here is a soul in the hands of God. The black, the drab, the uncertain and unknown is exchanged for a beam of sunlight, the Father's kiss for the prodigal returning. The glass through which he sees darkly is thrown to the ground. Who needs a glass when the reality is standing before you, when you are looking at that which is perfect? Peter becomes known as he is known. The childish things of time, sense, touch and feel are being laid on one side, as a bandage removed from once blind eyes which now see.

Great discoveries have taken us into new areas. In medicine, history and geography closed doors have suddenly been opened to us. So it was with Peter. This one of the twelve received new light and life. It moved him up a gear into a new spiritual dimension. No longer the lowlands, no longer the up and down of the waves, he reached into another world. That which is planted by the Lord will grow for He plants it in a beam of celestial light. It was almost a step up from Dark Age to Golden Age, from steam to electricity and on to nuclear power. The entrance of His word gives light.[7]

The keys of the Kingdom

To those who are born again (John 3:7), the keys of the Kingdom are handed. They are found on the ring of the love of God which is worldwide. You can open up the way to others because you yourself have had a revelation of Jesus Christ. That insight will fit every lock and open every door. In the Old Testament and in Revelation 3:7 the word 'key' or 'keys' means 'an opener'. Human nature might be a closer of prison doors but the Gospel opens them wide (1 Chronicles 9:27). In the Septuagint version of the Old Testament Scriptures the same Greek word for key is translated 'opening' (Judges 3:25). Every door has a key, and those keys are given to Peter and to every believer. There is that power within you to assist others into freedom. By testimony and presenting Jesus you open the door into the Church. When God gives anyone a revelation of Jesus that person goes through the open door and discovers that there is life on the other side. 'The keys of the House of David will be given to Christ' (Revelation 1:18; 3:7). He will lubricate them until they turn rusty locks and the creaking doors will open. The keys of any city were laid on the shoulders of a conqueror. First the sword was given, the crown was taken and then the keys placed in his hands. It meant the freedom of the city. The receiving of our symbolic key means the same. There was no place that the conqueror could not go, no door that could not be unlocked. This authority is given to all who are part of the true Church. We are all disciples with Peter. Cephas, in the Holy Spirit, has the keys to bind and loose, to open and to close. He opened the door to the Gentiles, to Dorcas, to those gathered in Acts 2 and 3. He opened doors to the Samaritans. What you loose on earth will be loosed in Heaven and what you bind on earth will be bound in Heaven.[8] This is spiritual warfare. Get the victory on earth before you seek it in the Heavenlies. We can only deal with the heavenlies when they come down to earth. Peter, along with all who believe, has been given vital keys. God has the key and He gives that key to you to help you to help another through a locked door and out of a prison.

Christ is the Key

Christ, the son of the Living God is the Key to every door, the door down into death and the door up into Heaven which John saw opened in Revelation 4:1. Peter's ministry from now on was to be a discovery of the keys which had been given to him by Jesus. Every situation was a closed door but he was armed with the keys as found in the power of God and centred in the crown of Christ. The key was the stamping of the Lordship and authority of Jesus onto and into every obstacle. In Jesus needs can be met. In any realm, He is the remedy. He comes as bread to the hungry, light to the blind, strength to the weak, water to the thirsty, peace to the perplexed. He is a Door to all those who are shut in, but He is the Key as well. He opens what no man can open and He closes that which no man can close. No man can alter what He has done. These keys need not be rusty or difficult to carry. They need fresh oil daily from the Messiah's plentiful supply. One drop of oil is worth a million hands seeking to turn that which will not be turned, to open that which will not be opened.

John Bunyan saw Christian in Doubting Castle. Bypass Meadow led to it. Christian reached into his bosom for the key of promise. When he turned it in the lock the door sprang open and he was set free to travel on the Straight and Narrow Way.

The One who said, 'Behold I stand at the door and knock' (Revelation 3:20), and the Greek tense is 'I am still standing and still knocking', He knocks out of courtesy. Once anyone says, 'Yes', then He turns the key and doors which cannot be opened from the inside are opened from the outside by Jesus Christ. When you have knocked long enough the key will be provided for you. It will not always be presented on a velvet cushion or wrapped in golden cloth. The keys may weigh heavily but they develop the muscles and the stamina. The shoulder on which they lie are broadened. The man with the keys does not have to stand knocking for long. He takes the key which fits the lock, turns it and enters in and sups with all. The word used for the meal in Revelation 3:20, 'sup', is the word for the last meal of the day. The last opportunity may be being presented to the Church at Laodicea.

In Charlotte Bronte's novel, *Jane Eyre,* Jane arrives as teacher to the little girl, Miss Adela. The housekeeper, Mrs Fairfax, meets her. She has a large bunch of keys which she passes on to the servant of the house. On that keyring is a key to every door in the house. The servant with the keys becomes the mistress, able to enter into every room. They are referred to as 'the most housewifely bunch of keys you ever did see'.[9]

The power of the Church

To Cephas, his work was eternal. The gates of hell, of hades, shall not prevail against you. The gates, the powers of the unseen world that was dark and unknown to the Greeks will not prevail against the Church Terestrial, for it shall become the Church Celestial. The power of the unseen and unknown will not rob the Church, of which Peter is part. A hymn (by R. Lowry) says of Jesus arising from the dead: 'He tore the bars away'. If He has taken the keys of death and hades from Satan then He has no need to tear the bars away, He opens the door and, as at the earthquake at Philippi, they follow the leader out of the prisons.

If God grants you insight it is to release the captives. Peter saw Jesus as the Rock and it was on that Rock that the Church would be built. That conviction would lead to conversion. It opened up a worldwide area of work for God. There is no limit to nation, time or place in these keys. You must see Jesus as the Rock before you can build. That light must come into your life before you can turn the key in any lock. You must have revelation from God and confess Christ and in saving yourself through Christ you will save others.

There are many keys

In Acts 2, dreaming dreams, seeing visions, speaking in other languages were all part of the bunch of keys. As they spoke in new tongues they were declaring the wonderful works of God. They were used as keys into hearts. The Macedonian Call was given to Paul as a key to Europe. Each one of the disciples and apostles shared in the manifestation of the Spirit of God which shone into hearts that were as dark as caves in the hillside but as the light shone in were found to contain buried treasure. Archimedes said that if he could find a lever outside the world he could lift the world. That is a reality in Jesus Christ. He is the lever and He lifts all who come to Him. Jesus is the first step up and through. Here is such a lever in Peter, the Galilean with the rough exterior and thick accent.

On five occasions the words 'find' and 'found' are used in John Chapter One in verses 41, 41, 43, 45, 45. They had found Christ and Christ had found them. God loves to raise Adam out of the earth. From the fields and the back streets He seeks through such as Peter to build His Church. God chooses the materials. He knows where they are and He brings them to be built into this wonderful creation, of which Noah's Ark was a type. Wherever there is a problem, a broken life, a bleeding disjointed heart, there God seeks to work a miracle, bathing it in light. Here is the classroom for the student. The teaching, reaching, healing ability of God's Son is seen time and time again as the door is opened and the curtain drawn back, enabling us to take a look at Jesus and Peter. God will grant us times of Heaven on earth, times of refreshing, rain after the heat, but only to help us forward to the Kingdom of God. The word 'refreshing' is 'recovery of breath' and is used figuratively of revival. It is the arrival of relief troops to the beleaguered fort. We must wander into the same area, the same College as Cephas and take a seat alongside him, even if we feel we have to wear the Dunce's cap! John Baptist longed for the confirmation of whom Christ was, the confirmation which Peter so readily received. 'Are You He that should come or do we look for another?' (Luke 7:19,20).

Peter, part of a plan

It was the realisation that made Peter into a man of destiny. He was part of a plan just as much as a twinkling star hanging as part of God's decoration. Did he feel as Moses did in Exodus 3:2 when he saw the burning bush? What thoughts did Moses have as God hid him in the cleft of the rock and His glory passed by? The child is wandering through the garden gate for the first time. What happened to Jeremiah? To Isaiah? To Paul on the Damascus Road where he found the keys in the dust? These were the same happenings as experienced by Simon. They were partakers of the same revelation. Simon recognised that Jesus was about His Father's business. That business has many storehouses, many doors and windows. 'On this Rock I will build, and nothing shall prevail against it' (Matthew 16:18). They will all be rolled away even as the Resurrection Stone was rolled away. All the keys despite much grabbing by false cults will rise up and say 'Do yourselves no harm, we are all here'. Just one key of Heaven can open all the locks and bondages of hell, yet all the keys of hell cannot open one of Heaven's gates. They are open already! Jesus never lost a soul. He never lost a key. He never failed to turn a lock or change a prison into a palace, a prisoner into a prince. Be those gates of hell made of brass or the finest British Steel they will not prevail! They will only go under, crushed with an iron hand without a velvet glove. As we pray the Lord's Prayer—'Thy Kingdom come', we are asking for a handout of keys. The Gates of Gaza did not prevail when Samson carried them away framed as a picture with a living portrait of himself in the centre of that frame. The unseen gates of Patmos, those gates of sea water did not halt John's revelations nor stop him seeing wonderful things. We don't have to be a locksmith to have the keys. A man's gift of his life will make room for him.

The prevailing Church

The same word used for 'prevail' in Matthew 16:18 is used by Luke when writing his Gospel as he describes the crowds shouting and clamouring for the crucifixion and death of Jesus. 'And they prevailed' (Luke 23:23). Little did the devil realise that even the Cross would be turned into a key and through it many sons would be led into glory, not running away from the realm of death but marching out in orderly fashion as a disciplined army. No shout, no command to charge or attack from whatever depth of hell will ever dominate the Church. Its progress is mapped out by God.

In *Treasure Island* by Robert L. Stevenson, the power of a man is described as a fist (page 32, Cassel's publication). The fist is used as the map which the seekers, the pirates are looking for. They seek for Flint's fist to enable them to find the treasure. The Bible and the promises of God are God's fists, God's arm made bare, to lead us to the Cross which directs us to the treasure. The map—the Word—the fist is ours when attacking and overcoming Satan. The hand of Jesus is there, clenched to fight for us, after its openness on the Cross. There are shields in it for defence and shields for attack, keys to open doors and keys to lock doors. The powers of the unseen become very lean when dealing with the scope of this revelation. They have only the light of hell with which to brighten their future, whilst the Church has the Light of the World! They are bound hand and foot and cast over the city wall into the darkness which surrounds them. Weak Peter is capable of binding the arm of the strong one!

A fresh glimpse of Jesus

A fresh glimpse of Jesus will take us into the world to preach the Gospel. When Peter looked on Jesus he wanted all to know who he had seen. He became town crier, trumpet sounder, blower from the walls of the city. One look at Christ will send you into all the world to preach the Gospel. It will give you extra legs, extra zeal. It will grant you disciple fortitude, fire and power. I can believe in a Pope who performs miracles, as Peter did, who inspires men, as Peter did, who walks on water and gives out miracle bread and fish, just like Peter. Jesus is the anointed One to turn the key. As the Son is seen, declare with Peter the fullness of the vision, the commitment.

Every one of the thirteen Resurrection appearances of Jesus were meant to be windows of light. They brought joy and peace. They laid Satan low. He who struggles, triumphs. Anointing and Sonship alongside the Father will always give victory, make us more than conquerors. The pages of everyday happenings in the life of Simon need to become part of our diaries. Jesus is always the Rock which shows the way (1 Samuel 20:19), meaning 'that which shows the way'. The pointing finger and the open hand, a milestone pointing out the direction.

The strength and durability of Christ

The Old Testament commandments were written on rock, tablets of stone, but that rock was smashed and had to be renewed. This Rock, Christ Jesus, is never broken, although many are broken by Him. He needs no renewing. He ever lives to make intercession for us. That revelation which was given to Peter's patriarchs can never be destroyed. You cannot destroy that which is spirit. The Bible has been burned, buried, torn in pieces, scattered far and wide, hidden in loaves of bread and in barrels, yet it lives and abides for ever. The Bible is the casket which enshrines the manifestation. Whole Churches in Russia and China have but one page of a Bible to read from. Jesus builds the Church, ever to prevail, never to disappear.

It must have been a marvellous sight when the hymn which contains so much about the Church, *Onward, Christian Soldiers*, was sung for the first time as the children marched through Horbury, near Wakefield, West Yorkshire. It was written by the Vicar for the children to sing at Whitsuntide as they passed from one Church to the other.

> Thrones and Kings may perish,
> Kingdoms rise and wane,
> But the Church of Jesus
> Constant will remain....

He is not speaking of buildings but people and the revelation within. It is not simply flesh and blood, it cannot die with man, you can never say the Last Rites over the Church. It will never need a wreath or a coffin. It is not tottering towards a hole in the ground. It is awaiting a call from the skies!

This revelation is what Paul received on the Damascus Road. From that light came every other light. It lit every part of his life. Everything he wrote, asked, thought or did was a product of that shining light. 'For me to live is Christ'—he wrote it and he meant it. Stones were used to bury the past and to build the future. Stones tell a story. The light shines on this stone. Certain Churches have a window built in a particular place and the sunlight comes through that window and falls on the altar, bathing it in light placing a halo around it. The altar appears as a priceless treasure seen behind a ray of light.

The true Church

Rocks and stones always formed the altars. They were places of victory and memory. Jesus Christ is all of these things. One pioneer worker testified, 'I heard that Jesus said, "I will build My Church", so I let Him do it!' This is the first time that the Greek word for Church—Ecclesia—appears. That which is drawn together. It must not simply be a cold rock but a calling Rock, a speaking Rock. There must be power in it to perform that which is promised. It is not on the wisdom or knowledge of men that Jesus builds. He places piece with piece and stone with stone, snugly fitting them together as a wise Master Builder. He does not build with wood, straw, rubble, silver or gold or such precious things of earth which attract the mind and leave the heart unadorned. He builds with the precious things which are part of faith—love, trust, kindness, commitment and faithfulness. All are held in the revelation of God and deposited on the Rock for safe keeping. 'He is no fool who gives what he cannot keep, to keep what he cannot give.'

Certain suggestions arise from the words Peter uttered. Certain things are suggested when Jesus said, 'I will build My Church'...

(a) Whenever, wherever or whatever Peter builds, Jesus will be there— *'I will build My Church'.*

When Peter preached in Acts 2:14–17, Jesus was there to add to the Church, to welcome the people in. At the household of Cornelius, Jesus was there. When Peter fell asleep at Joppa, Jesus was there to give him a dream. When Peter was in prison, Jesus was there. When he went down to Samaria with John in Acts 8, Jesus was there. As he recounted the happenings among the Gentiles and was not readily accepted, Jesus was there building His Church. Peter never went anywhere where Jesus was not. He had said, 'Lo, I am with you always,' every way and through every situation. People are saved at every time of the year, in every season. God's trees are always bearing fruit and they are always in season. When Mungo Park discovered a little flower way out where no man had ever been he was seen to stop and think—'God has been here already.'

(b) Jesus was saying to Peter— *'Don't build on other rocks.'* Don't waste time with timeless and wasteful ventures! Build on the real thing. It is stone upon Rock but it will be lively stones! Remember My story in Matthew 7:24. All other foundations, be they ever so bright and dazzling even as Caesar's Temple of white marble, will not do. The day will come when they will be no more. The Church of Jesus, commenced by Jesus, is the only Institution that has outlasted, outlaughed and outmanoeuvred them all. Babel was high but it failed; Babylon with its hanging gardens, one of the Seven Wonders of the World, failed. Where is it today? The Egyptian Pyramids only housed dead Pharaohs and rotting bones. Mausoleums will become whited sepulchres, full of dead men's bones. Where is the Temple of Diana? Where are the Inca civilisations today, the Aztecs, and such? There are many ways, but only One Way. 'There is no other Name given among men whereby we must be saved' (Acts 4:12). Many doors, but One Door, yet that Door has two sides. I am on the inside—on which side are you? Many truths, but One Truth—'Many will come in My Name saying, I am the Christ.' Where the eagles fly there will be carcasses, empty claims which mean nothing at all, repeated as often as a carcass appearing in the desert.

Other religions and cults are sand, not Rock. Mohammed, Joseph Smith, Confucius, the Watchtower workers, mystic religions of the East, Mormons, all other faiths, east, west, north and south, outside of Christianity are other rocks, naked, blind and miserable, the blind leaders of the blind, heading for the ditch. God in His mercy has placed a Rock between the nations and that ditch. Whatever others claim to be, act as if they make no claim at all! They are songs without the bird, melodies without the instrument, mere copies.

(c) Jesus would spearhead the attack. *'I will build My Church.'* I will always be at the front of the battle. There will be no tent at the rear where He can retire. He will tend to the sick and the wounded. Jesus provided the first stone, the first revelation, and He will produce the last, plus all the ones in between. Unless they are touched as He touched and prayed over the loaves and fishes, they will not have His fingerprints on them. There will be no impression of God on them. Unless the Father draws them, they cannot come. We are co-labourers, pulling the shafts, shoulders at the wheel, fellow workers. One plants, one sows, one ploughs, one clears the ground, and God gives the increase. The increase has to come from Him because increase is life, and the Son has life in Himself. 'I will always be first in and last out. If I open the door, I must close it.'

(d) *It was a sure phrase and a sound saying.* He had said He would raise up a destroyed Temple. When the Scribes and Pharisees had ended all their interpretations Jesus said, 'But I say unto you'. How was He going to build His Church if He was going to be crucified? The very fact that He was going to die meant that He was going to build. Dying was not an ending. He is the Omega. In all believers there would be a different method of building. As He died all who were to be part of this Church had to die. They had to take up their Cross daily, as found in the verses after Matthew 16:18. What Jesus said about Heaven, what He said at all times, was worth accepting and building life on.

(e)   There are centralised affections and a fixed Centre. *'Upon this Rock I will build My Church.'* Not on the edge of it, but at the centre of it. It will not slide off or be washed off. The fall of it will not be great when the floods and winds arrive with hammers of destruction or whispers of decay. When we have solid faith and conviction Jesus will build. The moment we believe He begins to build. One man said he was converted in the seconds between standing and kneeling before Christ. At that point in time the timeless element was introduced and Jesus began to build. Where there is dedication Jesus will build. The very things we hold He will take and use to build. Charlotte Elliott wrote 'Take my silver and my gold, not a mite would I withhold', yet she was convicted about some jewellery she possessed, but which in reality possessed her. She sold it and, from that moment, new light shone in her soul. Jesus had begun to build a little more. The man who built the first aeroplane, even the Wright Brothers and Amy Johnson who were to fly so far, had to start on earth. There had to be a starting point.

(f)   *Start where you are and see the potential.* 'I will build My Church.' Jesus is building it, not you! How can any individual do the work of God? Certain ministries belong to the Holy Spirit. There are furrows in a field which are God's furrows. We do the reaping. Jesus did not ask the disciples to commence sowing, He asked them to reap and to pray that the Lord of the harvest will send forth more reapers into the field. The field is large enough for every worker, every reaper. Boaz still makes a place for Ruth and leaves corn for her.

'Can any good thing come from Nazareth?' Can the quick Galilean temper avail anything? Can Jesus work here as

He has worked elsewhere? While some walk around in fear and doubt, Jesus is building in other areas where there is true faith. He may not work many miracles because of their unbelief, but when He finds faith, He uses that faith to build with.

The heroes of Hebrews 11 were all fully used up for God. In fact, if you read the Gospels, two of them came back for a second time, Elijah and Moses talking with Jesus in the Mount. He built on the tears of Jeremiah. He built on the farming figures of speech used by Amos. He built on the faithfulness of Daniel and on his administrative abilities. He built on the carpentry of Noah and the education of Moses. God can even build on our ignorance, when the wisdom of revelation becomes propagation. Whatever is rough, rocky, difficult, uncultured, rejected, there I will prove you all wrong by building My Church! God has done it worldwide, time and time again. When men have finished, then God has begun. Jesus used John Mark, whose name means 'the hammer', to build with. Each disciple represented a tool by which they were recognised. One a hammer, one a saw, another an aul, yet another a staff, and so on.

The Inner Cities, the broken tenements, the vice dens and drug holes, there He must build and do His most noble work, not in the finery of clothing or the pearls and silks, but among those who are needing, wanting and waiting to be helped. He serves them as Martha served. He breaks open His best alabaster box, as Mary did. He appears to come from the tomb, as Lazarus. He gives His mites, as the widow. He surrenders His loaves and fishes gladly. His donkey is there for anyone to use. In sprawling Suburbia and in Green Belt, along country lanes or in the mansion He will build. Satan catches society by using the extremes of riches or poverty, sackcloth or silk, and he can twist both into bonds which bind. Whether debt or dowry he does not mind. Peter builds in Jerusalem, in Samaria, in Joppa, in the tannery.

(g)   *Commence at the bottom. Starting with Christ.* He is the great example for all things. He lays down His life and takes it up. He loses it to find it. He is ready to fire an arrow at the target.

The risk is taken, the prize won. If you start at the start you may well finish at the finish! Humility is a good station to start. There will be many stops on the way to load and unload. If you build on the Rock with the Rock you will start and finish with the Rock. All that is built by Peter is given over to Christ, the Lord of the Church. Jesus is saying to Peter, 'On this Rock there are no religious ceremonies, no altars of silver or gold, no trappings, no cloths and velvets.'

(h) *Jesus has sealed the promise.* He sealed it with His own blood on a Cross. It was sealed with seven seals within and without. We have no need to weep because none is worthy to build. Jesus is wanting Peter the imitator to bring them to Him. Bring them and leave them with Christ. 'They tell Him of her.' When Jesus took hold of Peter it was another link in the long chain, not a chain which binds but a chain which adorns. The Acts of the Apostles records the acts of the Holy Spirit through the early believers. It is a book about building. If you want a book on building up the Church, on the Principles involved, read Acts. It will move you into action. You cannot fall into the fire and not be burned. Some of the spirit of Acts will enter into you. The acts went on in Rome, Corinth, Thessalonica, Galatia, Collosse, Samaria, Cappadocia, Pamphylia, places where the Church was established.

(i) *Here is the formula for growth*—not gimmicks, not the new or the appealing, there was to be no ceremony. Let Christ be your ceremony! A rock is a naked thing, a mineral formed by nature. 'Where two or three are gathered together' (Matthew 18:20), there is a growing congregation! It is more than numbers, it is characters who are blood-washed. You can prove lots of things from numbers. From a census taken some years ago it was proved that half of the married people in London were men, and half were women! That same census declared that all those under twelve years of age were probably children!

It is not a Church as an organisation, it is part of a living organism. No revelation—no growth. There are, sadly, some people who do not believe in the Church today. We need to tell them that Peter believed in it. Jesus believed in it! Jesus put blood, sweat and tears into it. Peter lost his life in it. Jesus loved the Church and He died for it. Peter longed to see it without spot, wrinkle or blemish. The Church grows when it grows up!

Note: This is one of the 'Wills' of Jesus.

'I WILL build My Church.'
'I WILL send you another Comforter.'
'I WILL receive you unto Myself.'
'I WILL come again.'

For Peter there was no denomination, race, colour or creed. Selected or reserved pulpits were unheard of. Jesus builds with the matter which surrounds Him. Can you think of a more cosmopolitan crowd than the disciples? Love for Him and from Him brought them together as spokes in a wheel, closer as they reach the Centre. Jacob used a rock for a pillow and had a dream about a staircase going into and out of Heaven with angels ascending and descending. David slips a stone into a sling and kills a giant. Moses sits on a rock with Hur and Aaron holding his hands, and Israel win a war!

In Southport, Lancashire, there is a large oblong War Memorial with the words, 'All ye who mark this place, tell Britain.' Let us, with Peter and all believers, tell the world that Jesus has died so all may live. Upon that Rock He will build His Church. You, like Peter, are a light leading to the Church. You are a door into the Church. The Church is not just a building, it is a Body, a Bride and a Building, all presenting further aspects of the Church of Jesus Christ. Jesus is the Key to turn the lock. The Key to open every door. That door stands before you, closed.

Notes

[1] Ephesians 2:20; Revelation 21:14,19
[2] Ephesians 2:22
[3] Romans 8:15; Galatians 4:6
[4] Psalm 18:28

5 Matthew 7:24
6 Genesis 28:18,22
7 Psalm 119:130
8 Matthew 16:19; 18:18
9 Bronte, C., *Jane Eyre*, p 110 (Wordsworth)

CHAPTER

10

Commitment to Christ

It seemed, initially, as if everyone would crowd around Jesus Christ. He would be the attraction, a great Leader of the crowd. When the challenging and the testing was put into operation, however, there were those who could not stand up to it and would be blown over in the draught. They hung back, afraid.[1] Peter had to be made into a soldier, a disciple. 'Will You at this time restore the Kingdom "unto" Israel?' Little did they realise that He had to restore the Kingdom 'into' Israel! Will You at this time restore Israel with all its power and conquering ability, with all its former glory? There was emphasis on the 'here' and 'now', it was what Jesus would do at this moment.

Many believe that Mark's Gospel should really be the Gospel of Peter. Many of the facts contained in that Gospel came from Peter, and from Mary, the mother of Jesus. Mark uses the word 'straightway' some forty times, used in such words as 'immediately' and 'anon'. It is the Gospel of the young man, of the immediate. It must happen now. The things of the Spirit, eternal workings, the nature of God is as the mills of God which grind exceedingly slow and small. Sometimes, like Peter, we want it all potted. Instant coffee, instant tea, instant potato, ready meals, instant action!

Christianity makes serious demands

The demands of Christianity are many. The crowds came to see, to rush at things and they wanted Messiah to do the same. They came for what they could get, not what they could give. They came, as the Romans to the Coliseum, to see the spectacular show. They were part of the loaves and fishes crowd, wanting miracles but not the character or the discipline of the normal Christian life. They were the miracle-multitude!

They had been told that they must eat the bread and drink the blood of Jesus Christ. Drinking the blood was part of their discipleship, that is why, in the formative years, Christians were accused of cannibalism. They didn't mind having a Jesus who did not rock the boat, a Jesus who calmed stormy seas, raised the dead or walked on water, a Jesus of story book dimensions. They wanted a sword but not a cutting edge. They required all the benefits without paying the contributions. The miracle aspect of Jesus cost them nothing. People don't mind a Cross-less Christianity. They don't mind having to run the race, as long as it doesn't stretch legs or pull muscles. It would have been so easy for Peter to become part of that spirit, the same spirit that is still in Churches today, hidden in a boat, a clandestine worshipper at home, on holiday—constant holidays, never there when needed, not having the commitment required to further the work of Christ locally. We can all be taken up with something without giving anything up as a contribution to the cause. The hand that gives must stretch to grasp. We have two hands, one to take, another to give.

The Son of God was not calling people to eat and drink in a human way. He was calling those who would become such a part of Him that He would be like meat and drink to their hungry souls. They, with Peter, would be lost in Him, as food and drink are lost in the body. He is calling Peter to love Him so much that he would literally eat His flesh and drink His blood, breathe His breath and walk His way. It is commitment that Jesus requires. We can love Him as part of a crowd, from a pew, from a cloister, but it has to be love from the heart, to be as He was in the world. To consume flesh and blood was another way of saying, 'Live on Me. Live in Me. Live off Me. Live by My means—by all means, "live".'

The challenge of change

Cephas had to face up to the challenge of change. He could not remain hidden in the crowd. He could no longer be a grain of corn in a sack of corn. He had to follow on to know more about the Galilean Leader or slip unnoticed forever from His influence, walking off the pages of the New Testament, out of history. There is a crowd within us all. There is one of self, one of riot, one unruly, one of anger, one of clamour. To walk away from Jesus would have seen the rocklike nature of Peter crumbling into sand. God had greater plans for Peter. There are certain ways in which the King draws His disciple away from the crowd and makes him stand on his own.

There are many teachings in John 6:66–70. John's commentary is a word on Matthew 16:13; Mark 8:27; Luke 9:18. The words are slightly different but the outcome is just as wholesome. The words in John could well have been spoken by Peter, the man who loves to be the spokesperson.

Jesus is wanting to challenge, to change ideas, attitudes and reasonings. One Church was so cold that it was decided to have central heating installed. A dear old lady objected on the grounds that it would desecrate the House of the Lord. However, the date was fixed for the installation and switching on. On the Sunday the old dear started to sweat. As the service progressed, she sweated more and more until, at the end, she looked as if she had been out in the rain. As the Minister approached her, he knew exactly what she was going to say...'It's that new-fangled heating, it is too warm for me. I told you we shouldn't have had it.' 'Madam,' said the Minister, speaking as only a Minister can speak, in rather a funereal voice, 'the heating isn't on. At the last minute the engineer could not make it. He is coming next week!'

The choice was crowd or cross

If Simon went with the crowd then Jesus would be crowded out. Even the woman with the issue of blood had to stretch her hand out of the crowd to touch Him.[2] If Peter followed Jesus then that would lead to discipleship and on to apostleship. It was the many footprints of the crowd, leading everywhere and treading underfoot those things which had been planted by the Lord, or it was following in the footsteps of Jesus. This was Peter's decision, and it was he who informed us that Jesus has left footprints to follow,[3] as many footprints as opportunities which run across our path. The Master's footprints are set in rocks. No blowing wind can cover these. It must be a choice path deciding the way we walk, talk and the mark we make in life. That decision determines our destiny. We are not quickened to be blown out, we believe in the ashes being fanned into a flame.

John 6:67, Jesus will ask of every believer, do you want to leave me? The waters ahead will get deeper. Will light leave the Light? The Christ who holds the Light will show us the way. We must become the instrument of His will, sometimes musical, other times practical and skilful, even mechanical, always useful. He fills the cup, makes the bed in sickness, shields my eyes, speaks my language. He is my sort of Man. What shall tear us apart? Nothing shall separate us from the love of God. Greater is He in Peter than that which influences the crowd. Whom or what shall pluck me from His grasp? 'None shall pluck you from My hand' (John 10:28,29). The head which has found repose on His breast will not leave. The soul which has found its peace will not venture into the peaceless presence of panic.

There are easy options

Jesus is offering Peter and the eleven an exit. Is there a wedge, a sharp rock, a jolt, which will bowl him over and away from the presence of Jesus? There were those who went away and walked no more with the Christ. The rich young ruler in Luke 18:23; Demas, using the world as an open door, but it was the door to the slaughterhouse and the sales pen in the cattle market.[4] Is Simon the magician's mind really on the world to come? Do the words and teachings of Jesus matter more than the works of Jesus? If he never witnessed another miracle would he still go on? Is Cephas about to become the Wise Man in the parable the unwise virgin in Matthew 25:1? Is he about to bury his talent and go away sorrowful? Could his cup of joy turn out to be a barrow of sorrows, picked up in Satan's garden? The storm is brewing, coming from the mouth of Jesus, whose voice is likened in the Book of Revelation 1:15 to the sound of many waters. Some are washed away, some are blown out to sea, some are swept off their feet for the wrong reasons. There are those with Peter who will never hear Jesus speak again, never look into His face or see another miracle formed from His hands. For them the sun is setting even while it is still day. The night has come and no man can work. Leave Christ and you put out the light. The darkness is deeper than the darkness of hell without the light of a single flame present. It was time to go fishing, not to be counting, cleaning, mending nets.

Christianity is hourly, daily

Christianity throughout the life of Peter had to be hourly, daily, monthly, yearly. Taking up the Cross daily, and following Christ. It may not always be clear where they are going, but they had to discover the Person they had come to. If we have to make the choice again, as Peter did, would it be the same? Peter chose Christ again and again. The lovely verse in John 3:7 is where it says, 'You must be born "again" ' —when we really come to Jesus there are many choices but each choice begins and ends with Him. Peter is here to stay. He must say to Jesus, 'I will never leave You nor forsake You.' Peter has taken off his coat, he is staying. He has found a place in the heart of Holiness and a closeness of comfort. Winds may blow, but he is in love with Love. Peter is like the weathercock, whichever way the wind blows, it remains perched aloft in the same place. It always spins round to its proper place.

The royalty and loyalty of love

The title of this Chapter could have been 'The Loyalty of Love'. This is what Jesus is really drawing from Peter, loyalty of love, proving that many waters cannot drown it and death cannot kill it. All the discouragements cannot overcome it. Is Peter like Caleb wholly following the Lord? Will Peter be remembered among those whose hearts were faithful and whose homes followed Him? Will he go on as a horse charging into battle, or as the eagle falling like a stone onto its prey? There is that commitment which is crucial in a crisis. We all have to step over walls, over hurdles, placed there sometimes by Satan to trip us up, and allowed by God to fortify us. He is always at the other side waiting to catch us if we should fall or falter. Stepping over the high walls of Jericho as if they were leaves scattered by the autumn winds. Everyone who follows the Friend must see Him as their Anchorage, a place to come and stay forever. Jesus is life! Wait until the pains of growth and the groanings of future glory begin to become part of living! In Galatians 6:2,5, different words are used for a burden. One is a soldiers pack while the other is the word used for carrying water. This life is thinking, being, knowing, acting, telling Jesus Christ, identified with Him in death and in life. It is being so like Christ that, when they talk of Peter, they speak of Christ and when they speak of Christ they talk of Peter. That is the relationship of life in Jesus Christ. That is the pearl which Satan would snatch from us if it were not sealed in a ring and on the hand of Jesus Christ. Peter, along with all who follow Jesus, will be disciplined by the fact that they are following Him. It is then that we discover what life in Christ really means. Spiritual life is not true unless it can be questioned, pulled and stretched. 'For me to live is Christ, to die is gain.' There has to be a dying now for a gaining. Like the corn of wheat falling alone in the ground. If it does then it brings forth a whole family, whether in a Roman prison, on a remote Island, in the midst of a crowd or the Gaza Desert, for them to live is Christ. It is seeing, knowing, recognising Jesus in all situations. Every colour is the colour of Christ, every contour is seen as part of Him. We cannot be cut off from Him. Boats can be cast adrift, nets can break, but the Word of the Lord endures for ever. Even computerised sputnics and rockets can go off course and explode showering the earth with metal confetti. The disciple who follows the Lord will not and cannot drift off course. There is only one Way and one Course. He will not be cast where God is not. There is no sea so deep or sky so high as not to know the working, moving presence of Jesus. Life means life of God in Christ to all who are believers, with Peter as the test cast. It is knowing, not mentally, but experientially, the Omnipresent, Omniscient, Omnipotent, His splendour, glory and beauty as the garments of Aaron the High Priest.

Jesus opens the door to this little lamb of the flock and Peter moves nearer to the side of the Shepherd, realising all the dangers which lie beyond His shadow, the scorchings of the sun where there is no shade. The words Simon used are those of the slave in the Old Testament, 'I love my Master, I will not go out free' (Exodus

21:5,6). 'I will dwell in the House of the Lord forever' (Psalm 23:6).
I will abide under the cover of His Lordship. This is the ship that
every disciple in fellowship must sail in.

Jesus is a life of discovery

There are many origins of life, forms of life which are known. Jesus
is the Well of spiritual life. People have come from all Ages to draw
from Him, and the waters have never yet failed. He has that which
we need to make us what He is. Jesus, for life, God's Life. Jesus is
the Word of Life. He is the Word on life. He is the Word through
life, directing and carrying it on forever. 'Come unto Me, come
after Me', did not mean that Cephas then had to go it alone. Go
with Me and help all those who are weary and heavy laden. I will
help with the burden. I will be that other hand. The Spirit 'helps'
in our weaknesses (Romans 8:26). 'Helps' describes someone taking hold of the other end. The real presence is God. Jesus shares
your responsibility.

Eternal life is a journey of discovery. The Beatitudes in Matthew 5 fit into this new life, it is the very essence of Eternal life. Salt
which has not lost its savour. That essence is always with us, just as
fire and flame are always together. Like the New Jerusalem, the
length, depth and breadth are the same. It is a fulfilment of Psalm
91:1, dwelling in the secret place of the Most High and abiding
under the shadow of the Almighty. The Living Bible calls the Most
High, the God of gods. There will be times when we are pushed
back to Headquarters, needing to be refreshed by being reminded
of Who Christ is. Our destiny needs to be brought before us often,
to displace other visions. It is life lived in the power and the
presence and activated by the promise of Jesus to give eternal life to
all who are called and who come. It may be life on the cutting edge,
but if Jesus is holding the weapon of war, I need fear no evil. It is
life in the forefront of the battle and the heart of the Kingdom.

The words of Eternal life lead to the works of life. Every word
of Jesus is pregnant with life. Every miracle was a new breath.
Dead souls raised into the breath of God.

There is no other way

'You only have the words of Eternal life' (John 6:68). We have received that assurance which is like the sunshine, brilliant among the clouds. What are you building your life on? What kind of materials are you using? Wood? Straw? Hay? Stubble? Brick? Sand? Base metals? or Dross?[5] If Cephas gave what he was to another, would the other person be better or would he be held back? Would they be improved? Life is more than the things we eat, what we say or what we do, it is what we are. Some things are spiritually discerned. Peter says 'You only have the words.' You only, not things, places, times but Jesus Christ. Being at one with God, unable to discover where branch joins the trunk. Jesus has and is the Word of Life. He is the secret of living.

As children we had secret dens. Peter would have his secrets, his favourite places, secret pathways, tunnels, doors. Like the wardrobe in the Tales of Narnia by C.S. Lewis. Secret is another word for precious. As Peter writes to suffering believers he mentions that 'unto us who believe, Jesus is precious' (1 Peter 2:7). Jesus is the Way, the Path of Life. Peter is challenged to walk His Way and to speak His Truths.

There was a person in the Market Place at Gainsborough in Lincolnshire who was challenged about Christ and Eternal life. The questioner was given short shrift. The woman then went on to pick up two cabbages, both the same price, and weighed one in each hand to see which was the better bargain. She gave more time considering which cabbage to purchase than she did to Jesus Christ.

Christianity means choices

There was a choice to make that would take them to Heaven. There is no other way, no other door. Ritualistic religion would never meet the depths within. Christ in a life and a life in Christ makes for completion, for perfection. The devil painted the Christian life in the deepest black, the most hideous of colours, placed as a dark November day in an attempt to make Christianity boring. Peter cannot leave the El Shaddai, the many breasted God, for another bosom. He is not looking for the life of the Sadducee, Pharisee,

Doctor of Law or the interpreters of the law. He does not want the teachings of Plato or the war-like life of Alexander the Great. There is no life among the bleached bones of history or on the dusty shelves of libraries and museums. He no longer wants a life on the ocean wave. There is no desire for the ceremonial, and the historical is dead and buried. Peter is wanting God. He has learned not to take from or add to the life which Jesus offers. That life is abundant life in all its fullness. To add or subtract from that would be as adding or subtracting from the Word of God. The old life for Peter is as a capsized vessel, a deserted fishing smack, a broken net. To have life at all, means Jesus. Let Him do His work and there will be the smell of fresh paint daily added to the canvas. Peter has found the Secret. It is Jesus. The Secret has to work in every Peter, Matthew, Mark, John. It is a discovery of principles to live and to die by. Jesus was the highest form of life on earth, the life of Heaven on the earth.

New life keeps us alive

It is this secret of life which does not let us walk away from Jesus. The secret keeps us close to Him. Verse 68, 'You have the Words and we have seen the works of Eternal life. No man can do these miracles except God be with Him.' I am staying with the One who is holding the light and showing the way through the darkness. No one else adds to life the same aspects as Jesus Christ. He is life, and more. Jesus, for Peter, captivates and capitalises life.

In verse 69, with Peter as the spokesman, we have come to believe and we are still believing, we still believe as in John 6:29. We have come to know and still know (Greek tense). There has been a rearranging of the life of Peter, but there has been no loss of confidence. The essence of that life for Peter was as fresh as when he first believed, when he first met with Jesus, that first look, those first words. The first challenge had remained. The choice is still Christ.

Never cease walking with God

'Walked no more' (John 6:66). Went not in the company of Jesus. His strides were too large for them to follow. The demands of the foot soldier were too great, but Peter stayed with Him, stayed to believe and to receive. There were some who stepped out of the sunlight and into the shadow. They were walking away with a patch over one eye, pretending that Jesus had never been. To Peter, life with Jesus was ever increasing, ever following onwards, out-wards, upwards. To walk no more suggests rebellion, or even just religion, a returning to the old ways, the old wells. A step back from AD to BC.

Peter had received the total essence in Jesus Christ. His fullness had entered in. It can be challenged but not altered. It will not melt in the heat or be lost as salt in water, or blown away with the dust. The strong wind may blow through a scented garden, but it will spread that scent over the wall to freshen the dark alleyways. Let the beauty of Jesus be seen!

You, as Peter was, are different. Holiness means to be as different from others as Churches are from houses. Does that new life smell like the bread of Heaven? That was Peter's answer.

Jesus Christ is all

Words of Life. Bread of Life. Water of Life. Tree of Life. Jesus was all these things to His followers, and it kept Peter in refreshment from start to finish. Bread to eat, water to drink, light to see, life to live. Life was meant to be forever. Peter is making all these discov-eries. The quality of life cannot be watered down. Contained in it is the better self of every person who ever came to Christ. '...will carry it to completion' (Philippians 1:6).[6] You may crucify it but it will rise again after three days, not diminished but as an oil light having received replenishment. It is that which is victorious in Peter, at the end. It is this tug of life which takes him on and lifts him up. There are many opportunities to go back, as in verse 66, but there are more avenues which suggest going on.

In a certain Church there is a Cross-shaped window filled with stained glass, crimson in colour and, when the sun shines, if you stand in the right place, your form is filled with red blood in the shape of that Cross. With the Light and Blood and the Cross we are filled with something outside of ourselves. The constant contact with Jesus does its work. There is a small light gleaming in the soul of Peter. He understands a little of the Charter of Christ. The transformation is working. The life of Christ is not only needed in miracle power but in the rowing of a boat or in the catching of fish. This life is our inheritance. The life we have now is the down payment, the engagement, the promise of the future. 'Pure and undefiled, beyond reach of change and decay' (1 Peter 1:4, Living Bible). 'And God in His mighty power will make sure that you get there safely to receive it because you are trusting in Him' (v 5).

The character of Eternal life

The characteristics of this Eternal life as found in the words 'know' and 'believe' (John 6:69). Peter had to believe before he could know. He had to commit himself before the eyes of his understanding were opened. Cephas has a light all of his own, even as we do. He has a life to live, a devotion before God and to God. Every lighthouse has a different light so that confusion doesn't reign on the choppy waters of the sea. Ships know which light they are making contact with. Peter the fisherman had made some small and some large catches in his time. There must have been joy and sadness on his return trips. Sometimes the sweat beads were more than the fish! Yet of all he had ever felt and known there was no feeling and excitement like belonging to Jesus Christ. This life was far better than the greatest catch of fish either by natural or miraculous means!

We are all free agents

There were no whips or harness to help Peter to stay with Christ, no chains binding or fastening him to Christ. It was a matter of delight and of choice, the spirit of Ruth to Naomi—Let thy God be my God and thy people my people. Where you die I will die.[7]

No-one will be allowed to drift beyond His love and care. There will be no hiding place where His eye cannot see. Peter will never go where Jesus cannot or will not come, and neither will we. Even when drifting, if you examine the boat and look for the Seaman's Cushion which was always reserved for a guest traveller, you will find Jesus seated there, if not sleeping, then commanding the waters! Every word is a miracle tool in the life of Jesus. More than water has to be turned into wine. There must be more than the multiplication of fish or the breaking open of an alabaster box of ointment. These things must happen in the life of the follower. Peter has to be affected in order to become effectual. Jesus must discover all that is in Peter. He knows what is in the mountains, the seas, now He must know what is in this disciple. The greatest journey Jesus ever makes is into lives, it is a voyage of discovery for within all of us are new worlds to be conquered and mapped out. Will Peter go away? Will he stand, rise or fall? Will he run or falter? One gun is as good as another in the holster, one soldier as good as the next in the barracks. Angels are watching. Heaven waits with bated breath. Will a free agent, a man with a free choice, still choose God? There must be no turning to one side, unless that be to the side of Jesus Christ. Peter must be willing to obey as a free agent in response to the greatest love in the Universe.

To whom shall we go for Eternal life? Eternal life is found in Jesus. Who can smooth the rough, straighten that which is bent, but Jesus Christ. Must the instrument go to another for tuning? The crowd went to the natural teachers of the day. Peter would stay where the grace of God had led him and placed him. The deep things of God are here, deeper, wider, broader than the Galilean Sea. The crowd dispersed. So far as we know we do not hear of them or see them again. Perhaps they became a part of the crowd clamouring for His destruction, 'Crucify Him!'. They became as melting snow on the mountains. Peter's influence was only just beginning, theirs was fused out.

This is the beginning of the Gospel of Peter the Apostle, a servant of Jesus Christ. For this cause also Jesus Christ came into the world. This was all part of the saving of a sinner. When Peter came to Christ it was as real and assuring as an animal coming into the Ark which Noah built. To follow the Lamb of God is the surest thing in the Universe. When the stars, sun and moon cease to shine, He still has light, is still the Light of the World. He will forever remain the Bright and Morning Star.

This is leading to Matthew 16:17 and that great enunciation of revelation. If you want anything to follow light, give it light to follow.

Peter has spoken. To follow on, to know the Lord, to continue following the Christ who followed and found Peter, naked, blind and miserable, but who seeks to lead him to the place of rest, forever.

Notes

[1] John 6:66–70
[2] Luke 8:43,44
[3] 1 Peter 2:21
[4] 2 Timothy 4:10
[5] 1 Corinthians 3:12–14
[6] NIV
[7] Ruth 1:16

11

To Conquer and To Control

In Matthew 16:21–23, and Mark 8:31–33 there is a gathering of gloom, a certain darkness, not seen but felt, settling over the area. The hordes of hell are mustering for the final onslaught. Word has gone out to far and near, and the Armageddon in the life of Christ is being arranged. The sad thing is that Peter is used as chief spokesman. The very one chosen of Christ is used by Satan, but Jesus turns the tables and uses the occasion to place a silver lining in the cloud.

The opposition did not come from temple courts, priests, Scribes or Pharisees, it came through the one under training, the one close to Christ who had witnessed so many miracles. The shadow of the Cross was deepening, the sun in the life of Jesus was sinking and the night was coming when no man could work. The Evil One must get in the killer punch whilst there was still enough light. The clouds were gathering but those same clouds would be taken and formed into a crown by God and from those clouds voices would speak confirming the Sonship of Jesus. The weakness of human flesh was side by side with the strength of the purposes of God.[1] It would be the triumph of right over wrong, good over evil. Those shadows would prove to be the Shadow of the Almighty God, the God of gods.

It was some six months before the actual crucifixion of Jesus Christ and at all costs and by whatever method Satan must stop

Him reaching the Cross. Once at that place He takes with Him the sacred plan for the salvation of the world. Satan will use one human to destroy God's plan of peace for all. God and Satan have their eyes on Peter, one for good, the other for evil. Peter still thought that Jesus was ready to be crowned an earthly Monarch, to bring freedom to the Jewish people. As a true Jonah and a Jew he had no concept of a worldwide kingdom. His world commenced and ended with the Jewish nation. He had his own concept of a zealous, youthful, powerful overcoming Messiah, one riding into Jerusalem with all the pomp and ceremony of an earthly king. His concept was kingship, not Sonship. Jesus had not only to open the eyes of the blind, but of this disciple also. To strip away these thoughts from Peter He had to do it in an abrasive manner. He had to teach Peter that there was to be a certain rudeness about His reign that did not include the silver spoon and the studded brooch. His reign was to be largely from a Cross, not from under an earthly crown or inside a purple gown. It was not going to be from an earthly glittering throne, a donkey would be more fitting. Let the world have its toys of silk and its ceremony, its pomp and pride, but that was far from the Kingdom of Jesus Christ. How could Peter's mind be opened to accept this concept of Christ? The Cross was wooden and crude. Those in rich apparel are in King's Palaces, but to get into human hearts is a different matter. It is easy to bow the knee, not so easy to bow the heart. Bows can be bent, but on releasing the arrow they return and are bent again. They go from the arch to the bend and back again quite easily. Those riding milk-white steeds belonging to the Household Cavalry are earthly companies of soldiers who have no place in the Kingdom of Heaven. There is no gilded carriage for Jesus when He goes out, it is on foot. When He rides it is on a donkey. The magnificent Man on a bony machine— and a borrowed one at that! So was His Tomb. When He preaches it is from the wayside, there are no steps up to His pulpit. He looks out over flowers and fields even as He speaks. The finery of Jesus is within the heart. The workings of His hands are seen in lives changed—a matter of character and conduct, not a thing of the Open Day or the Gala Garden Party. There are no side shows with Him. Peter cannot understand this. The natural man cannot. The fleshly mind cannot grasp these things. Cephas is still very much the son of Jonas, and not a son of God.

Life can be tough in temptations

When things get tough it is very easy to step out. During the Temptation of Jesus in the Wilderness, doors were opened before Him which were not doors at all but false ways into worship, false ideas about God. The easy way out was suggested to Jesus, but He refused. He wanted to help those who had a difficult way to walk in the future. When people cry and are hurt, see blood flowing, feel nails banged into flesh, a crown of thorns rammed onto a head, Jesus suffered that they might find a compassionate Christ Who has been there. If Jesus was going to bruise Satan's head with His heel,[2] then He would have to climb high. The heel of Jesus was big enough for the head of Satan!

Jesus became the Door, in John 10:9, the Door in every temptation and discouragement, there to offer a way through by receiving the sunshine of His strength to help destroy the shadows. The only way out is through. The only way of escape for Jesus, and Peter, is by the Cross. This theology was difficult teaching. It was bait with a hook that this crumbling character Peter had to swallow.

Peter, when he asked Jesus not to suffer the Cross, was substituting an earthly loaf for Heavenly Bread. He was asking Jesus to accept that He could not bear the Cross. He could bear the universe, but not the Cross. The very mould He was operating in would be smashed and He would be squeezed into another mould, that of conformity to the world, having taken the easy option.[3]

God does work in spite of men

In Acts 16, when the Philippian jailer was released it says, 'All the doors were opened, everyone's bands were loosed.' There was not one human finger to turn a key or lift a latch, God did it through an earthquake. Some doors, if the source of the opening agency is not God, can lead back into the very dungeon from which one is seeking to escape. They lead into the far country and foreign fields, near the cliff edge and the signpost with 'Calamity' written on it is well hidden! Peter was suggesting a doctrine of devils! It was the door leading to darkness and the road to ruin, formed in rock. Simon, in trying to be friendly, becomes the foe, seeking to turn

Jesus aside from His purpose, tripping Him up. The woman reached out and touched His garment but not so tightly that He could not go on in the purposes of God. Cephas became the invisible trip wire. Men can and have tripped others up with words, hurting or healing words, words of bondage or liberty.[4] By his words Job kept men on their feet.

Miracles are not maturity

Peter had recently received a revelation of who Jesus really was. He should still have been dazzled by that revelation, yet the light is dimmed into darkness. There are deep teachings in what happened, great revelations and deep insights do not necessarily fully form the character. Miracles have nothing to do with maturity. Israel witnessed so many, yet still perished in the Wilderness. A ship which has been to sea many times gives no guarantee of future safety from sinking. You can know who Jesus is and still say, do and think the wrong things. There is the Thomas, the twin nature in all of us, sometimes a mixture of the sublime and the ridiculous rather than the sublime and the meticulous, more brain, less brawn! We can be persecuting the Church as Saul did clutching letters in one hand and stoning Christians with the other. We can enjoy the peaks of Pisgah and still have a certain valley of death running through our minds and hearts, capable of dizzy heights or dismal failure. We crawl with the snail and we soar with the eagle. When we are in Rome we do as Rome does and fall in with the fashions of the day. Peter is giving a full display of the texture of human nature, the failings of flesh and blood. He had known the heights of divine inspiration, such leadings of God and yet he also knew temptations from evil sources. The one who had been banned and chased away. 'Away from me Satan!...then the devil left Him' returned in Peter. Belial is always looking for a very blunt instrument to do his most pernicious work. He finds work for working hands. Anything that is loose and lying empty will be taken and used for his own inglory. Unwise heads are soon placed on healthy bodies. He is a prince at this sort of thing, a master of his work. There is a price that Peter is called to pay his penance in a rebuke. This is not the glory of the Kingdom of which Jesus spoke.

Jesus always worked with the Father

I have often wond'ered, if Jesus had listened to the voice of reason, knowledge, Satan or Peter, what would have been the end of the matter? The worlds might have become part of a gladiatorial contest, the universe being the Colliseum. Great sparks of friction could have been witnessed as falling stars. Men would have seen great portents in the sky above with fire and vapour, earthquakes with crashing rocks, pillars of smoke where there was no fire. It would have seemed as if the Day of Judgement had arrived without any form of escape, because there would have been no Cross. If there is no Cross, judgement falls and never finishes. Nothing would have been fulfilled. Thank God that Jesus did not listen to the suggestions, or thought only of Himself but, because he loved others He saved them. In saving Himself He would have lost them. His grip on things would have gone. God knows what He is doing! He knows the best and sometimes the only way of forwarding what He wants to do. I need to follow Him. Human nature at times seems to be cast afloat in an open boat and before Jesus comes walking to us on the waters we are looking for a landing place, any strip of land will do. It may be cannibal infested, mosquitoes may be holding a conference there, even prehistoric monsters may exist in the area, but it matters not, we still go for it. We are bent on the desire. God is not like that. You can never apply the thoughts of men and stamp the thoughts of God with them. How can you bring that which is higher than the Heavens down to the level of base human thinking? The adviser is saying, because you are the Lord of Glory this should not happen to You. Your position should grant You privilege. As a Christian these things should not come to you. The reverse is the truth. He is the Lord and because we are Christians these things will come to refine our faith until it is as pure gold with the hallmark of Heaven stamped firmly upon it, not to bruise or destroy but to testify to its content. The sufferings, unexpected trials, questionings and suggestions are not the pitiless blows of the hammer on the rock, there is a design in all things. The hand which holds the chisel will smooth the surface. There is a design of Eternal nature if God is involved.

We can wallow in self pity

The life of Peter, although he was about to poison the Master's
soup, had more design to it than a drop of rain falling into an
ocean. You, with him, will be baptised in suffering and rejection.
Here is the carnal mind and the unspiritual nature joined to flesh
forever working together to overthrow Jesus. The mob, the crowd
are here, even before Jesus has been tried. The human mind always
craves to be let off and to be satisfied. The more it is at the centre
the happier it becomes. How can I make myself and my cause more
secure? Peter wraps himself around as with a fisherman's coat, with
false consolation and reasonings. The whole argument is found in
Matthew 16:22 (KJV). 'Never, Lord. Be it far from Thee. May the
gods help You!' Pity yourself. Huddle your wounded self into a
corner and cry. Have a pity party. Here is a pool of pity which, if
added to, could become an ocean! All sailing craft would sink in it,
the only fish caught would be red herrings! Let's have a 'symptom
swap shop'. That is what Peter in his weak human nature is
suggesting and which the Divine nature in Jesus is refusing. Jesus
never wanted that pity. Peter's love and obedience with friendship—yes, but Jesus does not need the pity of this one or of the
thousands of angels at the right hand of God to help Him through.
He ultimately used good honest human sweat as a witness to His
blood, He did not need human emotion. Jesus wants obedience, the
obedience that He learned through suffering. At this point the son
of Jonas enters into another ministry, he becomes almost, I say
almost, a disciple of the damned! The apostle of the adversary! A
disciple of the devil! Yes, it is possible to sell your soul to the devil.
It is even possible to lend it to him or give it to him and it is wielded
like the proverbial pronged fork. If human weakness did not yield
to Satan then Satan would have no instruments of war and his
arsenal would be empty. He would have no compatriots, no guer-
rillas, no mercenaries. This is door mat discipleship. The devil
walking all over Peter. Self pity is a great weapon in the hands of
Satan. Many have been slain with it. Peter is doing his best, but his
motives are wrong in asking Jesus to give quarter to natural feelings. The banks of the human heart are ready to burst. Later, as the
two walked the Emmaus Road, self pity walked with them...we
had hoped...we thought.[5] It is as if a trap is well concealed ready

to be sprung and unseat Christ from the purposes of God. Jesus saw right through it and side stepped it.

Satan is always lingering in the shadows, ready and fully armed for war. Peter becomes not only the spokesman for the twelve but lends his powers of speech to the devil. He is transformed into a messenger of misery,

'Lord, throw the towel in.'

'Peter, the battle, the fight hasn't even started yet!'

The true nature of devotion

In 1 Corinthians 13:5, love is not moody, it does not wallow in despair, it believes all and hopes all, it never founders in self pity. We can drown in our own tears, badly burned by their scalding heat. In your own situation you can be hemmed in on every side, closed up. It takes a word from Jesus to alter things. You can literally hang yourself through self pity. Jesus converts self pity into true love and compassion. It is time for Simon to take a fresh look at Jesus, to listen and to learn afresh.

Peter began to imitate Jesus in an unreal sense. He became a shadow of what he had seen Jesus do. He had heard Him rebuke the winds and the waves and that same ministry is turned inward, if it be a ministry at all, to Jesus Christ. Jesus was being treated as a leper, as someone deaf and dumb, needing healing and cleansing, so He is rebuked.

The will of God becomes as sounding brass and tinkling cymbal when pity takes over. It takes from the spiritual into the realm of the emotional, to lock you up there and throw away the key. We become as the seed in the parable in Matthew which perished for lack of depth. Pity will not take us through trial, it will leave us stranded and marooned as on an island. No man is an island unto himself. Pity always leaves us earthbound. It turns no eye to Heaven, the emphasis is always on the here and now.

Self pity has many converts

It was the beginning of the questioning process as Peter began to chide Jesus. The Children of Israel did the same with Moses as they began to dig their heels in. The same word for 'rebuke' is used in Mark 10:48, they 'charged' him to hold his tongue. Self pity silences the voice of the Saviour, turning Jesus into a statue, an idol, eyes which see not, ears that hear not and a mouth that speaks not. The voice of pity is sometimes much louder than the truth, sealing the tomb with seven seals and putting wax into the ears. We become deaf and blind to everything except our own beliefs. The words of Jesus become hollow, empty, echoing words, the Book of God just another book. The ministry and the mission of Jesus becomes that which is localised and idolised rather than worshipped. The Happening of the Ages which affects the worlds both now and in the future becomes something very parochial if pity holds sway. Self pity does not allow Peter to take one more step with his Friend. Each tear of self pity is another weapon formed against Christ and if you look into such tears you would see the image of yourself in each one. Multiplication of tears means the multiplication of your own image. This is part of the strategem of the devil, these emotions become his servants.

C.H. Spurgeon comments: 'He felt that the doctrine, the things Jesus was saying would not serve the cause very well.' Peter's place is always to follow, never to lead Jesus Christ. God must lead and man must follow.

The question that must be asked is what is the reason for this reasonable approach? Is it love for the Lord or is it pity? If it is pity then as that emotion dries up leaving no distinguishing mark it will utterly fail. It will be as the crow which seeks to sing as a nightingale. Love never fails, it remains. Pity stands and looks whilst true compassion rolls up its sleeves, moving out in all directions as an overflow of a heart that is full of love. There was nothing so negative or paralysing as the sheer pity in Peter. It leaves us like the one borne of four, carried along as the lame duck of the party.[6]

A picture shown on television during the Winter Olympics of 1992 showed a text that read from John 3:16. A viewer rang to ask what it meant. The Bible can become just a book of Chapters, numbers and verses. Christianity is more than that.

The word is a seed

As the Messiah taught the word, that word was as seed; some of it fell by the wayside when it came to Peter. His heart was as that stony ground, that seed in the soil which withered and lacked moisture. He did not always let things sink down into his heart. He was neither ready to die or to live. Like us, he might be ready tomorrow! At this time he was seeking an easy option. Tomorrow is still as far off as it has ever been once each new day dawns. Procrastination is not only the highwayman of time, it is also the arranger of it. Teaching and reaching will never move us or touch us if pity closes the door and bars the way. It takes that part of us and uses it for its own glory and gratification. There are many happenings of nature, some good, some bad, that will tell you to pity yourself. It is the picture of the violinist playing music into his own soul, the physician healing himself only. It appeals to the immature in all of us. Jesus came to more than save us from sin, He came to save us from self, manifested in a thousand ways. Self, always trying to trip up the purpose of God before it has a chance to arrive and survive.

There is an old proverb which says: 'The best teaching turns ear into eye, what you hear, you see, and when you see what needs doing you do it.'

A child bought a Bible for his Grandad. He knew he should write something in the flyleaf, but didn't know what to actually write, so he took up one of his Grandad's books and copied the words written on the first page. When Grandad read the words he was more than surprised for the child had written 'With the Compliments of the Author'. Every word in the Bible is a word from the Author—with His compliments! We need to know the Author, Maker and Sustainer of all things. We need to step out of the self portrait of Peter's denial. We pity ourselves without recognising it. What shawl and rocking is to a baby pity becomes to us, a sort of spiritual soother. Peter needed a Jesus big enough and strong enough by his side to recognise self pity and to break its power, converting it into something majestic like washing one another's feet or distributing the miracle loaves to those who are hungry.

Self pity dethrones Christ

Self pity dethrones Christ, crucifies Him afresh. It breaks the plan of God even as the Commandments were broken at the feet of Moses. The Ark that Noah built was built from gopher wood, strong, reliable, not soon given to decay. That cannot be said of this element of self pity. You cannot walk on water if you are swimming in pity. Apollyon has gained subtle victories throughout the ages. As the serpent was more subtle than any other creature, so also is Satan. Whilst we are looking for the wiles of the devil he is using something else. As we watch the front door, he climbs in through the back window. In scepticism, modernism, spiritualism and every other 'ism' he has done his work, but his best work has been done through self pity.

The Gospel according to Peter's old nature

It would have been life and redemption according to Peter if Jesus had listened to him! Very stormy and choppy waters indeed. A Gospel without a crucifixion, always turning back or to one side when the going got tough. 'Come ye apart and rest awhile' would have been the everyday doctrine, taking us from vital work at vital moments. There would have been no shedding of blood. The modernist would have rejoiced! How different are the messages which followed, after Peter's maturing in Acts 2 and 3! In the Acts you see the grown Peter, the galvanised, the glorified Peter.

Dr James Strong, commenting on: 'Be it far from thee', says avoid the calamity. This is not the word of faith. There was no calamity in the Cross, it was a willing act to fulfil a Divine mission, the mission of the Messiah. Peter understood with a child's mind as if he cannot fully comprehend, cannot accept. When we, as with Peter, are brought to that place where we accept it all, then we know we have grown out of pity. He still saw the happening as things which came to Jesus arranged by men. In Acts 2:23 Peter has it absolutely right. 'This man was handed over to you by God's set purpose and foreknowledge and you, with the help of wicked men, put Him to death by nailing Him to the Cross' (NIV). God at work and men fulfilling the deed. In Acts, Peter sees it as God at work behind everything allowing everything.

Cephas, in Matthew 16, was like a man going to war, troops running all over the place, firing wildly into the air. No real stratagem for battle, no real target or victory. To gain a victory you need to have an object. Peter is never afraid to manifest any emotion, from terror to pity. Peter throws a stone at the window through which we see Heaven and seeks to shatter it. Men get taken up with that which surrounds, rather than the view. Jesus Christ is smitten where it hurts the most, His involvement with the Cross and the Eternal welfare of mankind. Pity never brings the Cross nearer, it takes it further away. It never brings to the feet of Jesus but leaves us, like Mary in the garden, crying and asking the supposed gardener where Jesus is (John 20:11). Through sheer emotion it turns Christianity into a religion. Christ becomes a prophet, accomplishing nothing of real value. Peter is acting as a Fifth Columnist. He is working for another agent.

The character of Christ

Looking at the texture of a suit some mature tailors are able to state whose brand it is, where it was made and the quality of it. Did this which happened to Jesus through Peter come from Heaven or hell? Jesus knew! He takes it within His power and limits its effect as antidote limits the power of poison. Pity will always cause redemption to stop short. Instead of a leap it will produce the limp of Jacob as the sun arose upon him when he had been wrestling with God.[7] The crying eye should never take the place of the breaking heart. A lesser way is presented by Peter to Jesus Christ, but His feet refuse to tread it. Take a lesser way out, not full surrender or obedience. This is how intentions crumble into dust, the very dust where Satan glides on his belly. The message is turn aside, blow out the light and go to sleep. The sky at night would be incomplete if one star was missing! If Jesus had not fully followed the Father in perfection and to perfection then cracks would have appeared, signs of decay and change. The worm of earth would have destroyed the ripest, richest piece of fruit of the Tree of God. Everything Jesus touched would not have turned to gold, as in Greek Mythology, but it would have gone from trust to rust. To the human mind that which was presented through Cephas might have added up, might have found a lodging place, but it did not add up to fulfilment and completion in the Divine Mind. What Peter said was soft centre and off centre! The fisherman's way, the human way and God's ways are far apart. Jesus is invited to take a step backward like some frightened snail, to crawl into his shell.

A teacher asked the class of young children the following

question. If five sheep were in a field and two got out, how many would be left? Some muttered one thing, some another. The teacher said: three sheep would be left. One boy put his hand up and said, 'Miss, there would be none left. My father is a shepherd and he says if two get out, all the rest will follow. You see Miss, you may know all about sums, but we know all about sheep.'

It was so important for Jesus not to listen to the devil's voice of human reasoning. If He had listened then the very door of the sheep, the Gate, would have been shattered and the little flock, of which Peter was a part, would have left the pasture, the very heart of Christ. Human suggestion, human reasoning, human desirability will never erect the Cross or drive the nails in the hands and feet of Jesus. Pity would never have thrust a spear into His side, it would have used the spear as a staff on which to lean. Our feet plod the plateau whilst He moves in another dimension. Peter could only see the now and the outward form it produced, the natural aspect. Spiritual things are spiritually discerned. Take away all the elements of the Gospel—the Cross, the shedding of blood being the central elements—and all that is left is chaff. Jesus kept real and was real, in order that something real might be presented to us. The birds that snatched away the seeds sown in Matthew 13 had drunk at the pool of pity before flying there. That which was sown preached and taught was not allowed to take root. The Crown of Thorns is snatched from His head and replaced by the soft cap, often a night cap.

The minds of men

Matthew 16:22,23, is the mind of men and not the mind of God, carnal conduct reasoned out of weak will. Maybe Peter had a boat ready with sails prepared to make a dash for the open sea, but that would not have solved anything because feelings can be like reefs, hidden just below the surface. We cannot add to or take from the purposes of God as some ship having its cargo thrown overboard because a storm threatens. We cannot arrange the sun or clouds. The wind does a far better job of planting than we ever do as we follow instructions on a packet of seeds. If we remove one piece from its proper place we ruin the act of God. Peter was embarrassed. God never intends embarrassment to replace the glory look.

There are choices in Christianity. The choice sometimes can be the difference between chalk and cheese, whilst on other occasions it is far more subtle, the choice between white and grey, or off-white.

Old age does not mean maturity

The heart of Peter has been under the good ministry and influence of Jesus for a number of years yet there are still many deficiencies. It is remarkable that the Church in the Book of Revelation which had John the Apostle of love as its Pastor should be accused of leaving their first love. In the Garden of Gethsemane the easy way out was to say 'here is a sword' (Matthew 26:51,52). It is easier to chop up a few obstacles rather than face them, yet in the facing is the strengthening of the inner life. In resisting is the making. In withstanding is the strengthening. Any old room would not do for the Last Supper! It had to be a particular lad with bread and fish, a particular woman with the choice alabaster box would break it open; the donkey on which Jesus was to ride into Jerusalem had to be His choice! If God chooses and if the choices are left to Him then they will fit the need.

When dear old Billy Bray, the Cornish prince, went to a man and the man said, 'The Lord has told me to give you this suit,' the man asked, 'Will it fit you?' Billy replied, 'If the Lord has sent it, it is sure to fit.' It did! It did! On one occasion Billy made a bid at an auction for a piece of greatly needed furniture. He was very disappointed when someone bid more than he did, but he followed the cart and when it arrived at its destination they were unable to get the piece of furniture in the house for which it had been purchased. Billy offered his original price and the man readily accepted! It all fitted in at the end. Sometimes the glory of a thing is seeing the matter through to the end.

The death of Jesus wasn't a matter of convenience

The life and death of Jesus, as Peter was to witness, was not a matter of convenience but of conviction. It was not choosing the paths which would run downhill, alongside sweet sounding streams and passing through flower filled meadows. Jesus was flint like and unflinching. He did not need ropes or nails to keep Him on the Cross.

In Philippians 2:5, note the difference between the mind of Christ and the mind of man. Self pity will always cover the iron fist with the velvet glove, yet Jesus said 'must' go through Jerusalem and Samaria; 'must' go through with it; 'must' suffer many things; 'must' be rejected of men; 'must' rise again from the dead! Many a 'must' has defeated many a lust. Peter must understand. Jesus said, 'Let these sayings of Mine sink down into your ears.' 'He that has ears should use them' (Luke 9:44), so translates J. B. Phillips. Peter must understand. Peter must follow Jesus to the end, to hell and back, come high water or deep water. Peter must get to Heaven, but not like a thief or robber. There are no back doors into Heaven.

The prayer of Jesus in Matthew 6:13: 'Lead us not into temptation', lead us not, arrange it not, yet arrange our escape from evil. God will use temptation, as He uses all things.

The old sailing vessels used Trade Winds, taking the strong winds in their sails to help them to their destination. There is help for Peter and as we join the queue there is help for us in making the right choices. There is no path of duty for self pity. It floods with tears and washes out that which has already been revealed. It washes away good intentions before they are carried through to fulfilment. It is this same essence of self pity which would have kept Abraham in the Ur of the Chaldees; Noah would have created the umbrella rather than build the Ark—Moses would have enjoyed the riches and pleasures of Egypt and so perished with them. There would have been no mothers in Israel and no leader to blow the trumpet to rally the people. Men of faith would not have prevailed. Hebrews Chapter eleven would never have been written because the walls of Jericho would not have fallen. Rahab the harlot would never have been rescued, nor would she have been in the lineage of Christ, Matthew Chapter One. Mouths of lions would never have been closed if the men of faith had acted on pity alone. You cannot build for God, Peter, on that which drips from the eye. It cannot be wrapped in a handkerchief. There must be a birth in the heart of that which is required by God. What does God require of you, Cephas? 'To act justly, to love mercy, to walk humbly with your God' (Micah 6:8). It costs something to continue. There was imprisonment, beatings, mockings and scourgings awaiting Jesus, and Peter. It cost Jesus His life.

The retreating nature

There was something of the nature of retreat in Simon. Backward steps are always into the unknown, because you cannot see what is behind you. 'Let us go to the house of Mary, Martha and Lazarus, it is safer and more comfortable there. Martha has the reputation of making the best meals in the area.' The fair-weather Christian must, sooner or later, face a storm of flood proportions. Self does not like or want the Cross. It would eject it from the memory as a nightmare, spue it out of its mouth. The Cross was never meant to be draped in silk or velvet, to be perfumed, to smell like a rose garden, gilded and clothed with soft light, gentle to the eye and soft to the touch.

Jesus knew when to accept and when to reject criticism, but Peter did not. The soft option was the only option to Peter, yet it was really an optical illusion. The easy way was the only way, he thought. We would all prefer to stay on the Mount of Transfiguration. It is even recorded of Mary, the mother of Jesus, that 'the angel departed from her' (Luke 1:38). We cannot live constantly with angels. 'He was with the wild beasts and angels came and ministered unto Him' (Mark 1:13). We would always be in the Upper Room with fire falling, cascading glory and speaking in eloquent tongues the wonderful works of God, but there is a whole world perishing outside that room. We would live in the atmosphere of the miracle power of Jesus. No one would willingly go down to Gaza where it is desert, or even to the bad company at Samaria, but Philip the Evangelist went and there was revival.[8] We have no desire to stand where the stones were thrown at Stephen and see, as he falls, covered by stones, how they form an altar of sacrifice from which he ascended into Heaven. Let it come to these, but not to me! That is the language and the love of pity. Let the cannibals have their flesh, but not mine!

During the 1940/45 War a lady used to pray 'Dear Lord, don't let the bombs drop on me, but bless those they do drop on!'

When Bramwell Booth, the son of the founder of the Salvation Army was at school, a group of youths decided they would knock

Jesus Christ and religion out of his soul. They took hold of him and constantly swung his young body against a tree until it was badly bruised, yet they did not succeed. There is always that which, though working humanly against us the Bible describes as our 'light' affliction and which is actually working for us an exceeding weight of Eternal glory.

We have built-in self preservation and that is good, yet it must be controlled and kept in its proper place. It must not be allowed to dominate Jesus Christ and His claims on your life. 'This will never happen to You' (Matthew 16:22)—not now, not then, not ever. The statement was as Eternal as the new nature and the Nature of God. Eternal life and the kiss of reconciliation does not grant us immunity against the onslaughts of the devil. God allows the devil to send the storms so that He can calm them and show us the rainbow.

Let God share His care

William Carey likened Missionary work to going down a mine. He would pray, 'God I will go down, if you hold the ropes.' Even in the most severe temptation we have to acknowledge that God, the God who holds the ropes also knows the ropes. When Paul was lowered over the wall of Damascus in a basket there had to be rope holders. The time for calling a prayer meeting had to be suspended whilst practical considerations were undertaken. They lowered Paul on the end of a rope, but it was really God who held the ropes.[9] Paul thought this was so important that he mentions it again in 2 Corinthians 11:33.

Instead of thinking about our own situation, our own circumstances, how it will affect me, get to grips with the words 'will the work of Jesus be affected for good or evil by my decision and comment?' Take up your Cross and follow Me. The Cross empties us of self pity. The emotional believer desires to follow Jesus but first needs to be excused to bury the dead. Peter needed a good dip in the cold waters of the Jordan to arouse his conscience to the facts as they were happening. Don't cry yourself to sleep! Arise and be aroused for the Philistines are upon you!

The Cross must challenge and change

The Cross removes the stone of stumbling from the path. It places us in the race mentioned in Hebrews 12. It makes us look at Jesus. Pity needed a miracle to convert it into praise. The buried talent becomes the testimony of truth. Pity is transformed into plenty to fill the empty, clothe the poor, help the needy. It is self pity which says, be warmed and filled and go your way. That is faith without works, rather than faith that works! Peter needs to take up the Cross daily and follow Jesus right through to the end, bitter or sweet. He must take the next step into opportunity.

Pity cannot arrange a life, for you will never mature under its administration. All sunshine may make a desert, but tears and pity will make a deep well, a stormy sea. Your hand will never reach up and touch the moon, you will never reach out and get near enough to the sun for it to warm you through and through. Pity never forges fellowship links, it takes but never gives, always wanting attention, becoming a circle or fallen halo at your feet. Peter, through Christ, stepped from the unreal into the real. Jesus did not say, 'Those who will come to me will be well dressed, filled and blessed and have the largest car in the drive.' He did say, 'Who will come after me?' Like a deer panting for water after the chase, or a man who has heard the cry of a child in distress running to the water's edge, discarding clothing as he runs. 'Laying aside the weight and the sin which so easily "upsets" (deliberate mistake) beset us' (Hebrews 12:1). Nothing else matters. That is a true picture of following Jesus Christ. 'Draw me unto You and I will run after You.'

Jesus saw the self pity in Peter as if it were Satan in human form. He saw it as it was, a Satanic attack. It was the closing of the gate, the end of the day.

Remember, all this followed Matthew 16:16, a most glorious revelation. Heaven had come down to earth, and hell then followed up from beneath. To Peter the comparison was that of Jesus being led into the wilderness to be tempted of the devil. If it is not a wilderness then you can be sure that Satan will turn it into one. Each piece of temptation, although seemingly a wilderness, can blossom as a rose garden. There can be growth as we resist in the

Name of our Leader. By my God I have run through a troop and leapt over a wall.

From Peter's immature suggestions we have the deeper teaching of Christ the teaching of Cross-bearing, what it means, what is done and how it prevails when all else fails. To get up and go on is glory indeed. Reach for the stars! Grasp one and pin it on your coat!

Jesus did what one famous artist was known to do. When anyone gave him a handkerchief with a spot or ink stain on it, he would draw round the mark, turning it into something beautiful.

Notes

1 Luke 9:35
2 Genesis 3:15
3 Romans 12:2
4 Job 4:4
5 Luke 24:21
6 Mark 2:3
7 Genesis 32:31
8 Acts 8:5
9 Acts 9:25

12

Paying the Bill

When the Temple needed maintenance it was done by way of a certain tax which had to be levied and paid according to the Law of God.[1] There was no escape from the tax for devoted Jews. Matthew 17:24–27 records Jesus paying this tax. There were those who would question not only the credentials of Jesus but also His motives, attitudes and devotion. Jesus had to be as one with the people even in the payment of Temple Tax. By doing that He became ordinary, yet the manner in which he received and paid the money made Him extraordinary! It did something in the heart of Peter. It placed a coin there, metal with the stamp of Sovereignty on it. Jesus is still teaching the Son of Jonas, developing him into a Son of God. The child of circumstance is being formed into one born of grace, not just one of the human race. Peter has to learn how grace is always greater than the law of demand or command. It is more blessed to give than to receive.

Taxes must be paid

The tax had to be paid by certain people. They were levied on the people of the land but the sons of the king, the royal retinue, were normally exempt. Peter had earlier informed Jesus that He was the Christ, the Son of the Living God and Jesus could, as the Son of

God and Lord of the Temple, have been declared exempt. However, until He was recognised for Whom He was, He paid the amount due to the Temple Priests. This coin and miracle was the last investment that God would make in the old system. That is grace, when God's final act is a miracle! It was the final payment. The sad thing is that the glory of God which had been so splendid in the Temple was reduced to coin of the realm.

The need for the Temple Tax

The Temple Tax was to be paid by Levites, Israelites, Proselytes and the free. Strangers were not expected to pay it. In 78 BC the tax became compulsory and land and buildings could be sequestered if the tax was not paid. Jesus had no land, no buildings, no bed and no claim to earth's handouts. 'The foxes have holes, the birds of the air have nests, but the Son of Man had nowhere to lay His head' (Luke 9:58). Jesus was borrowed from Heaven and everything He had was of a borrowed nature. Even the payment of the Temple Tax was borrowed from a fish. The whole of creation was the purse of Jesus Christ. His pockets were the living things created by God and the power of God held all the gifts which He needed. The open mouth of the fish was a purse, as was the open hand of the young lad with bread and fish. What appealed to Cephas was the ability Jesus had to dip His hand into the sea and take what He needed. He took everyday things, common ordinary things. Jesus knew that you have to pay your own way through life. Certain demands are made to make the payment of tithe or of tax. The work of God can only function as we finance it. We give, and God does the rest. We must operate beyond demand. We must give enough for two. In giving, however small or large, we must give ourselves also. Jesus could have taken all the fish, yet He only took one.

The Temple involved many expenses: wood, oil, incense, materials, metals, repairs, cleansing, paying of servants, all needed payment. Peter witnessed the unstinting hand of Jesus giving to the work of the Temple. In fact, He gave enough for two people. He gave out of His poverty, out of His emptiness came forth a fullness. He took from that which needed no upkeep in order to pay for that which did. God finds loose change where it is never lost. His 'petty cash' is never petty!

In olden times it was the duty of the ruler to pay all expenses but now this requirement had passed to the State. The Jewish nation had to attend to its own finances and this, in turn, was implemented by Temple officials. The actual half shekel was the equivalent of two denarii, and was levied on those from the age of twenty years. It represented two days wages. Booths were set up for payment of the tax and those manning the booths were to ensure that the tax was implemented, collected and paid, albeit sometimes reluctantly, particularly by Jews from abroad who received little help from the Temple.

Jesus did not create the coin, He simply found a gold fish and redirected what was already in existence. If all the world was directed to the needs of others, then there would be no poverty or Third World countries.

Consult Christ before answering

Peter had been asked the all important question—'Does your Master pay Temple taxes?' Campbell Morgan writes: 'The way in which the question was framed suggests a criticism.' Peter stepped in with a sword of words! The answer was an immediate defence of Jesus. We don't know if Jesus had or did pay the tax. He might have been too poor. He who was rich came into poverty on our behalf. He would rather perform a miracle than dodge the issue, offend the stomach of a fish rather than men!

Peter answered without consulting Jesus. His answer was in the coinage of the world around him. The answer which Jesus gave was cast in silver and met the need. When will this leader of the twelve realise that not every answer is the correct one? Sometimes we say things in defence which are no defence at all. Simon had to learn to listen to what Jesus was saying. When faced with difficult questions we need to learn certain lessons by entering the school of Christ. The lesson of truth through trust be understood. Peter does not have all the answers. He doesn't seem to have any! The answer was still being created by Jesus Christ and when and where it was ready then this leader of men would be sent to collect it. We have heard of the talking ass, but what about the talking fish? God using a fish as a donkey, a beast of burden, or as one of the ravens which carried food parcels to Elijah.[2] The coin which is supplied need not always be in the palm of a human hand. This time it was in the soft mouth of a fish—a 'gold fish' indeed! The payment or the answer was not in the mind of a man. Peter would never have looked to something so familiar as the sea and fish.

God has as many coins as fish

In Grimm's *Fairy Tales*,[3] we read the story of the fisherman and his wife and a fish which granted them many requests, turning their humble home into a castle. Every time they had a need they went to the fish. In the same book is the story of the White Snake, where a fish deposits a mussel at the feet of a needy one and in the mussel is a lost ring which saves a life when returned. These stories are but shadows of the real happenings in *The Growing Pains of Peter*.

A Minister and his wife suffered great poverty and need. Their children were requesting ice creams and various other things which were on sale at the Fete they were attending. Dad's wages were so small that Church mice could hardly exist on them! Before they had left home that morning they had prayed and asked God to supply their needs that day. At a coffee stall they purchased cups of coffee and, as they were drinking, they began to feel metal bits in their mouths. Had the fillings fallen from their teeth? Had dentistry gone wrong? They had heard of 'biting the bullet' but this was ridiculous. They emptied the rest of the cup onto the ground and to their utter amazement it was filled with money, lots and lots of silver pieces! Treasure ships had been located! Proverbial coins in a fountain! The children could now buy the ice cream for which they had longed. Suddenly it had become coffee cup Christianity, the place where God had hidden treasures for them! If by some chance the stall owner had placed his money in that plastic cup and it had been inadvertently filled with coffee—well, I cannot tell, they cannot tell—they could only thank God for meeting their needs.

We give dull answers to questions. We need to learn to let God provide His own answers. He does it in such miraculous ways. He replies with coin of the realm, with what is acceptable. The money was not encased in seaweed, it was in a wallet of water and met the need. It had no trace of rust, nor was it out of date.

Peter was told to fish, not to swim, we know from a previous experience that he wasn't too good at swimming! He was not told to fight with a sword either, as we shall discover.

There is no empty pocket when God spends. He hangs His purses on trees, he puts pips in them and calls them apples, he puts wings on them, calls them birds and they are there as the stars of the night. He places them in deep waters.

Jesus sees and meets every need

Jesus looked into the future. He understood what was going to happen. The fish was fully loaded, a small Jonah with a coin hidden within its body. A treasure chest wrapped in water, not to be opened until the shadow of Peter complete with line appeared over the edge of the water. That line was to be the finishing line for the fish. The coin had seemed to be some kind of food to the fish. Imagine sending your tithe to Church in a live fish!

The sons did not pay the Tax, yet Jesus did. The Temple was the House of the Father, and Jesus in a special sense was the Son of the Father, yet He went the extra mile, He set the example. Lest we become a stumbling block to them, we will do it. Jesus paid many a debt He did not owe. He is never wanting, only waits as the King's Treasurer to be called to settle the affairs of State. He was not a debt collector but a debt payer.

God could have arranged for the fish to surface in the Temple fountain and spit the coin into the offering box but there had to be human involvement and responsibility, through Peter. There had to be human evidence of a Divine act. That is why we have the Gospel records and why the term 'eye witnesses' is used in Luke 1:2 (KJV).

Dr Richard Glover, writing in his commentary on Matthew, says, 'The priest and the Rabbis did not pay the Tax. All that Jesus was and fulfilled said that He should not pay it. He paid it not of command, but out of grace.'

During my younger days I had an adopted Granny who would take me out and, whatever it cost, she would always pay the fare from her purse. It never seemed to be empty.

Princess Ann, as a little girl, came into the presence of a stranger and was asked, 'Who are you?' In her youthful innocence she replied, 'I am nobody, but my mother is the Queen of England.'

There is such a fullness in God

Throughout the life of Peter there are places and incidents where the hand of God opens as a fish's mouth with a coin in it. Our hands open only to reveal empty palms, but God reveals something more. His hands are full hands. They are our last appeal for a need to be met. He does not give a stone when we need bread. If Temple Tax is required, then Temple Tax is provided. Not in wagons with wheels but in fish with fins. Jesus took from one part of Creation and contributed something to another part. One lent to the other. The order of the day was reversed. Once the Monarch had been responsible for the upkeep of the Temple, as in the days of David and Solomon. Now the King supplied the need from His fish. God has reserves in fish stocks! It was a matter of one lending to the other. The fish became the coach or 'roach' of Royalty. The sea gave up more than its dead. The Widow's Mite was found in the stomach of the fish. Here was a minute Jonah swallowed by the fish waiting to be released to preach a message into the heart of Peter. God will provide—Jehovah Jireh.

Jesus used fish many times to reveal His Lordship. Have you noticed how often parts of natural creation lend to one another without expecting repayment? They contribute to each other. The human body and its many functions is a perfect example.

God pays exceedingly good wages to fishermen. The miracle, like those of Moses and Aaron in Egypt was at the end of a rod and line. Cephas had to throw in a line, but after that the outcome was the responsibility of God. Cephas must do that which was reasonable. God did that which was beyond all reasonable doubt.

If only Jesus could get the fish ministry into Peter! God had a fish in the ministry. He wants to get Simon involved in the same way, to do the same thing with the same commitment. Serving Jesus is not simply silver and gold, it is giving such as we have. Finance can cancel a debt but the man in the ministry can believe God to cancel out any sin, having the total assurance that Jesus had paid the price. If only we could surface with coins in our mouths everytime we arise from the depths of gloom and sorrow! When

Peter is taken on the line, what has he to give? Only that which Jesus has provided.

Through the Holy Spirit, 1 Corinthians 12 and 14, Jesus saw beyond the Temple. He heard the whispers in the background. Every wind interprets every conversation to Him. What mouth does not say or ear does not hear, He listens to and, entering into the conversation, He is prepared to act. His gaze in the Spirit was such that He could see beyond land and into the sea. The fish was pinpointed. He knew where it would swim and where it would be at the precise moment that Peter threw in the line. The sea was a large shop window for the Son of God! It reminds me of restaurants where the fish are swimming in the tank and you choose the one you would like for dinner! It was the first fish which Peter must take up. People are looking for many fish, while Jesus is interested in one.

Note: it was the only miracle of this nature. A thousand rods may take a thousand fish on other occasions, but this was of miraculous proportions. Normally men could labour all night and take nothing. The rod of God always takes a miracle. It always has coins and fish. Not every fish contained a coin but the one which did was the one which Jesus knew all about. Peter must not spend time with empty fish. He must receive those which God sends onto the end of his line.

Peter played his part

Peter had to play his part, he had to cast a line. When Peter acted, so did God. Fish are going to be caught, but only as Peter casts the line. When he throws the lines which bind him into the sea to be buried he has a catch of one fish. At one end of the line was Peter and Jesus. On both ends of the line there was a miracle—Peter on one end and the fish with the coin in its mouth on the other. The fish became the natural emblem of Christianity. This happens when we walk and work together. The rod and hook and line were the words of Jesus. The fish in the water has life and progress. Peter, in Jesus, like the fish in the sea.

God never sends us on errands which are unfruitful. For Peter there must be as much obedience in the Feeding of the Five Thousand, the Raising of the dead, as in the catching of a coin carp. There is always fulfilment at the end of the journey. Peter did a normal thing which produced an abnormal result. Every miracle of Jesus had a coin in the centre. There were many aspects of His manifested glory, as in John 2:1–11. When we read of Old Testament miracles or hear about modern day ones, each is like a nut with a sweet centre. We feed on bread and quails, drink water from the Smitten Rock as we listen to testimony of the miraculous. Here is another alabaster box, just as precious and still containing a rich aroma. This fish, along with the two fishes and the loaves of bread was multiplied to meet the needs of at least two—Jesus and Cephas. The offering that was given put new oil and light into Temple worship. Giving always does. It purchased far more than the thirty pieces of silver which Judas grabbed. He discovered that the bag was not large enough to hold it. He had nowhere to hide it. Life for Peter is the same life which we live. God's provision into a life. What God does when He acts provides enough for two, and more than two.

The coin that God wants He clothes with fleshly fish. He puts skin and bone around it and sends it to the end of the rod of Peter. This was not just a fisherman's story to be told at the local public house as the beer flows.

Near to where I live in Manchester there is a Public House called The Roach Bank Inn. The humorous thing about the sign hanging outside is that it shows a man who has just caught a fish. He is standing on a jutting piece of rock and there is a waterfall in the background. The fish is wider than the stream it came from, higher than the waterfall and, as the fisherman holds it up for all to see, it is bigger than he is! The fish fills the whole picture, just as some 'fishy' stories from fishermen do!

Obedience has its ample rewards

At the end of the walk and obedience of faith there are 'catches', fish swimming. God never sends any disciple where the fish are not biting. The liberal interpretation and the modernist theory to this miracle is that Peter sold the fish and paid the Temple Tax. Can you imagine any Jew paying four denarii for one fish? I think not when I consider the Jewish tradition of frugality.

Peter was told to cast a hook, not throw in a net. God allows the hook for the one and the net for many. Sometimes Peter turns hooks and lines into nets and complicates things.

Evangelism pays a debt

Peter received a new commission in this happening—to pay the debt of Jesus. Every time we whisper a word we are paying the debt of Jesus. Whenever and wherever evangelism is undertaken we speak of a debt which has been paid as we tell of that happening on the Cross. Jesus told His Father that He would rescue men and women, and we help Him as we seek to evangelise. There is a debt, to love one another and to tell people of that redeeming love. Cancelled debt in caught fish! The payment of the penalty. One had to be caught, to be taken, leaving its natural element, just as Jesus left the heights of Heaven.

In John 21, when they came after the toiling and the catching, Jesus had fish already on the fire. I wonder where He obtained them? Did they come to swim in the water of life? Was there some attraction to a hand more powerful than any sea?

There is enough for others in what Jesus is and has for them. Enough for me, and for you. The follower of Christ who puts Jesus first will find enough for 'Me' and 'thee'. All needs are met in His Lordship. He always has enough for Himself and for others. The lame man is given a straight walk. To the poor He gives riches, based on what He has and is. The leper receives cleansing. 'Go your way and sin no more' is based on the Holiness of Christ. The Nicodemuses receive the New Birth. Those seeking forgiveness receive the same from the wholeness of His nature. Those who need to believe receive from the faith of Jesus Christ. The blind received sight, the dead received life. Every star receives its light from Him. He is all those things that we are not, and we become what He is.

What satisfies God will satisfy Peter. What comes from Christ will be enough and to spare. Jesus looked at the world of need as He hung from the Cross, suspended more by love than by the nails, and His actions were a deed to the dead.

He who broke the loaves and fishes and met the needs of so many will take His life and scatter it amongst us, satisfying us with a satisfaction beyond words. His Life, His Death, His Atonement, His Resurrection, His Second Coming is enough for me, and for you. John 1:16, we have received grace to replace grace, measure alongside measure, enough for enough. There is enough in Jesus to meet the needs at birth and at death.

It is God who can bring two ends together in Jesus Christ. Jesus has fully paid and satisfied all demands. He has paid the debt of every Peter, James, John and every other believer. The 'whosoever' of John 3:16 is because of His payment. Not the payment from the mouth of a fish, but from a heart that was broken through suffering on a Cross.

Notes

[1] Exodus 30:13; 38:26
[2] 1 Kings 17:6
[3] p 100 (Wordsworth)

CHAPTER

13

Breaking With Tradition

There are challenges in life for which we have no understanding. Here, in Matthew 14:22–32, the Gospel writer allows the curtain to be lifted and we are able to see within the veil. Whilst the disciples were struggling with the sea, Jesus Christ is in a mountain grappling in prayer on their behalf. There is a mountain in each disciple which needs to be conquered. Every stroke of the blade into the sea is answered by a word of prayer from the lips of Jesus Christ. No sea overwhelms Him, no ship ever sank that He was Captain of!

This is almost the inverted story of Jonah and the whale. The only whale is in one named Simon, Son of Jonas with his whale-sized audacity and pronouncements—though all forsake You, I never will.

How limitless is the Lord?

Earlier Messiah had multiplied the fish but the question might still be asked, Can He control the fish in the waters? Is He the Christ of power in parts of Creation or is He the Lord of all Creation? What happens here illustrates that He is Supreme Lord of all. Every knee had to bow before Jesus during His earthly ministry, including the knee of Peter, the Apostle in the making. The Apostate must become Apostle. If only the knees of Peter might bow and by the stature of Christ he would measure how small he really was! Most happenings will control most men. Calamities can make cowards. We are as straws in the stream or the oar floating loose from the boat. Not so with Christ. He is the Master of all. He regulates happenings and incidents. They do not carry Him, He carries them. There are no 'sudden' storms in the life of Jesus. Waves and wind do not buffet Him. Lightning does not strike Him. They are all part of His weaponry, part of His choice as to what and when He will use those things surrounding men until they worship Him as the Lord of every realm.

Peter must recognise Jesus as the Lord of every realm. One of those realms is the heart of Cephas which many times is as a sea with tornado blowing, ships battered on the hard rocks, cargo lost overboard.

The disciples were about to take water. It was as if an unseen hand were ready to crush and crash their boat. The waves were about to lash them to death. Memories of Israel in Egypt and the Taskmaster sprang to mind, but where was Moses? Peter was in the middle of the muddle. He was to witness more of the majesty and power of Christ and this would, in turn, affect his heart and life forever.

In John 6:15, the crowd had been ready to make Christ the king. King of what? He can be crowned for the wrong reasons. Jesus can perform miracles but unless there is that calm obedience and prompt action to His word then He is no King at all. He is only the King in imagination.

There are sudden changes in life

It was just a fishing boat having another battle with a storm. The same thing had happened many times. The contour of the land provided a channel for the wind to blow through, to whip the water into waves. The wind was creative, began to play with the water as a child with a toy. At first there was no Presence of Jesus, no voice, no miracle power as they struggled with the watery serpent coiling its body around them. No God at hand to help. The sea is so great and their boat is so small, they lack a real oar on which to pull, that of faith in God. Just a struggling boat as a cork bobbing up and down. How difficult! How black and empty! So much sea to swallow before land is seen.

The disciples with Cephas the fisherman leading, had set out on an adventure, a voyage of discovery more remarkable than the Pilgrim Fathers sailing from Plymouth, more than any Columbus. Yet the Cape of Storms would be renamed The Cape of Good Hope. The treasure sought by Christ was within Peter. There had to be development. Without a captain they were to make Christ Captain. Without a hope of escape He becomes the escape. Nowhere to go? Christ is the place to go. Facing the unknown alone? Nothing to hold on to? Everything is moved—everything except Jesus! For Simon it is an illustration of life, illustrating the power and care of Jesus Christ with perfect timing. Somewhere between the billows, the wind blowing and the oar touching the water Jesus appeared. As the wave lifted like some great black velvet curtain there stood the Son of Man, the Alpha of Ancient Mariners appearing as it were from the raised oar. They had deliberately been made to 'go it alone' because Jesus needed to discover what was in Peter in order to place within him that which was lacking. Peter was being fashioned on the Potter's wheel, and made into a fine vessel of distinction. It is the pressures which complete the vessel. Rising from the lump of clay—the lurching boat—is a form serene and beautiful. At the end of the storm Peter is not what he was at the beginning. He steps from the storm washed, dressed, kept, fed and safe with Christ. Jesus has a new hold on him. Peter had to sink in order for Jesus to reveal His care in rescue. Peter now has a greater capacity for Christ. There is no distance or mountain between them. They are side by side in the sea and then in the boat. Each step is side by side.

They were straining in training

The word 'constrained' (Matthew 14:22) is a very strong one, suggesting the animal being put into the shafts, the yoke being placed on the animal for the first time, or a saddle being gently placed in position. Jesus had said, 'My yoke is easy', i.e., well fitting. How will Peter react? Here are more pains which will enable him to grow. There was a plan to be unfolded, a deliberate attempt to place this disciple, along with the eleven, into the severest trial and test of their faith. Jesus does not always use fire. Sometimes it is through deep waters that He causes us to go. The trials of God are sometimes inconclusive, yet the triumphs of God are always conclusive. There are many paths to walk, many ways of trial, of God getting to know what is within us, our strengths and our weaknesses. When the oyster takes a piece of grit into its shell, it is pain to the oyster but pearl to man! Do we have the sweet wine, the waters of Pharphar within us, or is it bilge? Marah and Mary (bitterness) must mellow.

They were taught when to pray

How long could Peter pull on the oar, how long could he continue in that hurricane without crying out for help? Would his strong self will take him through or would he come to that moment when he submits as a fish does when freed from the net? Without a voice to listen to or footsteps to follow through the waves, or a shoulder to lean on, how would he fare? Peter knows that one soldier is as good as another when on parade, that one ship is as good as the next in dry dock. One disciple is as the rest when leaning on the bosom of Jesus.

To preserve something, to make it last longer, then dip it in salt. Let the salt do its work. Peter, after being challenged, is placed in salt water. Precious truths are being taught which need salt to preserve them in his life. The salt will keep the truth fresh. The lessons of life and faith are learned as the salt water whips over us and we are shaken as a tablecloth to loose the crumbs. The crumbs may be shaken from the cloth, but the print will remain.

Earlier miracles were soon forgotten

It was a time without a miracle. Jesus had fed the five thousand, but how would Peter fare without a miracle? Miracles are mighty but how mighty are we without them? Peter was revealed in the raw, a seaman without a sail or oar. Whatever delusions he had about himself, nevertheless he was still just Peter. Thomas was still Thomas and certainly future events would prove that Judas was still Judas.

The work of the Master in a life will never wash off. Jesus

never teaches by using powder paints. Weak faith is soon drowned, weak commitment is soon sunk. Any old fish will be taken using any old hook. Weakness, whether in character or in boat will be strongly tested in a storm. The rain does not only come down, the floods come up.[1]

There is nothing like a maelstrom to find out what you really believe, if you really believe. In a tempest weak things are washed away, the things which matter remain. Cephas would become a true Moses, whose name meant 'Drawn from many waters'.

For every disciple, including Cephas, it was the life of Noah with Jesus. Noah's Ark had no rudder. It needed none because God was inside it!

Jesus can be heard in a storm

The voice of Jesus was in the storm, more necessary than compass, sexton, map or oar. The safest place for the compass was in the hands of the Saviour. The heart of Jesus is the best map. When taking soundings, listen to the heartbeat of Christ. Matthew records this miracle as a desk disciple and office official. The sea journey probably affected him the most. Those waves were written deep into his memory, never to be forgotten! Even Peter who gave Mark many of the facts contained in his Gospel omits to mention the struggle, the fear, the difficulties and the walking on water. Walking on water leaves no footprints and Peter decides, rightly or wrongly, to leave it as it is.

There was a work taking place in Peter. The waves, the scenes and the power of Christ were all acting as the tool on the rock or marble, forming the image of Christ. Pressures and influences were present, doing their essential Eternal work.

Even as the disciples were struggling with water, Jesus was facing a mountain. The heart of Cephas, as with every disciple, was a mountain to be climbed and conquered. The banner of love needed to be planted firmly on the top as a signal of such conquering. For Jesus, praying for Peter was a mountainous journey, a lofty peak needing to be scaled. Every fault that Peter had was a mountainside to be climbed. The mountain for Jesus was that which was commonly called intercession, a place of quiet and solid meditation. There was no storm, no waves, no sinking ship between Jesus and God. Matthew Henry says, 'Although the Lord of Glory and the Owner of the Universe, yet on their behalf He presents Himself to God as a beggar begging for bread.' Peter, without doubt, was the topic of the mountain prayer. Prayer is like a mountain, quiet, strong, durable, lifting up from the sounds and sighs of earth.

The prayers of Jesus

The prayer of Jesus surrounds the sea He sustains. His prayers did not lessen the squall whilst He was in the mountain. God did not pull the plug out of the sea, neither was it allowed to flee before the face of the coming King. Having gained the answer, Jesus took that answer to the one encased with fear and saw it work at the very heart of the need. We know that, in type, there is a Man in the Heavenlies, praying for each one going through growing pains. Praying that they might develop from caterpillar to butterfly, from seed to fruit. Jesus was instructing the sea to put back its many waves where they belonged. Those hurting, wounding waves were taken and placed again into the bosom of the wind from whence they had come. This gives every follower of Jesus strength and hope when facing a whirlwind. It assures one and all, whatever the storms, wherever we are, whichever sea, that there is always an opportunity through the prayers of Jesus. Opportunity means 'open harbour'. In these sea situations Peter realises that every wave is flung in the will of God, and every wave has a prayer from Jesus riding on it. Matthew allows us to look into the diary of Jesus. Each wind whistles, each wave as it beat against the sides of the ship gave out the death knell, seeking to execute the sentence. The prayers of Christ surrounded the son of Jonas more than the waves of the sea, like the word 'helps' in Acts 27:17, 'frappings' passed under the ship to help during a time of violent storm. The same thought is in Hebrews 2:18, He is able to 'succour' those tempted.

It was more than praying which helped Peter, the much loved follower of Christ. It was a real presence, the Master's touch where it hurt the most. The hand which had been upraised and stretched out in prayer had to stretch again to catch Peter as he was sinking. Prayer became practise. Jesus prayed, then He walked to the need with the answer. He did not throw the answer into the sea, He threw Himself into the sea like an Anchor over the side of the ship and He did not sink or cry for help—He was Help.

Prayer brings calm and peace

Because someone prayed there was calm after the storm. There was a fair haven for Peter as the sure-footed Christ came from amongst the waves. Jesus, stilling the raging waters, was Jesus operating healing and placing everything where it should be in order to work in proper order. He didn't even have to speak to the sea. His presence was influence enough.

Peter was buffeted. The wind was contrary. The rowing was hard. A man of calmness, prayer and peace stepped in. When He came into the situation He shut out the wild wind and the storm. The disciples had been in a jungle of water. Every wave had taken on the shape of the hungry beast, springing at them with cutting claws. They were but lambs afloat at the mercy of the wind and waves until, through Jesus, they rested on the mercy of God.

The fact that Jesus makes intercession in Matthew 14:23 should give courage to the feeble and fainthearted. It should act as an oar, helm, sail, anchor and rudder to a floating, drifting boat. We need to be baptised with His prayers more than with the waters which surround us. We need His prayers, His presence and His promises in every storm.

The subject matter of Christ's prayers in John 17 would be the disciples and Peter. Jonah is in the boat. The sea is threshing the ship. Christ's prayers must become the sheet anchor. Peter had to wait and Jesus would come to him through the storm. When Jesus appeared it was not the end of the story, another chapter would be written. Peter is called into the cold water.

The challenge to be different

Cephas was the same as the other men in the boat. It was not so much the sea surrounding him as the sea within him which needed dealing with. There had to be a calm quietness of soul within. It was not the crowd left behind that needed ministry but the crowd within Peter, a Peter who tried to put his own oar into the sea and found it made things much worse. There is a crowd within him, of self, of fear, of tears and of fault. These make up a crowd which keeps Jesus on the outside. There are moments when the real danger is not in the sea or the boat but in Peter. There is no captain, no map or orders.

Jesus could have walked by,[2] but He bends His straight path into their whirlpool. The power Jesus was to display was not in calming a troubled sea. That was easy. It was controlling Peter that was the difficulty. Jesus comes to our struggles in order to make our strivings cease.

In Matthew 8:24 Peter is seen to be struggling and buffeted as the man with demons in Matthew 8:29 is thrown around. It must have been quite a hurricane to make a hardy fisherman fear. When Peter stepped out of the boat he was the only one of the twelve who stepped out. Jesus had called him on land to leave the boat, now He calls him on the sea to leave it.[3]

We are all called to Christ

Matthew 14:28,29 was a test for Jesus: 'If it is You, call me to Yourself.' Not to the boat, the waves, the depths, but to Jesus Himself. Other elements lost their grip on Peter's life. This was as Daniel in the lions' den or the Children of Israel crossing the Red Sea. Once eyes are fixed then feet are sure. There appeared to be a path of concrete between Jesus and the disciple. There is strength and length in the catch of Christ. His callings are His enablings. Peter would find Jesus under the sea and above the sea. When He called Peter it was from the old to the new, from the fellowship of the struggling and strangling to Christ, from death to life and from the shallowness of a boat to the depths of the sea. 'Be where I am, be as I am, get wet with Me.'

'Tell me to come to You' (verse 27). As Peter stepped out the gap between the two narrowed into a close fellowship. There had to be such a closeness that neither wind or wave could penetrate. In the shelter of His presence there is perfect calm. The sun never ceased to shine. There had never been a raging storm in the heart of Jesus. Where His shadow rests, waves bow in worship.

He called before he reached rock bottom

Peter did not wait to hit the bottom before he cried out in verse 30, 'Lord save me' (the Greek tense is 'do it quickly'). Had he continued to sink he would have completely lost sight of Jesus. The water reached his knees and he had been taught a lesson. 'Call while He may be found.' Cephas calls before things became worse, before the ship sinks and he disappears from sight he calls to the Lord. The man who sees attackers in the shape of wind and waves is a sensible man who puts the trumpet to his lips and gives a blast, rallying all the powers of Christ to his aid. These walls of water were as real as the walls of Jericho and must be brought down. The arms of the Saviour reached to where Peter was. They always do. Peter, sinking, appealed to the calm Captain, and Jesus, in saving him, saved others in the same situation. He surrendered His whole life stretched to bridge the gap between Himself and Peter. What a picture of the Calvary to come!

Why do we doubt?

Verse 31 of King James Bible asks: 'Why did you doubt?' The same word for doubt is used in Matthew 28:17 meaning 'pulled two ways'. Peter was now being pulled Christ's way. When he was pulled by the giant sea the troubles began to multiply and he began to sink. You cannot have your feet on the Rock and on the sea at the same time in a gale and hope to maintain that position for any length of time. The whole commitment of Cephas was in his cry. It had to be heard above every other noise. The place itself was marked forever in the heart of this disciple.

If you travel to the Lake District, on the edge of Lake Windermere you will see a small Cross erected by a family in remembrance of a loved one who died in those waters at the very place where the Cross is. Such was in Simon's heart.

The pull from below was greater than the drag from above. We all tend to gravitate towards our centre. Peter went down, but Jesus did not go down with him! Jesus retained His position. A hole was made in the sea to receive Simon the Son of Jonas, but there was a larger space in the heart of Jesus for him. He was not only plunging into the depths of the sea, but also moving deeper into

Jesus. You can only sink as far as the hand of Jesus. There is a sort of shelf which runs through our troubles, rather like the golden bar which ran through the boards of the Tabernacle.[4] He made the bar to 'shoot' right through the middle of them. Peter sent out his S.O.S. (Save Our Souls) and as he began to sink he cried out to the only one who wasn't sinking and to the only place which he knew offered refuge. Jesus could have calmed everything, but it would have been less of an adventure. The disciple becomes an Apostle standing as a rock in the sea. With the help of Jesus he did what Jesus did, he walked on water. They had to walk together back to the boat. The journey back was much easier than stepping over the side of the boat. It is always easier looking back, retracing steps when we have conquered. Neither King Canute or the so-called prophet John Wroe of Wakefield accomplished what Peter did. Both tried to control the seas, and one tried to walk on water but failed because there was no Christ in the water calling him to His side.

It was not the cry of fear in verse 26 which claimed the help of Christ. It was the cry of seeking, of wanting to be where Jesus was. That cry was the whimper of the child and it made a louder noise in the hearing of Christ than any storm. It was a sob from the heart: 'I am a failure—be my success.'

Never lose your sense of God's presence

Peter must never lose his sense of God. We awaken every morning to the rapture of His smile. We pass each day conscious of His presence. We close our eyes at night under the breath of His benediction. Peter has to be on guard against anything which will dim his vision of Christ. We must not wait to cry out until the next step has *Ichabod*—the glory has departed—written all over it. Paul speaks of being knocked down but not being knocked out.[5]

Jesus had prayed before He faced the storm and He did not sink. We are never told that Peter prayed, only that he began to sink.

The hand (verse 32) which lifted him to the water's surface and brought him back to where he had been earlier in verse 22, was a sure, strong hand, it was the hand of the Pilot and was better than the hands of the other eleven disciples. The wetness did not cause that hand to lose its strength or ability. Simon did not slip between the fingers.

Cephas became like Alice in Wonderland[6] who fell into a pond with all manner of creatures in it, birds, animals, Duck, Dodo and Eaglet and several rather curious creatures. One cry and they all flew away. Only those things which would help others were left and Alice led them onto dry land. How many has this sinking disciple led onto dry land? Some sinking for the third time have caught hold of something that Peter said or did. The action of Jesus has been swift to their aid at a time of plunging into a sea of grief. How many have been helped back to Christ as they have slipped and slithered over the side of the ship? We will never know. Many have been helped to safety and held in safety because this one wave-walker taught that when we begin to sink we cry unto the Lord whose hand is larger and safer than any sea, whose words are louder and more powerful than crashing waves. Words enter inside, waves only splash on the outside, splashing themselves out of existence as they strike a solid object.

Being baptised afresh

Peter had his wayward feet baptised again when he began to sink. Feet washing wasn't only done with bowl and towel, it was done with sea and with the power of the Son of God. The sweat of the old paths and the deposits of disobedience had to be washed off. There were things that day which drowned, cast into the sea of His forgiveness and forgetfulness, never to be remembered against Peter as he touched new depths and reached for new heights.

The New Testament Church

The boat became a floating Church. It had all the hallmarks of the New Testament Church where every convert was lifted from a sea of iniquity. It was a true Bethel on the waves as they bowed before Jesus Christ. A true 'Logos' and 'Doulos'. When they worshipped Jesus they were acknowledging the winner in the war of the waves. This was no nebulous Neptune. The congregation had been converted as Jesus lifted Peter and calmed the fears in their lives. When Jesus walked back to the ship the waves of the sea like the prickles of the porcupine fell flat and smooth. The winds and strong waves were taken into His hands and squeezed dry. The disciples witnessed a conversion of the sea. They had been first hand witnesses of Jesus at work, of all that He began to do. There was deep harmony in that boat. Peter went out over the side and they made room for him as he returned bringing Jesus into the boat with him.

This boat was as every Church should be—*a growing company* as Cephas and Jesus stepped into it. The best member a Church has is Jesus Christ! *It was a calm, peaceful Church,* lacking the clamour of the waves. *It was a moving Church,* they were going somewhere. It had a Captain and they faced the future with His strength, the strength of the Conqueror in the midst. *Every member was a witness* to the miraculous power.

The wind grew weary and ceased acting as a tyrant. It had wearied itself as some hunting dog in the presence of the Master of the Hunt. No quarry had been taken that day, there would be no stories of ships driven to suicide by strong winds. You can huff and puff but the Rock will not be blown down. The wind and the sea gave up the battle. Jesus had conquered the elements, now He needs to conquer the eagerness of Peter and turn zeal into deeper love, as deep as the surrounding sea. There needs to be that in Peter which would not capsize with fear or be driven by the impetuous. Jesus had to bring the sinking and the erring into a place of total surrender in worship. It was to take many happenings in the past and many storms in the future. It would take much water and strong winds until sail was hoisted into God's wind.

The true 'ship'

They came into the ship. Every word ending in 'ship' finds its full cognisance in this one word—fellowship, friendship, partnership, relationship, membership—but the best word of all is discipleship!

Along the Scottish coast as one travels in a boat you will suddenly see a Gospel text freshly painted on the side of a cliff for everyone to receive as if perched from a pulpit. The cliff becomes a preacher of the love of God, for written are the words: 'God is Love'. One day a young child straying to the edge of this cliff fell but was not killed. The parents were so thankful that they vowed they would have the words painted on the cliff edge and apply fresh paint when needed, as a token of their thankfulness that their child survived. Whenever we fall, at the end of everything, when things seem hopeless, we can write 'God is Love'.

William Cowper, the hymn writer, was planning to commit suicide. He asked the driver of the carriage he was in to take him to London Bridge where he intended to jump and to end it all, but the carriage became lost in a thick fog and, after travelling for some time it stopped, not knowing where they were. Cowper said, 'I might as well get out here.' To his utter amazement he was outside his own front door! He went into his house and lived for many years after this incident. He wrote, 'God moves in a mysterious way, His wonders to perform.'

Love takes through every storm

Love is greater than trial. It was to Peter. It is that which is stamped on every pain, the greatest soother of all. It is healing, health, hope in storm. The love of Jesus for this one disciple and therefore all disciples was deeper, wider than any sea. Sea might dry up but the love of God never will. Rather a sparrow taking the liquid from the sea little by little, taste by taste, drying it up completely than the love of God disappear. Faith and hope may disappear, but love remains.

When men first learned to sail ships during a storm they thought that the gods were angry and would make an offering to appease them. Their ships even had god-shaped prows, each ship sporting the image of their own god carved on the boat. They would throw a felon overboard, tie one to the rigging or mast as an offering to the gods. The old life of Peter was offered as he stepped into the sea and there and then it was buried in the waves. Baptism was here for him. There had to be a death, burial and resurrection. When this happens great calm prevails and victory is assured. There had to be that surrender of self in the Growing Pains of Peter.

Notes

[1] Matthew 7:25
[2] Mark 6:48
[3] Matthew 4:18–20
[4] Exodus 36:33 (KJV)
[5] 2 Corinthians 6:9 (J.B. Phillips)
[6] Carrol, L., *Alice in Wonderland*, p 17 (Wordsworth)

CHAPTER

14

A Reasonable Explanation

The parable, or short story, was at the very heart of the ministry of Jesus Christ. Many times He used earthly stories to unfold Heavenly meanings. The parable was His way of revealing truth to the discerning. Figures of speech and loaded metaphors were His method of preaching, diamonds with many facets flashing forth brilliance.

The term 'Parable' appears some forty times in the New Testament. Mustard seeds, birds, Prodigal son, all were parables. A parable is that which is thrown alongside. We can use it as a measure of Heavenly likeness in earth's stories. The parabolical will always defeat the diabolical!

Jesus told a number of parables in Matthew Chapter 15, and Simon Peter wanted a full and frank explanation as to their inner meanings. Life can be like a parable, a maze, yet designed and patterned if viewed from above, full of shapes, signs and sounds which need interpreting by the Accoustic Engineer. Cephas needs an interpretation of life, shot through with light from the lips of the Light of the World. He needed a word of knowledge and a word of wisdom to apply that knowledge.

Peter again is the spokesman.[1] His were the questions and reasonings of a natural man. What troubled him needed to be broken small enough to feed the little fledgling not yet ready for flight into fight or might.

Jesus was at hand so many times to give an explanation. Those on the Emmaus Road needed an exposition and Jesus unfolded to them the secrets of God. The years were peeled back and all that they contained was revealed to the disciples. Jesus always holds the torch. That which had remained secret and hidden was revealed by Jesus Christ through the light of His knowledge and wisdom.

The explanations we require are requited

Peter said, 'Tell us the parable' (verse 15). Talk to Jesus for He is the listening Christ. Peter found that to be true. In Matthew 15 there are a number of parables against hypocrisy, double standards and shallow teaching. The blind do not lead the blind when Jesus is leading them. There are no false plantings when He sows the seed. These are words of the Wise, knocking at the heart's door of Cephas.

Peter comes to Jesus as a child, desiring an explanation for everything. Who? Who? What for? When? As Creator He has supreme knowledge of what He has said in parable form. He wants to explain it to Peter fully so that the teaching would keep him from tares, blindness, ditch discipleship.

Peter realises that if nothing is asked then nothing is answered. God's Son is the Words and the Meaning. There is not one thing that He doesn't understand. Peter went to Jesus when he wanted to consult the Word of God. For explanations of life we need the source and centre of life. When we are afraid of misspelling or misinterpreting, then go to Jesus. If you have got hold of the wrong end of the stick, go to Jesus. What seemed cloudy and dense to Peter when he came to Christ became sunshine and clarity. When Peter says, 'So help me God', Jesus tells the truth, for He is God. Every word of explanation was a doorway for Shepherd and sheep to go in and out and find pasture.

When C.H. Spurgeon wanted to produce parables in book form he called them *Salt Cellars*. Each parable contains some wit, some spice, some flavouring, a tang. The radiancy of Jesus was better than daylight, wiser to Peter than all the wisdom of men. Moses, the man trained in all the wisdom of Egypt: Daniel, trained as a statesman in Babylon, and Solomon arrayed in all his glory was not arrayed like one of the words which Jesus spoke to His disciple. They are all closed books, but He is the open page containing the answers. There was no requirement to work it out, to make a final guess. Ordinary words were crowned with the celestial. From each word comes a thousand pathways to Heaven.

Why we sometimes ask questions

Verse 16 gives the answer to why they wanted an explanation at all. Are you without understanding? Eyes closed and ears stopped? The meaning of the Greek word can allow it to mean, 'Are you a weapon without a point? Can you not strike the target? Are you off-course with your understanding? Is there no penetration into the things which I am saying to you? They were without spiritual insight. The arrow falling short of the target found in the word 'sinned' (Romans 3:23). All disciples can be blinkered, dull of mind and hard of heart when wanting to understand what God is saying in pearl form, as it were, and yet hearing it as a pebble in a parable.

C.H. Spurgeon wrote: 'Even the College of the Apostles failed to grapple with it. He who uttered the dark saying could best interpret it.' Jesus is the giver and the interpreter of all things which are seen as a shadow or through a glass darkly.

The inspiration and interpretation of life

'Let him keep silent if there is no interpreter present' (1 Corinthians 14:28). There is in Jesus! 'Lo, I am with you always. I am the full interpretation of all things. Others are shadows whilst I am sunshine. Others guess, and I am that about which they are guessing. Others work it out, but I am that which they are working out.' Peter didn't stay huddled in a corner trying to work it all out. He went to the Index of the world, the Concordance of Christianity, Jesus Christ. If Jesus didn't know what He meant then the disciples certainly would not know. Their knowledge, particularly the knowledge that Cephas had, was being brought to birth. There was a sort of renaissance taking place, old things were passing away and behold, all things were being made new. The explanations of life are not difficult to understand. We, in our darkness, see no light at the end of the tunnel because we look at the walls and not at the way ahead. We, with Peter, seem to have veiled and shackled minds. 'Let this mind be in you which was also in Christ Jesus. In understanding be men' (Philippians 2:5). In malice, be children. Peter begins to understand what Jesus is saying.

Jesus can deal with every parable in your life. Any dark enigmatic catastrophy, anything which is not readily understood. When there is no interpreter, there is Jesus Christ. He is the interpretation of every foreign tongue, every vision, dream, and dark saying. He is the mother tongue speaking through the Father in a diversity of tongues, sometimes of men, sometimes through angels.

Everything seems so marvellous, then suddenly there is that which encroaches upon our own happiest moment, that which stabs happiness with pain, lacerates laughter until it is torn into shreds. What was once healthy is found bleeding and dying, about to be buried alive with problems. Laws and ceremonies were one problem. Water which had been turned into wine was another. Fruit, long since dead, reappearing as fossils. Should they eat with unwashed hands? There are things which are presented to us which encroach on life, closing doors. We have to recognise the hand which is sliding them into the life. What was a grain of sand can become a mountain and what was a mustard seed, the smallest of all seeds, can become a tree. Goliath was once a small child! Fibres become rope, sand, when heated, becomes a pane of glass. If a person cannot understand then striking that person on the head with a heavy encyclopaedia will make him see stars, not increase his knowledge. He will need a doctor and not simply an answer! The best and surest answers about life come from Him in whom are hidden all the treasures of wisdom and knowledge.[2]

The interpretation in these verses is connected with both outward and inner experiences. It is guarding the heart to ensure that what happened in the life of the Apostle Paul does not happen to us. Paul says of some: 'They came in sideways' (Galatians 2:4), 'unawares'.

What is life saying to you?

Jesus told the parable of the tares which were sown in the night.[3] Growth in the night is like the tide coming in. Even at the final

Judgement there will be goats and sheep. The Kingdom is likened unto a fishing net full of all manner of fish. There is a whole list of those things seeking to spoil your heart, to bind you as they did Samson, gently, quietly lest they disturb your peace and rest in Jesus. There is a silent working which needs to be understood. What is life saying to the disciples at this time? They want to know where they stand. Where are we in this? Peter, willing to learn, needed to know who was opening and closing the doors. Was it right to practise this or that? If more followed the example of Jesus would we have less of this and more of that? To know and to be assured, to have anything and everything interpreted by the glow of the Light of the World keeps us from stumbling. Those who follow Him will not walk in darkness. We sink until we come to the One who is solid Rock. Jesus is Light and He is the window for the darkness of Peter. He is speech for our dumbness. Sometimes, when I am in the Church building without lights and I want to open a door, I aim for the chink of light shining through the keyhole. The key fills the light and the door is opened. Peter had to use the light he had, but he also had to use the Light which had a grip on him. There are some things which come to blow the light out. We need that which comes in the Name of the Lord, the true Light which comes into our world is not comprehended by the darkness. We have eyes but we see not, we have ears but do not hear. There is a discernment which is spiritual and which comes to us as we mature. If Jesus is the door, let Him be the Door. If He is Light, let Him be Light. If He is Truth or Life then let Him be what He is. Give Him freedom of expression, let Him roam freely in and out of pasture. God does not only bless others, He blesses Jesus and us in Him. Christianity is Jesus in all His fullness and achievement. His service is still to open the eyes of the blind and to grant a sound, healthy thinking mind.

Life can be a kaleidoscope

If men were to come from outerspace at different seasons of the year and then had to describe earth to someone from another world, how different their explanations would be. Science is sometimes like that. It depends from which angle you come and along which avenue you travel towards a conclusion. There are things which creep in and which need chasing out. Cephas, with Jesus, is equal to anything. Life can bowl us over but then that allows Jesus to get underneath us. He is so humble that He is on the floor even as we fall. No two days, no two problems are the same but the One Who says, 'I change not. The same Yesterday, Today and Forever' can deal with everything. We struggle as we stand on both feet but Jesus conquers on His knees in prayer. What we cannot handle with both hands He manages to control even when two hands are nailed to a Cross. He treads the tempter down with feet that are nailed to that same Cross.

There will always be thorns on the branch and we shall never fully understand them. All children go through different stages. I know of one little cotton bud of colour who would say something and then add for good measure, 'and dat is dat'. Another phase the child went through was to say NO to everything. The same child would also say the opposite to anything that was said. If you said YES, it said NO, and so on. Even though the child was contradicting itself, it seemed pleased to do it! Immature, as many Christian converts are!

What troubles you, matters to Him

Cast all your care on Him. Had Peter learned this? When you cast all your care on Him you make room for more of Him in your life. Christ will crush care. Care will seek to crucify Christ afresh. Care thrown (cast away as a sickness) leads to Christ on the Throne. These are vital lessons for the leader among men. The thoughts and ideas of men needed removing so that the teaching of Christ might rest in the heart.

> Cast care aside, lean on thy Guide,
> His boundless mercy will provide.
> Trust, and the trusting soul shall see,
> That Christ is all in all to thee.

A tale told in the dark is an enigma, that which is shrouded in darkness. Yet the light for that darkness, that enigma, Peter, realises is in Jesus Christ. Jesus was shut in with Simon. We want to break open the roof, do all manner of climbing and scaling when all the time the door is open. Jesus is the Light at the end of the tunnel. There is no need to live today by the light of tomorrow. Today's light must not be switched off because of tomorrow's darkness. Why should your life continue to be a tunnel? When you are faced with the unknown you turn and cling to the known. 'The hand of God is better than a known way.' If you follow that hand you will come to the heart—from finger tip to heart beat.

On another occasion Cephas had said: 'To whom shall we go? Only You have the words of Eternal life' (John 6:68). For the spokesman of the twelve there has to be utter conviction that there is nowhere else to go. Where else could you go? What else could you do? To beg, I am ashamed.

There is greater power in Jesus

Question: 'Will you at this time restore the Kingdom unto Israel?' There is the envelopment of darkness. We are shrouded in mystery. We hear that enigma speaking to us, 'Behold, I show you a mystery.' At the appearance of the Lord the smile of knowledge spreads across the unknown. Peter could have asked, 'what is happening to me?' He did not need to match wolf with wolf, but wolf with lamb. The only way to match up to what Satan may try to do is to bring David to Goliath. Bring your lions to Daniel or Samson or even Benaiah.[4] If you have not the strength to wrestle with them, then bring the lions to Daniel and have their mouths sealed. Bring them to Jesus, for He will make the lion and the lamb to lie down together. If we brought the problem whilst it was still at the cub stage of growth it would never develop into a lion.

When they brought other questions concerning the dividing of an inheritance, Jesus said, 'Who made Me a judge or ruler over you?' (Luke 12:14). The Leader did not mind explaining His own Creation. He is the Designer, Upholder and Sustainer of the Universe.[5] Jesus came to give light of the knowledge of the glory of God.

That which Jesus brings into a life, He is able to explain. He is the original manuscript, in Hebrew, Greek and Aramaic. If the colloquial is best, He will use that. He is the Appendix and the Dictionary, the Concordance to Greek and Hebrew, to character and conduct. All of the answers are with Him. All the promises of God are Yes and Yes in Christ Jesus.

There must be relating in questioning

We have our own dark areas and we expect Jesus to give us the answers to questions He has never asked. If Jesus is not saying, then I am not asking! Peter is not waiting for the morning, the dawning is in Jesus Christ. We come to problems with clouded eyes and we see, hear and know not what God is saying to us. When Jesus was spoken to by the Father, some thought it was thunder. We need the flashes of lightning and the rains. Let Jesus roll the stone away and flood the tomb with light, banishing the darkness within this Cross-bearer. The answers come not from books or learning, not even from visiting country after country, but from Light itself. Leaning on Jesus leaves us marked forever. It is not just an impression, but we are impressed.

The best sermons and expositions come from Jesus Christ. Matthew 5 is a prime example and explanation of Christian action.

Luke 24:27 Jesus explained everything to them, putting everything in its place. When we are newly converted it is rather like going into a new house. We don't quite know where to put anything. I once saw a jigsaw puzzle and if you were able to position a rose in the centre then everything else fitted into the pattern, forming a beautiful garden around the rose itself. If Jesus is at the centre, the circumference will be right. In Peter's mind it was as if everything had fallen from the shelves and Jesus came and put everything where it belonged. He translated from a foreign tongue. He was not simply the Translator but also the Interpreter. When Nehemiah preached as he built the Temple he gave the interpretation of what was written. If it is an unknown tongue, pray for the interpretation.

Weariness can lead to questioning

Jesus asked those disappointed weary travellers 'What manner of 'communications' are these you are having with one another?' (Luke 24:17). The words 'communications between one another' means, according to John Trapp, throwing the ball to one another.

Then, in Luke 24:27, He expounded unto them in all the Scriptures the things concerning Himself. Jesus is preaching on Jesus! The Monarch speaking on the Monarchy!

Judges 14:12 is a riddle, a hidden saying. Jesus was doing this when explaining this parable. It was the expounding of a riddle. They were in darkness travelling from Jerusalem to Emmaus, about to exchange the city for a village. Some of Lot's experience was going to be theirs. '...the little place' (Genesis 19:20) Zoar. Jesus had to tell Peter and all the disciples so much more about Heaven then hell and this is illustrated in the things that happened to Simon of Cyrene, fresh from the country and pressed into service, to be remembered for ever! Jesus adds permanence to that which is defined as transient. He expounded to them the things which they did not understand. 'I am on the outside looking in, above looking down, underneath looking up. I am inside but as the door leading out.' Jesus speaks into any situation. His sayings and His words are not matched by Simon listening. He became dull of hearing after the first sentence sometimes. What enriched Peter and the people was that which was like honey from the Honeycomb, proceeding as gracious words out of His mouth. Those words lack nothing, they are pungent and to the point, having a beauty and a form. Having Jesus we have all. All things are yours. It wasn't what friends, Scribes, Pharisees or Saducees said, but what Jesus said. There might be those who are tempted to speak on the Rise and Fall of the Roman Empire and who sound quite impressive, until we bring to the podium Edward Gibbon who wrote his famous book on the subject. The local bricklayer might think he is alright until he looks at the work of Sir Christopher Wren or Nehemiah or Bezaleel. I am not going to read a book, listen to a record or watch a television set if the real living person can come alongside me and help me!

Jesus tells us what to do

As Jesus spoke, the Greek alphabet formed into words as soldiers on parade. There was a word of creation for Peter, a word of authority coming into him. Others may speak and we listen and are left weighing what has been said. When Jesus speaks we do not weigh what is said, we ourselves are weighed, judged, challenged and changed. We do not listen in order to applaud, we listen so that we may fall down and worship, not the gift but the Giver.

To know that you know and to have received the answer from the depths of the heart of God is assurance indeed. You need no other signature on the paper.

As Jesus performed a miracle through His word to sickness and blindness, as disease fled, and as He spoke to Peter darkness and ignorance were thrust through, so there was trust. One is always richer for having listened to the Master. Hear His words alone, and forget the rest. No man ever spake like this Man. He spoke to Mary in the Garden and a fresh Genesis 1:2 took place in her heart. 'They say... but I say unto you' (Matthew 11:22,24).

At the Wedding of Cana in Galilee 'Whatever He says to you, do it' (John 2:5). Water is turned into wine. The scholar is with the Master. Very often Jesus has to take us to the Alpha in order that we may be led to the Omega. His word deals with all that is in the heart. Within the heart there is confusion, questions unanswered, many doubts and fears. We are like the matted wool on the back of the sheep yet when Jesus speaks that wool shapes into a beautiful garment. We understand, we know that this is the Messiah, the King of Israel. We watch the way others walk, we follow Jesus in His footsteps and, as we travel, we turn to speak to those by our side who are walking in the same way to the Celestial City. Suddenly we realise that the one we are speaking to as we follow Jesus is Peter the Apostle. We are part of the growing pains.

Notes

[1] Matthew 15:15–20
[2] Colossians 2:3
[3] Matthew 13:25
[4] 2 Samuel 23:20
[5] Colossians 1:16,17
[6] 2 Corinthians 1:20

CHAPTER

15

Building Around
the Glory

The great moment of Caesarea Philippi was followed by the great hour on the Mount of Transfiguration. It is thought that the time spent in the mountain of such distinction followed Peter's confession and revelation 'You are the Christ, the Son of the Living God.' Tradition states that it was Mount Tabor, but there is more evidence to suggest that it was probably Mount Hermon which the Sidonians called 'A coat of mail'. The source of the River Jordan was on its slopes and it was about fourteen miles from Caesarea Philippi. Psalm 89:12 describes it as the Holy Mount. Hermon was at the centre of the Promised Land, the highest peak in Galilee.[1] It was there as a monument of conquest, part of the border area. Psalm 133:3 noted its heavy dew. Joshua 12:5 records how Israel had conquered its king. It was part of the war dowry of Israel.[2] It had been the seat of Baal worship.

It was with this as a backdrop that Jesus led the three disciples, Peter, James and John up the mountain through happenings and religious suggestions into something which was to make history, something which had never happened before. Walking with Jesus, even scaling a mountain does have its compensation and glorification. We exalt something through elevation. God allowed Jesus to ascend to the place where Peter could see His true glory. Everywhere Jesus went He set alight with life and made it relevant to the day and the hour. There was to be a Holy glow placed into that mountain making it into a stage on which God would place the actors whose parts were for real because Jesus was always real. Such happenings served as light to the soul of Peter, quickening his desire to follow and to serve Jesus Christ. At the climax the difficulty was not in getting them up the mountain but down again! They wanted to stay there, or at least Peter did.

The inner nature of Christ

The Mount of Transfiguration was given so that they might see the inner nature of Christ aglow in His outer body to encourage them on the way and to strengthen Jesus Himself on His way to the Cross. Hidden resources were revealed. There was more to Jesus than they thought. The treasure chest containing all the treasures of wisdom, might, knowledge and righteousness and in which dwelt the fullness of the Godhead bodily,[3] was thrown wide open for eyes to see and minds to know. He was transfigured before them. As Jesus prayed, He glowed, like a shooting star or rising moon. If seeing is believing, then this was believing and seeing, so far as Peter was concerned. What could have been an ordinary mountain climb turned into something spectacular and Cephas went on in the power of it for many years. He mentioned it later in 2 Peter 1:18, as if the light was still shining on the page. It was as if a hand from Heaven was gilding the lily. The picture, framed by the mountain, seemed to contain luminous paint, the Light within had been switched on. The Light which had always been there began to beam outwardly. The picture that film directors of modern times have presented in glowing 'spacemen' was a reality in Jesus Christ. As the burning bush had flamed with fire and was not consumed, so the Christ, the Son of the Living God was before Peter. Without the human form of Jesus to shield that glory the eyes of the watchers might have fallen from their sockets as buttons. The ears of the listeners would have melted like wax.

There was no more glorious Synod! They were all in attendance—the Father, the Son, the Holy Spirit, Moses, Elijah! Peter, James and John are Apostles of the same Church. All the representatives of all the Ages gathered within the shouting voice and seeing eye of Peter.

Hearts are changed by glory

When Peter is writing to help others in their growing pains he mentions the fact—'When we were with Him in the Holy mount'. His pure mind of remembrance is filled with the glory. It did something to the heart of Peter, that glow of glory illuminated that which was within him. There was a substance revealed there and then which stayed with Peter and he mentions it as an encouragement to others who are trying to climb the mount of glory...keep going, keep climbing, keep pressing upward and you, too, may see His glory. Though Peter is long gone into the presence of the Lord the glory is still there for all who have struggles to see. At the end of the path of pain there is a light to lighten the next valley. We all need the light of His glory to take into the valley, to help the crowd, to see a young boy delivered from demon possession. The way is hard, the steps steep. The Transfiguration of Christ taking place as they watched meant something. It illuminated all the past happenings, punctuated all the writing and the thinking. Peter is saying, 'We arrived. We saw the glory, and lived to tell the tale. Go higher, follow Jesus all the way until you see that glory in your circle of friends.' The glory of God is in more than mountain top revelations, it is in our daily living, each happening that comes to pass. It is glory which can be taken and multiplied to correct situations and heal lives. Glory in the nature of Jesus the Son of God with healing in His wings. Whether in the mountain Hermon, Tabor or the valley, each happening is a miracle formed to bring glory into the heart. There is part of the glory of God in all that He allows, adding weight to us, the Eternal weight and glory which is ours. When a feather is turned into a wing or a tadpole into a frog, that is glory. The glory of the child is the old man. The very thing which Jesus denied the Scribes and Pharisees was granted to the disciples in this mountain. The glowing of His form was a sign from Heaven. The 'inner circle' as it were, was taken up into the mountain to crown it with human voices and faces. The feet of the disciples were meant to walk all over the highest realm of earth in order to state that humanity can live where the glory is and to take that glory via the Gospel to others. To this servant of the Cross it meant that whatever the difficulties, however hard the climb, Jesus was not diminished. He still had His glow. The brightest torch or lantern in the

220 The Growing Pains of Peter

Garden of Gethsemane was Jesus. He was the outshining of God's splendour, the express Image of His person.[4]

We need Jesus to lead us

With Jesus leading we can climb every mountain, ford every stream, follow every rainbow, for He is our Dream. With Him we can enter into new revelations. Peter's heart was enlarged. God was revealing the fame of His Son in glory, not in a newspaper or history book but in that which will last for ever. A place had to be made for the outshining of that glory among the small band of the Inner Circle. Moments of Majesty and days of demonstrated glory. It wasn't all climbing, sleeping or struggling, it was progress seen in the depths of a Jewish night. Peter's life lacked the glory of Christ before the Transfiguration but afterwards it never would. There are even more mountain peaks because one peep at glory is not enough. There had to be radiators of glory in earth's cold moments, among bare rugged rocks. That which shines through Christ must shine into Peter. Jesus was not crucified on this mountain but on Mount Calvary. Each mountain mouths a new message, brings another challenge. There is gold in them thar hills! It is gold of a different quality than that which men revere. The disciples saw, heard and recorded something that this world cannot purchase.

We all have our peaks and troughs

There are mountain peaks in the Christian life. There are stones and ditches, hills and valleys, but there are mountain tops to attain. The truths of Hermon are to be grappled with, the harp strings of Hermon to be played—Apostles are in the making! The disciples were the little Church on the mountain top, reminiscent of the positioning of some of our Cathedrals. Normally little grows on mountain tops but here the glory of Jesus Christ is glowing. Followers become disciples through climbing mountains! Giftings are developed in glory. Jesus was unique. Small minds are enlarged, those with a limited knowledge of Him became an unlimited company! This mountain was as different from Sinai as law is from grace. What had belched fire at Sinai became glowing glory at this place. Command and Law was seen in this shining Light. The fire had fallen on the altar when all was ready in the Old Testament, but now the fire and the glow and the glory does not come down from above, in Jesus it shines out from within. Peter is discovering that the path of the just shines more and more until the perfect day. It was another dimension revealed through Christ. The Light was switched on. The touch of the mountain rock acted as the switch and He became a Lamp unto their feet. Heaven itself will be a world of other dimensions.

The inner glory of Jesus Christ

The word used for 'shining' (Mark 9:3), means 'no fuller shining'. It is bleach-white. Soap and washing could not match it. It describes a garment with all the oil and soil removed. Jesus was clean within. Pat Boone, the Gospel singer, had the nickname of 'toothpaste' because of his clean life.

The same word was used of polished surfaces, answering to the laver in the Old Testament, built out of brass and lined with brass mirrors.[5] If Cephas had been close enough he would have seen his reflection as in a mirror. The word can describe lightning and twinkling stars, and also the sleek movements of a horse (Vincent, New Testament Words). When a spear was thrown and the sun caught the metal tip it shone. The face of Christ was as the sun, His garments as light. Daylight appeared at night. Daylight appeared and the darkness comprehended it not. The word used for the transformation of Christ describes pure white belts similar to those worn by soldiers which were whitened by having pipe clay rubbed on them. It holds a description of pure water. As white as snow. 'We were eye witnesses of His majesty' (2 Peter 1:16). The mountain became His Throne with three soldiers surrounding it— Peter, James and John. God kissed His Son and from those lips a gentle breeze fanned the coals within Christ and He began to glow, the fire burned. The crown He wore, His garments, the sceptre in His hand, the golden sandals on His feet were all of light, of glory.

Seeing things through the glory

The view from the top of most mountains is breathtaking. Other worlds can be seen. What the finger of nature has performed in valleys and hills is visible, but these things that we see, know and appreciate do not surround us, they are with us in Jesus Christ. He is the ultimate. There is that in Him and about Him which was breathtaking for Peter. Here was the beauty of Jesus drawn in light. No artist could paint this scene, although many have attempted to do so. Here was something God had not created—His Son. The clouds had divided and, instead of the moon shining through it was the essential character of Jesus Christ. The glow which was in Him shone right through. The higher we go with Jesus the brighter the prospect. Here was the Ray of Hope, the Rainbow of Promise. If you desire to see the Christ glorified, the inner nature of God revealed to you, 'Show me Thy glory' (Exodus 33:18), then be prepared to climb and to stay with Jesus. Be ready for visions, manifestations and dreams whilst you are awake! There can be glows of glory and visions of Heaven even in a mountain situation. If a burden is as large as a mountain then enter into it with Jesus Christ and you will see Heaven in and through it all. Somewhere between lifting the burden and placing it at His feet you will witness glory as a burning and shining light. This was mountain cast into the sea of His glory.[6] Muddy footmarks as they travel forward will be filled with the glory of God. The Beatitudes were given on a mountainside. Even the Ark ended its journey on a mountain top! Ararat, meaning 'Holy Ground', according to Fausset. After the flood God had finally brought His chosen few (Noah and his family) into holiness. On Hermon Peter entered the Tabernacle of His glory.

I have often wondered why this manifestation of the nature of Jesus was not seen in the valley or the town. The disciples had to look at what happened and then take it down into the valley in order that the glow, the glory, the Shekinah of God would be shared amongst the people in the delivering of the sick, feeding the poor, opening the eyes of the blind. Every miracle, every healing, every answer to prayer is a manifestation of the glory of God. They saw the glory in its entirety. Even Creation itself had been but shadows of glory.

The need for His glory

It was as if a mirror had been placed before the disciples and Jesus was transfigured before their eyes. He was greater and more glorious than a vein of silver or gold in any rock formation. We need the glowing Christ to help us maintain the spiritual glow of Romans 12:11. Darkness and dreariness can shine! The silver plough blade can come out of the furrow. The ordinary and rock-like can and will shine with light from Jesus Christ. God will be God in the fullness of His nature, for wherever Jesus is taken and accepted He gives forth such light that it touches the depths of darkness in every adherent.

It reminds me of the words of Graham Kendrick's hymn:

> Shine Jesus shine,
> fill this land with the Father's glory.

We talk of taking this land for Jesus, yet it is the glory shining through us which will take it. We do it when we have seen the glory of the Son, when we are living the life which Peter saw before him as an example. There He stood in all His shining glory. Those who were uncertain before are certain now, those who had lost their way could now find that way again. Shine on, shine on in Majesty...clothed with light as with a garment...Grace, glowing in the human race. As He glows there is light and help in that radiancy. There are enrichments which move across barriers and into realms that we know not. By the light which came from His body the veil of death and the future was lifted, and the disciples were able to peep inside. The glory always moves over the denominational fences erected by men. It touched all those present, whatever their beliefs. It was inclusive of all ages. It is larger and more complete than Peter, James or John. Their eyes turned towards Jesus Christ whatever their convictions might have been. Where that glory is, there we see Moses and Elijah in a new light. They are at home in the glory of God. Peter wanted that also, that is why he wanted to build, to add permanence, but that would have privatised the glory, shutting it up in some tabernacle. In the light of that glory those long since dead are alive and well, still walking, still talking, communication lines are still open. They are not worn out, decomposed, but still intelligent, knowing the future. They talk of Exodus, Moses and Israel leaving Egypt, their theme the Cross, bathed in glory. They were not in a hole in the ground but on a mountain! Risen in death they were in fellowship with Jesus holding conversation with Him. This must have exploded much of the thinking and teaching of Simon and those who did not believe in the resurrection of life after death.

Jesus is the centre of all worlds

Peter is convinced that Jesus is the Centre of this world and the world to come. He had important things to discuss, even with the saints of long ago. Memory and recognition is intact in the glory of the Son. This was better than the finger of God writing with fire in the rock or placing commands onto slates. Peter was lifted up into something new. Not everything old is useless and cast on one side. All things are refreshed and receive new light in the glory.

Moses is not striking the rock, Elijah is no longer in the chariot. Now they are in the same area, influenced by Jesus Christ. He has glory for every Age. He is the glory of every Age. The living and the dead, the ascending and the descending are still within His grasp. His fellowship is celestial and terrestrial, with those who have gone, with those who are here, those above and below. It reaches near and far, past and present. Jesus is there, adorned with glory, representing future days, those things about to be brought into the realm of human grasp. Jesus stood as a warrior, not yet wet with blood, but having returned from many wars and battles, adorned with medals. Moses and Elijah represented the days which are past, Moses the Law, Elijah the Prophets. Jesus adds to all things for He is all things unto all men. These two, of all men, were so close to God and draw near to Jesus Christ to discuss His death, His plans for the future. There was a design and an unseen presence at work allowing Jesus to be nailed to a Cross. His death was spoken of as a going out and a going on, a passing from one land to the Promised Land. If He gets there, then everyone who believes gets there!

Human frailty can dim the glory

Simon has been quiet for a long time. He breaks the fellowship of the Heavenly bodies with an earthly thought. He begins well, 'Lord', then he wants to build. There is a sense in which Peter was right. When we have seen the real glory of God we should want to do something, but not on a mountain top. Can you imagine the pilgrimages there would have been to the top of this mountain if Peter had been allowed to build? He spoke without thinking, but he never thinks without speaking. When you don't know what to say then don't say anything.

In verse 4, the best manuscripts read, 'I will make'...this was something which countered what God was doing. That day, in his blind zeal, closed to the glory of God, Peter would have commenced another denomination, another creation, another redemption. He did not fully realise that Christ was not for staying. Sit and be quiet was a difficult command for the activity in this man. God never wants to build other than on His revelations. He does not want us to build that which binds. Peter must not build that which would keep Jesus on earth. Build a booth and cover the glory, is unbelief, sectarianism. It is reminiscent of the Corinthian Church,[7] the three divisions of the Church before it was even built! Those who are lawful and rigid into the Moses tent! Those who are fiery Pentecostals—into the other! Those who want Jesus—into the first tent! Religion would never be complete until each tent had been visited and you had been sprinkled with Holy water. That sprinkling would have been the tears of Jesus spilling over because it would have been all so wrong. Jesus wanted the disciples to build in the valley, in the hearts of the people, not on the mountain top. Carry that glow with you, put it not into three tabernacles but into three thousand gathered as in Acts 2 and 3. Take it to Joppa, carry it to Patmos, take it to Lydia the seller of purple, and to the Philippian jailor. Let us not build tents, let us build lives and introduce Jesus to those lives.

The bright cloud answered to the glory emanating from Jesus. Even clouds on mountain tops can speak to us. One might ask, how can one of the twelve know the voice of God? 'Listen to Jesus' (Matthew 17:5). It is the voice which testifies of Jesus. We need the voice to calm our fears, to set us free.

The glory seen and voice heard must result in compassion shown

Any vision which does not result in Jesus touching a person is no vision at all. The clay is wet, the potter will mould it. One touch confirmed that He was real. A God who cannot touch cannot feel. Compassion without a finger has no hand. He was still in touch. The life of Jesus was God touching what He had become. The voice of Peter is soon lost in the voice of God. When God speaks He has wondrous things to say. It was that voice which stopped Peter establishing his own little three-tented kingdom. Verse 7 was God reaching out removing fear from the heart. There is no place for fear in glory. It told the heart of Peter that Jesus was still human enough to have a hand to touch and a heart to feel.

If you have seen the glory of the Lord, if you are part of the Inner Circle fellowship, if you have been up the mountain, had great visions and heard marvellous things, as John did on Patmos, you will be believed when the manner of your living reflects that glory. What works on the mountain top works in the valleys. What works in God's house works in every house.

Seeing and hearing Jesus only

Verse 8 (NIV) says, 'Get up and look up.' There is a message for Peter and for all of those of like nature who gather with him. That voice put Jesus back in control, when the nature of Peter might have taken over. That voice has to direct all who would see glory to a place where we see no man save Jesus only. That does not mean that God cannot use other men. It means that, after the Voice, there was no need for lesser men such as Moses and Elijah. What they were and accomplished fits perfectly into His glory. Take a look at glory as revealed in the Scriptures.[8] When we see no Man but Jesus only, that Image lives in us and from that we build and bless other people.

A man told D.L. Moody that he had spent three days in the Mount of Transfiguration and Moody quietly but knowingly asked him how many souls he had won to Christ. Glory is more than stars and good feelings, it can be an Oxfam parcel, deeds of kindness. God wraps many gifts with a ribbon of glory but the undiscerning eye can miss the message it conveys. All the glory of men and of this world if placed in a parcel would make a very small object indeed compared to the glory of Christ. That glory is so great that the Heaven of Heavens cannot contain it. It took a real full grown Man to reveal it and a mountain had to be used. It took the sky to hang the glory of God, like Christmas decorations as stars with clouds as balls of wool. It took a sea to reveal that glory. Even as the waters cover the sea the glory of God is in it. This is great thinking and action on the part of God. The prayer of Jesus was that they might see His glory where He is, having been made what He was as a man in touch with God.[9]

We have so misused the phrase, 'They saw no man save Jesus only.' It is as if we must not follow men or look at them, yet some followed Paul—as he followed Christ. That phrase was the rolling away of a stone. Moses and Elijah had gone. The volcanic eruption subsided. Each vision, each voice heard, every ministering miracle must bring Jesus back into His humanity. They saw no man, only Jesus. 'Then were the disciples glad when they saw the Lord' (John 20:20).

What Peter saw and was called to witness, we too are going to share.[10] We shall be changed. We shall have a body likened unto His glorious body. God is working within Peter and a body will clothe that new nature within him. They had witnessed a Resurrection, yet Jesus had not died. All these signs, sights and sounds set Peter's heart moving fast. See what Simon saw and do what he did, go into the valley, leave the ivory palace, minister into a needy situation with the power of God revealing His glory. Not only Jesus was transformed. The plan of God was that the disciples might also be transformed before Jesus. Peter must go down the Mount, as Moses did, not simply with a shining face but something in his heart that was God-given. There are things among the people which, having seen the glory of God, they could help to remedy. Seeing that glory gave great boldness to Peter. It made him realise that he was part of an everlasting cause. This Kingdom of God was not simply a matter of law or inspiration, it was Glory.

Notes

1 Matthew 17:1; Mark 9:2; Luke 9:28; Joshua 12:1
2 Judges 3:3; 1 Chronicles 5:23
3 Colossians 2:9
4 Hebrews 1:3
5 Exodus 30:18
6 Matthew 17:20
7 1 Corinthians 1:11–13
8 Hebrews 1:3
9 John 17:24
10 Colossians 3:4

16

The Towel, the Water, the Bowl, the Feet

There have been many comments on Christ's action of washing the feet of the disciples, recorded in John 13:1–17, but few have noted the action and reaction of Peter. The Creator of feet is seen stooping at His creation. The One who instructed the first foot on the first man to walk is seen peering into the sweat of men. From the sweat of the brow to the sweat of the feet, Jesus loved men and He loved this man Peter, the man of limited vision. How did it affect the son of Jonas as he saw the Lord of Glory with a towel around His waist washing feet? It must have had a profound effect on all the disciples, but especially on Peter. He was open to failure but also ready for success. Jesus had to lead him step by step to the washing bowl. His words were 'You shall never wash my feet—never in all Eternity', but Eternity did wash them, in Jesus. Jesus conquered this most resistant heart, saw it yield as the water washed away the last vestiges of rebellion, well hidden between the toes of the one who moved out of line when demands were laid on him. The towel, the water, the bowl were all more willing to respond to the Son of Man than this son of Jonas. The message from the actions of Jesus to Cephas was that you can conquer from a lowly position and with a towel. You can wash away anything that is between yourself and your brother. Using love as water anything hindering progress or the walk of the believer can be washed away. The first action, the first step came from the Saviour of men. Through humility you can make servants of all things, even toes! Those things you serve become your servants.

Was Simon dreaming? Kings usually wore golden girdles but Jesus takes a common towel as His dress of distinction and uses water, Adam's first beverage.

The towel becomes the emblem of Christianity

We are told that these actions took place the night before the Lord's death and they were in strife as to whom should be the greatest. John 14 to 17 gives us the teachings and happenings in the Upper Room which had been reserved for the Master to eat the Passover with His disciples. The High Priestly Prayer was discussed, the Promise of the Comforter had been given to them, battle orders had been received, yet the strange way in which to conquer all things amongst themselves, to be identified with Jesus was not a fishing boat or net, not a drawn sword, not even a broken box of alabaster ointment. It was a towel. How Peter's mind reacted we are not informed. Sufficient to say that here were strange weapons for a King establishing a Kingdom. A towel, a vessel of clay, water and feet.

On one of the Caribbean Islands when coconuts are cut from the tree just before they crash to the ground a man with a piece of sack towelling throws the cloth forward and it breaks the impact. If the coconut actually struck the ground it would crack open, but that touch with the towel preserves and keeps the coconut intact. The impact is conquered with a towel.

Jesus showed them the full extent of His love. It became basin-shaped to clean, towel-shaped to dry. His love ran like the water to hurting, dusty, dirty areas. All toes looked the same under the water as it washed away the dirt, removing all memory of where the feet had been. The evidence of straying was removed, the past washed away. The feet were presented as new born, baptised feet, rising in the newness of life. Had not the feet of every Israelite passed through waters of the Jordan and Jericho before entering the Promised Land?

Washing feet was an act that all could carry out. It did not make Jesus better than the rest, but the example was set for them to follow. When Jesus had performed the act, not a ceremony, He returned to His normal place among them. It was probably one of the finest deeds ever performed away from the Cross. The greatest deeds are often the most simple. It was necessary to teach Peter humility, that which he was refusing to receive from the hand of Jesus. Occasionally the things which Jesus did or said or the way He acted became too much for Peter to accept. His mind could not follow or his hand grasp. Jesus, robed with a towel was Christianity in all its glory. These were Kingdom Principles taught by Christ, acted out as a play with the towel as the curtain on the stage. It was to be humility and service, not the conquering hero as expected. There was no priestly gown. To towel the feet of others was what Jesus was expressing about the Christian faith. He had been used to the rough seas, the tough fisherman's existence. In Jesus we have service which not only pours water and washes feet but also dries those feet. The work He came to do was completed. Not one pair of feet did He refuse, not one life did He refuse to change by His power. Give a cup of cold water in His Name, fill a bowl from the wells of salvation, but do not stop there, bow low and wash feet. If the vessel is full it flows to the feet of others. This is the spirit of the Church, of Jesus Christ, and is in direct opposition to the spirit of the world. Compassion which ceases with a handshake is limited. The contrast between the teachings of Jesus and the teaching of the world is the contrast between a salty sea and a quiet pool. It was to be a ministry to dying feet, a service to those standing on one leg whilst the other foot was being washed. The water you have must be dirtied by the feet of others. You have to towel the dirty and the smelly. The water was poured over the toes and both feet were washed and dried. The work was completed in a spirit of humility. This wasn't the servant washing the feet of the Master, it was the Master washing the servant's feet. When the water was low then the tears of Jesus replenished the bowl. Toiling feet were cooled and refreshed. In Peter there had to be a refreshing ministry. For He often 'refreshed' me (2 Timothy 1:16). He cooled me down. He made me fresh again with soft breezes. As with Achilles' heel there was a part of Peter that he did not want to be washed, but if it was not washed then part of him would be weak and vulnerable for ever.

The lack of understanding

Verse 7—What I am doing you do not understand now, but you will one day. Peter still lacks understanding. His mind is as the fishing net with water going through the meshes. There is no light at the end of his tunnel, no dawn to his dark night. There are doctrines and ideas which have not yet penetrated the solid rock. Peter was wanting to make the act of humility more acceptable— wash my head and hands—wash every part of me! It was this very act of humility which made Peter part of Christ. Not only love but humility is the stamp of the Christian, willing to stoop at the feet of others in glad service, not simply being ministered to, but ministering. Jesus left the ranks of glory to become a servant. He made a choice and in doing so bows before His subjects. It is victory with a towel. When He washed their feet He threw in the towel and He won! He went to the bottom rung of the ladder in order that He might ascend to the top. The Son of God wrapped a foot in a towel, clothing it with what He gave 'As much as you have done it unto one of these, you have done it unto Me.' Washing, cleansing, touching, towelling—that which cannot do for itself.

Understanding the actions of Jesus

There must be an understanding of what Jesus had done (verses 13–14). Jesus is wanting to teach Peter to wash other people's feet. Not the face, but unseen, unsightly feet. Jesus set the example in everything from birth, childhood, youth, manhood and on to the Cross and Resurrection. Healing, praying, walking, speaking, He is the living Model and Peter must learn from Him. This wasn't textbook teaching, it was living action before the eyes of the student. In the humility of the Messiah there is that which does not only get under the skin it gets between the toes, into every crevice, neutralising every ounce of pride. There are teachings of Christ, teachings of the heart, things which need depositing in the heart. The inner motive, inner action, the compulsion from within. Jesus kneels at the feet which will kneel before Him in the future. He triumphs before it all happens! If in training Peter, then whatever you allow, whatever happens to you, will make it easier later on. The man who is humble has no problem with humility. Washed feet have no problem with grit. When you learn to laugh at yourself, to accept, to love the truth about yourself, that is humility. If there were no humility then all would have committed suicide long ago. Judas became suicidal.

We never want to submit

Peter did not want to submit. He did not, at this time, want a Jesus with an arched back dressed as a servant. This was not a fallen Adam's conception of a leader. His leader must be strong, abrasive, resolute. Jesus is teaching Cephas how he must act in His absence. The way up is the way down. If you commence with the feet you can rise to the heart. All things were given into His hands. The Son of God won with water. Jesus was not a servant in Name only, He was a servant. What He did was the overflow of the servant's heart as found in Philippians 2. He emptied Himself. All that water in the Vessel poured out, used up, marked the humility in the life of Jesus. When feet are being washed they are not walking away, not treading on others, not wandering. As He washed, so He controlled the next step, their destiny. To take shoes off, have feet washed means that you can start again. The feet can be turned in another direction, they can now follow on to know the Lord. The feet of Peter can be placed in the footprints of Jesus. All He did and was is there as an example. Each man must have his own towel.

The foot washing ministry

The lowest servant in the house of the East was called The Foot Washer. What a position with which Jesus commenced His ministry!

A young man appeared before the Missionary Council. He was educated, clever, sophisticated, but the Council had received a request for a servant. 'Will you forget everything else and go as a servant?' he was asked. The young man decided that he would. He went as a servant and was a great success. Serving and submitting to Christ.

As the water submitted to the bowl and the towel, the heart must respond to Jesus. This leader of men would act as a servant, submissive. Peter's problem was submission to service. He could serve, but could he accept the service of Jesus into his life? Peter was not consulted when Jesus wanted to wash his feet. It was service in the manner and at the time of the Master's choosing. Redemption, salvation, is the same, it is accepting what has already been accomplished. If Cephas is in default with one then he will be weak in the other. If he could not be trusted to wash feet he would not be trusted with any greater tokens of love. It was the Bowl for Beginners, but there would be an ocean later in his work for the Lord. If you can wash feet you can work in other spheres also.

It was necessary, before attending a feast, to take a bath. As you journeyed the feet became a magnet to sand particles and consequently at the home of the host the feet were washed. There was a participation of the owner's goods even before you tasted the food. If feet were not washed you did not sit at table, you went no further than the threshold of the house. This is the message of the Master to Peter. You can never come right in to the feast until you fully surrender, until the things which are hidden are washed away. Pieces of grit would cause trouble if left between the toes.

There are many services to be rendered but we have to be made ready to accept them through the example of Jesus Christ. He stood protocol on its head and Peter on his feet. It was more than gritty feet that needed hiding under the water. You cannot get lower than the feet. Jesus washes away those chaffing pieces with His tears. Washing the feet may not be a literal thing to us in the West but there are equivalent things we are called to accept from others. We must ensure that we have the humility to accept any blessings we are offered. Peter, if you don't lose your independent spirit you cannot be part of us. There will be no further step into the Kingdom if you do not submit now to the water. For the remainder of his days he would have had a limited vision. That is true for any member of the Church.

A guest would never be received without feet first being washed thoroughly, but the difference was that the host would never wash the feet, the servant would. Jesus is preaching even as He is pouring, I will have those with clean feet and dirty towels around Me. The marks of humility are branded on the body of service.

We must not accept lesser acts of grace

Peter would have had no difficulty in surrendering to a miracle or some great manifestation of glory. 'Let us build three Tabernacles', he had requested. There has to be a submission to the less spectacular. It is this which really enriches the soul, makes us worth our salt. Jesus won by throwing in the towel. Peter must win by allowing Jesus to perform those things in his life that he does not fully understand. There are many everyday things which Jesus wants to do for us but we need the humility to accept, even though we do not understand. We tend to limit Him as Peter did. It has to be acceptable to our way, to fall in with the order of our day. Any service must start where Jesus chooses. You cannot choose where, how, why and when you will serve God. Will you start at the dirty feet? Any service should be every service. You do not have to travel far to serve God; bend and bow in worship, the worship of washing another's feet. Jesus served the Father when He was in the Upper Room. The need became the altar at which He worshipped the Father.

One of the Caesar's of Rome commenced his life as a galley slave, rising in rank until he became Captain of the vessel and ultimately he ruled all Rome. Peter must start with the oar, rise higher than the waves, from cabin boy to Captain.

Our service must not contain partiality

Many feet need to be washed. There are those with sores in their souls. The disciples wanted to serve Jesus but some thought it would be in the waving of a sword or the plunging in of the knife, they would be as soldiers in an Army. In a way that was true. We must drink water from our own wells. There are services rendered right where the need is. Feet are walking by all the time and there are still some who would seek an opportunity to wash feet, claiming that there are none to wash! Look for legs and you will see feet. Seek evidence of weary feet needing to be washed. A shoe salesman was sent to a tribe which did not wear shoes. He sent a telex to his firm 'I cannot do anything here, they do not wear shoes.' Another salesman went to visit the same tribe and hurriedly sent a communication which said, 'Send as many shoes as you can, and as fast as you can, no-one here wears shoes!'

Peter is trying to tell Jesus how to do His job. Where, when and why He should do this or that. If Jesus had listened to him it would have destroyed the very act and washing the feet would have been lost in the bathing of the body. You could do that for yourself, Peter. Jesus is saying, 'Let me, as a servant to your humanity, take care of you. I want to get between your toes.' Each person coming with humility to have their feet washed in the presence of Christ must take shoes from their feet for as they stand in the presence and shadow of Jesus it is Holy ground.

The paths of righteousness

'This thing I do will help you to walk straight.' The devotion of the servant touches the points others miss. Peter has areas that need cleansing and which he does not want Jesus to concentrate on. The smelly, sweaty, bunioned, calloused, varicosed feet received the jems of Jesus in water and towel, the dedication of Christ. I have feet to wash that you know not of, an army marching. Foot washing places the feet near Christ for His inspection. 'They beheld His walk.' They were pointed in the direction of Jesus. Grace is like water, the sparkle of the water must get into the tired feet.

You, son of Jonas, have to see that men's feet are as important as any other part. The ministry granted to you, however lovely, however small, must be as the greatest act ever performed because I have sanctified it by My action. Wayward washed feet are acceptable to the Body of Christ. If they continue walking away, drown them with water; if they are cold then wrap them in a towel; if they are dirty, wash them. If you will not let Jesus perform small acts of grace He will not perform great ones. Many people want Jesus to do the whole thing, the great thing, but they are not ready in servant devotion to accept the smallest things, the washing of feet. Yet it is as much a part of the Divine intent as the creation of the worlds. When God looks down feet are important. Small acts of service are always seen.

As Jesus stoops He bends His back as He did on the cross. It took this Cross-like posture to fulfil His assistance in the life of Peter. One foot was placed over the bowl and water was poured.

There would have been a place where the water and towel would not have reached if Peter had not surrendered. God loves feet as much as faith, tears, sweat and blood. There is nothing common or unclean with Jesus. It was feet-first total commitment—all or nothing.

In verse 5 He dries the feet as He dries away the tears with that which is wrapped around Him. The towel is an extension of the heart. If Peter had refused to submit then the work of Jesus in his life would have stopped right there. His hand would have been withered, his eye blinded and he would have had crooked feet, unable to walk the distance.

Jesus washed everyone's feet

In verses 2 and 12 Jesus washed a traitor's feet and He must wash the feet of Peter. We are called not only to surrender to saints but also to those with a demonic disposition. That devotion must not stop or stick in human thinking. There was enough water in the bowl, enough humility in the heart to complete the work.

'Above all' (Colossians 3:14), as a towel or outer garment, as a girdle, 'put on charity' which will bind together. Peter wants to so display his humility, THOU shall not wash my feet, that he reduces the very thing he is seeking to promote. His was the pride, the arrogance.

Mohammed Ali travelling on an aeroplane was asked by the stewardess to fasten his seat belt. 'Superman doesn't need a seat belt,' he said. 'He doesn't need an aeroplane either,' the stewardess replied.

Every drop of water becomes a jem, every towel a seamless dress. It is a bowl of compassion. Some feet need more than one washing, they need a constant flowing fountain. Peter, if you have dirty feet and you will not allow God to wash them in the conventional way then He will see to it that you pass through deep waters in order to arrive at the other side with clean feet. Then, using the sun as a towel, He will soak up all the moisture. Flood and fire offer the same service. Jesus conquered by using water, not a flaming sword or great army. That one act more than ever made Peter a part of Christ. That towel was the red carpet into the very heart of

Jesus and all who would be royal must come and take it up. His death on the Cross would make Cephas even more a part of Him.

The posture of victory

Armies stand in order to conquer but Jesus knelt down. Were there some of His tears in that bowl of water? There were certainly kindnesses and good deeds. Rich water and a threadbare towel suddenly became as important as Gideon's fleece. At the back of every kind deed there is a bowed Christ in all of us. The statue of Philip Brooks, the great American preacher, shows the hands of Jesus resting on his shoulders as if to say, 'In all that he did and all that he was, Christ had His hands on him.' You can water thirsty feet. No-one will ever rival this ministry given to Peter, the servant of the Lord. Cooling overheated feet, washing away friction.

Jesus completed the task. The glory was in seeing it through. What Jesus did conquered Peter and accomplished all He wanted to do. It does not say that He used all the water or that the towel was too wet to be used again. No water? Wet the towel with your tears!

One man wanted to belittle Abraham Lincoln in front of other people and said, 'You polished my father's shoes.' The quick reply came, 'And didn't I polish them well!'

You need to see Jesus in every little deed, and every bowl of water and towel becomes His motif. When all talking fails then you can get inside a person's heart as you kneel with water and a towel. When great things have no appeal, use everyday things. The surrendered foot was but part of the surrendered heart. Small acts like foot washing became glorious acts in Heaven. Peter has to learn to help others walk to God and with God. As the shepherd must stoop to lift the lamb so must the pastor with his sheep. Try kneeling before them. If they are going to walk all over you, son of Jonas, make sure they have clean feet first!

Accept your ministry and it will minister to you

Whatever and wherever Jesus chooses to minister for you and in you be humble and gracious enough not to question but to accept. Once we have accepted small tokens then we shall feel clean.

Obedience is cleanliness. It was not a cleansing by blood which was required, it was deeper even than that and yet Jesus used a lesser substance than blood when He used water and towel. Jesus used ordinary water. It is the simplicities of life, water and cloth, the bare essentials which are messengers from God. 'Give us this day our daily bread.'

Francis of Assisi was riding along one day and, seeing a beggar covered in sores and smelly, was filled with compassion. Dismounting he flung his arms around the beggar, only to discover that he took on the form of Christ as he embraced him! The feet you wash can be crucified, hurt feet wearing the same sized sandals as the Saviour. Feet which have walked the Jericho Road, the Damascus Road and the Emmaus Road. Stories hidden in the grit.

An example to be copied like a child's first writing, to be traced over an outline. The test of a true widow was not some marvellous miracle but 'has she washed feet?' (1 Timothy 5:10).

The story of the Sad Prince says that he had all the toys he could wish for, yet he did not have happiness. A visitor wrote words which could only be read if the paper were brought to the fire. When the Prince placed the piece of paper near to the fire he read the words 'Do a kindness to someone every day.' He did and his life was changed.

That change is only discovered as we bend low, be humble and wash feet. The commands of Christ are best understood when baptised with fire. In the footprints we find the plan of God for our own lives. In washing the feet of another we find our own feet are clean.

These lessons are entering into the heart of Peter. They come in as water into the bowl and, as the water was poured over the foot for cleansing, so they will perform their good works in his life.

CHAPTER

17

Denying the Destroyer

Peter, in Luke 22:31–34, is the spokesman for the disciples. He is also the role model and when Satan desires to tempt Peter he tempts not only the disciples around Jesus but all who believe on His Name. When the stone is thrown into the centre of the pond the ripples travel far and wide. Something is happening and as Jesus draws back the curtain He allows Peter to see the truth.

When an artist is painting on canvas we see lines, colours blending and a picture emerging. Sometimes it is necessary to wait until the last few strokes are added in order to see the full drama unfolded but if you could climb into the head of the artist, know how he is thinking and feeling, then how different it would be. No waiting for that final splash of colour or the unveiling to recognise what was taking shape. How much fuller the understanding would be. Jesus does this for Peter, lets him see beyond the temptation to give him a better understanding, a fuller view. The wiles, the craftiness, the guile, the poison of the asp, the stratagem as if waging a war, deciding on troop movement, must be understood by the one in the shadow of Jesus. Satan has already claimed one soul in Judas Iscariot, but his nature means that he is never satisfied. Even when at the heart of the Christian life, even when in the Upper Room at the Last Supper by the side of Jesus, even those things do not bring exemption from satanic suggestion and temptation. To be well-rounded Christians we shall, as Cephas, be attacked from every angle, tempted in all quarters. This demon of darkness will push from behind and trip from the front. The ball and chain, used in mortal combat, had spikes all around to pierce from every angle as it was whirled round. Satan seeks to pierce Peter.

The whole armour of God is required

United Nations Forces in Bosnia wore bullet-proof vests with sides, back and front reinforced, whilst the British troops in 1993 had just the front and back reinforced. Consequently they were open to attack and penetration from the side. The whole armour of God is required for the Christian soldier (Ephesians 6:11,13), including Peter. Maturity is that which is seen and tested from every angle and which has passed through every stage of growth. All this is happening to Peter so that we might have courage when we are being crushed. It is reassuring to know that Peter was a man of like temptations. Maturity is to stand the test from all quarters but not to give quarter. What Peter went through has been left for us to collect. It was temptation to deny the Lord, to leave His cause and His army.

This temptation did not come from another brother. John did not lean too heavily on Peter. It came from within the heart of Peter, as a coiled snake, the voice of Satan, the music waiting to arouse it. The snake within answered to the claims of the snake without. Satan sought to use doubt and fear ingloriously to further the wicked ways and works of the kingdom of hell. The sludge and the slime he finds in the heart is used to build a wall between us and our God. It is even used to fill the ears of this believer so that he cannot hear the prayers of the Intermediary, the Interceding Christ. God cannot fail, but we can and Satan helps us to do it. Simon is but an apprentice learning the ropes, and he is tripped by them, left low, cold and deserted by everything. This man who was ready to go to prison, to face death, was not ready to walk a few more yards without denying Jesus. There was a prison within and Jesus required the keys to become a key figure in this conflict of the sentence of death. Every foul fiend would seek to occupy that prison and the darkness within it, awaiting His Majesty's pleasure.

Faithfulness in all circumstances

The early morning alarm in a feathery cock was to be more faithful and regular than Peter. It will even crow on the morning of its death, but not Peter. The cock had to crow and all Peter had to do was to be the Simon whom Jesus had made. How disappointing when the models you have made melt in the sun, or the baking sags just as it is being served. Some things are broken at birth whilst others reach the maturity of twig and bud then fail because the years of the cankerworm, locusts and caterpillar have arrived. Jesus sees and seeks success in every disciple. He believes in the believer just as much as any who invest in Shares believe in the Company. He believes in Peter, even as the Father believed in the Son.

Verse 31, is plural. He has desired to have Peter, to make a start with him and then go through the rest. There can be a domino effect in trials. Peter said, 'I go fishing' (John 21:3). They said, 'We will go with you.'

The wiles of the devil

Satan has desired to have you. It is the desire of lust. It is that which desires to conquer in order to kill. God will try Peter so that he might mature him, while the evil one will do it in order to break him.

Satan desired to have this member of the Inner Circle. The same thought is in Job 1:11,12. It places the tempted from all the Ages alongside the suffering of Job. The endurer will be better for having endured. Without the Cross there is no Crown. No temptation, no glorification. He will stand where once he fell, walk where once he crawled, run where once he could only hobble, coming in last. In Jesus the last shall be first.

Like our modern society, Satan is filled with desire. Whatever was virgin in Simon Satan wanted to violate. Evil designs were being worked out by Satan himself. The only desire Satan has is to break, kill and destroy. His shadow is dark, blotting out the light of the love of God. He is a dark cave, a narrow passage, and as we enter we are assaulted and robbed, left bleeding and dying on the Jericho road. Jesus had enough love for Peter to encircle him. Satan was allowed in that the love might grow larger and embrace all temptations. Jesus had enough love to spend time pleading for Peter. That which lies heavy on the heart of Peter causes Jesus to bend His knees in order to lift the burden from him. Those pleadings in prayers are the antidote to the poison and perplexities which the prince of darkness is suggesting.

Christ is with us in every temptation

Jesus wants Simon to realise that He understands. He wants Peter to know and to grow. There are times when Peter is stretched into being a saint and Jesus wants him to know that He is with him, just as He was in the sea when they walked on the waves. Jesus came as a Man that mankind might understand that in temptation God is no bystander, no flag fluttering on a pole far removed. Our only strength is in Jesus Christ. The weakness of God, if there was one, is more than enough for the attacks of Satan. The prayers of Jesus are stronger, of more lasting value than fleeting temptation. Satan may be as a roaring lion but Samson conquers lions—Daniel sees their mouths tightly shut. In Daniel's conquering he saved others who might have been in the lions den. Many times Satan falls into the pit he himself has digged and the saint of God is strengthened by his deliverance. The process of refining brings forth gold and silver, sometimes refined seven times. We might be knocked down, but never knocked out.

The desires of Jesus are quite different from those of Satan. Satan drags down, Jesus lifts up. Satan dethrones, while Jesus longs to enthrone. Satan would pierce with a sword, Jesus is for placing medals on the chest of the 'well done'. The plan of attack is revealed to Peter through the knowledge of Christ. To be forewarned is to be forearmed. To have the knowledge of the event before it takes place puts you in the first place.

God uses even the Evil One

Below, above and beyond every temptation there is the evil power of Satan which God can take and use for our good. The character of the tempter is the black curtain drawn across the stage as one passes through a crisis. Before Peter can be a man he must suffer in order to mature. He must be stretched to become a saint. To strengthen the brethren he must be made strong. Simon is still out of condition, at least physically. John could outrun him.[1]

Every farmer squeezes corn to see if it is ripening, to gauge the juices that are present, the colour and the texture. Does it pop under pressure? In reality the farmer is saying, when can I expect a harvest? The believer can expect testings to be answered by prayings. The trial from the heart of God is measured to our capability.

Satan sees the chaff, God sees the golden corn white unto harvest. There has been a planting by Satan and a planning by God in the life of Peter. It was an attack on Peter's relationship with Jesus, a trial of his faith, a rubbing of the file against his brittle spirit. It was a temptation to deny the Lord, to act as though there was no such Person as Jesus, to pretend that God does not care or exist. The disciples rubbed corn in their hands, and they plucked it, as the devil did with Peter. Their lives were to be plucked by Satan. Peter's life was being plucked and shredded, the outer cover torn away. Satan took hold of one small piece of Peter's life and it gave him a mighty grip. He locks onto those things which hang loosely. He seeks to reveal Peter in a bad light, the only light he knows, the shadowy world of hypocrisy.

Satan has the grip of hell and the hardness of the vice, but the touch of Jesus is gentle, sure, reassuring and altogether lovely. There is such a vast difference between the king of sin and the Altogether Lovely. God takes Satan's squeeze, uses it as a mould and from it emerges the true Christian. The destroyer of the faith will rub through circumstances and suggestion until he crumbles together, destroying, while the hand of God moulds. Three hundred pounds of pressure is required to tune some string instruments. Only then will fine melodies be heard and discordant sounds blend into Symphonies.

It must have been so strengthening to Peter to know that, before he even entered into the conflict, Jesus had been arranging his armour. He had been prayed for. Failure or success was not measured by Satan's beating stick but by the prayers of Christ.

The nature of temptation

Jesus wants to sift you as wheat from chaff, the same thought is in Matthew 3:12 the winnowing process and the corn taken on a fan-shaped shovel, tossed into the air and the wind from the fan blows away the chaff. Jesus wants to remove the chaff and keep what is good. The only answer to his puffing and blowing is Acts 2:2 where there was a sound of a mighty rushing wind, the Lord was on the attack! There was a suggestion that the servants of the Lord were like sheep blown over by the wind, rolling as balls of wool. Their safety was at the side of the Shepherd. There is shelter from every fierce wind, blizzard and blast at the side of Jesus.

Jesus Christ must discover the whole of the humanity of Peter. There is the thought that Simon was still full of hypocrisy. Jesus uses his old name, the one of old association when referring to him, He calls him Simon. Satan has put in a claim but limits and permissions are needed. Peter stood within Satan's reach, for the tempter always fishes in the shallow streams of our thinking, the places where he can claim ground in the old nature. Carnality and lust are old haunts for him. Rebellion is a rusty old sword but occasionally it is polished to a shine as it is used to cut believers. The weapons of his warfare are carnal. He comes from below, he knows no rules. There are no Queensberry Rules with Satan. He will strike Cephas whilst he is down. When he is up he will knock down, add insult to injury, applying more pressure. If he is given something to lean on, then lean he will. He desires in Peter, to take all that belongs to Jesus, to make it his own—conversion in reverse. He would do as he did with Judas.

Satan would dig and dig until he found sand, not the rock in Peter's nature. The chaff is just an outer rug, the surface. Satan wants to turn the inner wheat into chaff. He will discover and highlight weaknesses. If love covers a multitude of sins, then Satan uncovers that same multitude. Artists always depict him as having two horns and a two pronged spear. The two prongs are because he strikes twice, one to poke the other to push. Jesus is painted with His two hands together in prayer, very tender when dealing with people. Our only depth is the love of God, but Ephesians 3:18 speaks of the height, the depth, the length and the breadth of that love.

The love of Christ

God can use what Satan does in order to discover our strengths. Jesus wants to discover inner reserves, inner glory. Verse 1, had been in the plural 'you', but it moves into the singular—'Simon, I have prayed for you.' I love the world but I love you.

A little boy wrote the words: 'Tommy Smith loves the world.' Some time later he fell in love and he crossed out the word 'world' and wrote 'Mary'.

Severe temptation brings a revelation of Jesus who is praying whilst we are in the midst of the sea, in the mountain praying as we are struggling.

Peter must be rock-like above every temptation.[2] When we are tempted Jesus is still in love with us, loving every part of us. He still cares, still stands, stays standing with us. The Shepherd will never flee when the wolf comes. He is there with hands outstretched to catch as we fall.

I asked Him if He loved me and He answered Yes. I said, How much do you love me? He said not a word—just opened His arms wide and made the sign of the cross.

The prayers of Christ

'I have prayed for you,' is the plaster to the wound. I have prayed—from a root word meaning to bind, knit, tie. We are tied to Him, bound to Him through prayer. Jesus never prays that we might be lifted out of a situation, He prays that we might be taken through. His prayers tie the loose ends which would trip. He calmed the troubled waters but still left the boat where it was. He healed Peter's mother-in-law, but she remained in the house to minister. He expects His glory and majesty to be seen: 'Go home and tell them what great things God has done.'

The prayers of Jesus are called 'succour'.[3] He is able to succour the succumbed, like the frappings under a ship in a storm. With all our knots and tangles Jesus, in prayer, becomes entangled with us and produces calm. He puts the order of Heaven back into our lives, praying that your 'faith will fail not'. The same word for fail is used in Hebrews 1:12 of His years not failing. He helps our infirmities the things which limit us. We sit as the child on the lower end of the see-saw, suddenly another weight is placed on the other end to give perfect balance. Jesus takes hold of the heaviest end of the burden and lifts it with us. As that burden is lifted, so are we. Into our groanings He pours His glory.

Peter needed the helping heart of Jesus, the comfort of that heart. He had to have an understanding heart to help him with his pains. Only Jesus can make pain plain. (See Author's book *In Sickness and in Health*.)

John 17, the prayer of Christ for the Church was also heard in this context. In John 17 is the essence of what Jesus prayed when Peter was tempted—'That they may be where I am. That they might see My glory.' 'Protect them by the power of Thy Name, that none shall pluck them from My hand. I pray You will keep them while they are in the world that they may be one as We are One. As You have sent Me, I have sent them' (John 17:18). These are the prayers of Jesus for Peter and for all the Church, a branch on which to rest. The Heaven of Heavens cannot contain Peter's God. Satan is left with the bottomless pit.

Above the noise of battle and strife listen to the voice of One, not crying in the wilderness as John Baptist, but praying that Cephas will be true rock, through the assurance of the presence of Christ. There are whispers of the still small voice that Elijah heard and recognised. 'The Lord did speak unto Samuel' (1 Samuel 3:10). The Hebrew word meaning 'to lift back the hair and speak into the ear.' There must be more concentration on what the tempted are hearing rather than what is happening.

The believer's prayer

When anyone is tempted and cries out, even if only a weak cry for help, it sounds as the trumpets of Zion in Heaven. The hills of God are blasted with the anthem as the voice of Goliath in the Valley of Elah. It may be as the snapping of the twig yet it sounds like thunder in the gentle hearing of God and even before the arrows of temptation are loosed, God hears the feathers on the end blowing in the breeze. It is ears open to the cry of the young when God hears. God will help us and that right early, He will bring in the dawn.

When we seek the face of God that face is as small as the earth and as large as the universe. He hears our tears as they melt into the earth. In His ears they sound like the Niagara Falls! It is for you to strengthen your brethren. Let the light that is in you shine across their paths.

Through being strengthened, we strengthen others

Out of all this Peter was able to write in 1 Peter 5:8,9—'Be sober and watchful, for the enemy is as a lion.' 'The fiery trial of your faith (1 Peter 1:7). 'Cast all your care on Him for He cares for you' (1 Peter 5:7). The same Greek word is used in Luke 19:35 when it speaks of laying garments on a donkey. The root Greek word for casting comes from a word meaning to 'stitch'. Stitch all your cares to Him with a needle, fasten them with a nail from His Cross, a thorn from His Crown. Tribulation works patience and it makes for experience. It is the experiences which develop glory, and exceeding weight of eternal glory.

Later, during Peter's pastoral ministry, he is able to help those who are severely tempted. 'Be sober and watchful for your enemy is as a strong lion' (1 Peter 5:8,9). Lions take their prey usually at waterholes as they drink. Peter has looked into his own life and now, as an older man, he sees how Jesus dealt with him and he is able to comfort others with the same comfort he received. 'Add to your faith' (2 Peter 1:5).

These temptations, denying Satan his claims, will result in additional growth. Faith will have virtue added to it, knowledge will know temperance, patience will have Godliness. It is all part of Peter's Growing Pains and what he has learned he will pass on to others.

Notes

[1] John 20:4
[2] Mark 6:46−48
[3] Hebrews 2:18

18

Controlling the Impetus Nature

Matthew 26:37–45 leads to John 18:10,11. John names the man who was struck with the sharpened sword, Malchus, the servant boy of the High Priest. One record follows the other. The happenings in Gethsemane have been noted often but we need to realise how they helped Peter come through from Gethsemane into the daylight beyond and onto resurrection ground. The Garden of Olives must not be the place of assembling of troops or designation of sword practice, with human beings as targets. It was to be the arena for the development of human nature. Deep within the darkness of its shadows were the school rooms for disciples. Every shadow cast was part of the miracle ministry in their lives. Olives are pressed and human nature is to be pressed and squeezed dry. Through this process the white flame appears giving off an aroma of perfumed oil. What happened to Peter may have seemed to be in the dark but Jesus was standing by him all the time. Jesus would always stay, see a thing through to the end, for that is the true glory. Somewhere amongst the people, between the shouts and taunts of the rabble, we see Jesus Christ with the beams from the torches marking Him out condemned. The real battle in Gethsemane, after the battle in prayer, was the battle for Peter, the wandering sheep that was ready to gore with a sword. Certain things happen which, if not checked will use us. It is dangerous to carry a sword, or a grudge, to have a sharpness as if we have eaten razor blades. The tongue can be as a gleaming sword. To argue or to have some instrument of war ready we need to be trained soldiers. There is the temptation to fight your own war your own way. Jesus was thrown back on God. Peter, like the Saul of the Old Testament, leaned on his own sword. There is teaching here for this army of one—to lean on God. The action, the dedication, the strength used and the sure blow of removing an ear needs to be given to God. Jesus did not want an ear—He needs the whole body, soul and spirit to be presented willingly to Him, not piece by piece until we are no man at all.

The weapons of our warfare are not carnal

The Old Testament abounds with pictures of the sword being used as a weapon of destruction. 'Whose teeth are spears and arrows and their tongue a sharp sword' (Psalm 57:4). 'Who wet their tongue like a sword' (Psalm 64:3). What and how we say things can lop off ears, but how little the deaf and the wounded hear. Peter left the man wounded and deaf, but Jesus, in Luke 22:51, touched the ear and it was healed. So different was the touch of Jesus to the cold steel of the sword. One is an emissary of compassion, the other cold, hard cutting steel. It may glitter, but it should hold no attraction. Humility and meekness is to have the strength and opportunity for wrongdoing, for cutting ears into pieces, and yet resist that opportunity. This message has to penetrate the heart of Peter, who handles the sword as well as he uses his feet!

To speak one's mind can be a sword. It stops people hearing when we are wearing it and swinging it. Owners of swords used to give names to them after a battle where an enemy had been routed and the sword was bloodstained—one means the cutter, another, the stream of anguish—the beater—the deadly. What shall we name this sword? Clumsy, wild, debased, chopper? Cephas surrendered the ability to trust Him who could have called ten thousand angels, He who had sweat drops of blood. Jesus was wanting to make Peter sharper than a two-edged sword. The aim had to be the heart, the inner life of people. Give them your prayers, your blood, your sweat, but not your sword. The sword of conquest for Jesus was in a life given and crucified.

Jesus didn't grasp at glory

In the form of God, yet Jesus did not grasp for that position, which was His. That shines very bright at the heart of the glory of God. That weapon will be seen in Heaven. While Jesus is taken up with the Redemption of the world, the Son of Jonah can have his own little toy gleaming in the dark and think that he is doing the work of God. He has a kingdom all of his own, he is the border and the defence of it, he makes up the laws as he moves along. He must defend his land at the expense of another's blood, pain and hearing. God's Kingdom is built neither with sword, spear or hammer. The manifestation of its power is healing, not hurt. Part of Christ's Manifesto was—The deaf shall hear.

A General of a conquered army offered his hand to his conqueror. 'I said, your sword,' was the curt reply. This was one sword that Peter had never surrendered to Jesus.

> Force me to render up my sword
> and I shall conqueror be...

in that hymn the sword is spoken of as the will of man. As Jesus builds, Simon destroys. He who had ear trouble decides to remove the hearing aids of anothers!

Paul says, 'I am not as one who beats the air but I bring all things under subjection' (1 Corinthians 9:26). As a wrestler I get a grip on things.

Passing judgement on others

The sword is judicial. Peter held a Court of Law there and then and passed judgement on the first person to come within reach. The word sword can mean a short sword or even a knife. It comes from the word meaning war and is used figuratively of strife, a fight, a quarrel, a dispute. All these things become swords to Peter. Without a blast from the trumpet he moved into battle to engage the enemy. For maximum impact he should have waited for the order to charge! Had that order been given it would have been to love the young man, not to hurt him.

Learn from Peter. You cannot fight your way out of some

situations, you have to listen to the prayers of Jesus. Cephas had to learn to depend on the prayers of Jesus Christ—'I have prayed for you.'

The sword is like the flesh. If you would be made less of a man or woman then take up the sword. In each chop and thrust a man loses an ear and is made to look smaller. It is not long before good blankets are turned into patchwork quilts. This action of Simon made an awful mess of God's creation. Peter is looking around for helpers. He, too, would have mustered a crowd with sword and staves. Human thinking would have used him to match what the others were doing. Human thinking appeals to swordsmanship. The words of Jesus are: hang it up!

There is new light for all

There was a greater light in that Garden than the light of the lanterns casting evil shadows on ground and stone, it was the Light of the glory of God shining from Jesus Christ. The gleam of the sword was but dull when compared with that glory which gave sun, moon and stars their brilliance. Peter cannot keep Jesus intact by swinging a sword.

It is easy to swing the sword, to cry with Elijah: 'swing the axe, off with their heads' (1 Kings 18:40). The Queen in *Alice in Wonderland* chopped off heads for no reason.

The spiritual mode of victory

Jesus was offered two swords, but accepted neither.[1] He could have had an army of angels, but He chose not to. He had to conquer by way of surrender. There was only one sword for Jesus to use, the sword of self-surrender to the Father's wishes. He had come to suspend the sword of judgement. He surrendered His sword on the red velvet of His blood. Peter kept his sword hidden ready for the battle he expected.

Luke 22:51 tells of the healing of the mistake. Jesus stayed long enough to heal and to mend what Peter in his haste had torn. There is healing in your darkest hour, healing in your Gethsemane. There is a healing ministry following this one disciple. How graciously God grants us grace for grace. He heals what we have injured. We are found cutting the flowers and swinging the sword because we do not understand what He is trying to do.

Watching unto prayer

There is a certain discipline about watching and keeping your eyes open (see verses 38, 40 and 46). Some things are missing from Peter's writings because he slept. As he did so tares[*] were sown amongst the wheat. His knowledge became limited. There is a watchfulness about resting in God, letting God do the watching whilst we sleep. The teaching from Christ was how to handle a crisis. You don't do it by stirring the porridge with a sword. Did Peter desire to take the place of the Cherubim at the gate of the Garden of Eden, turning the sword every way in order to keep the approach to the Tree of Life sacred so that animal, creature or human could not come within smelling distance of the fruit on its branches?[2]

Luke 22:38 shows Jesus was blunting the point of death, about to tell the devil to put up his sword forever. Satan, through Peter, was attempting to make a final cut, a lasting impression, to make his mark on the creation of God and to cut Christ adrift forever. We need eyes anointed with eye salve to see the fullness of Jesus. Jesus on His knees is bigger than Peter on his feet or up a mountain. Jesus with hands together accomplishes far more than Cephas with a sword. The gun or bomb never win. If they did, those with the largest armies would rule the world.

There is a certain amount of watching needed in the Christian life. We miss much if we go through our Gethsemane with eyes closed. The choice is to go through a Gethsemane with a Cephas, or with Christ. Peter has a flag we can fight under, but it is sword-shaped. He leads the 'stab and grab' army. The flag of Jesus is His red blood shed for any and for many.

---

[*] The tare is like wheat in every aspect. It is so intertwined with the wheat, that to separate one from another would destroy both. The only difference is the ear of wheat bends in humility at the end of the stalk whereas the tare stands proudly upright.

When prayer is lacking

Peter could have prayed with Jesus. He could have been as Hur and Aaron, holding up the hands of Moses while Israel prevailed.[3] Like those who lowered Paul over the Damascus wall in a basket, he could have been holding the ropes whilst Jesus went over the side, but instead he took up a sword. The emblem of the military will only move ears, while the Cross of Christ will move hearts into the hands of God. A cut off ear is a deaf ear, has no head to control it and enters into the red of hell. It is a strange thing that the Lord of Heaven and earth, the Lord of glory relied on the prayers of little weak Peter, yet one mesh in the fishermen's net depends on the other. God's Son wanted Peter and the others to become a praying band. Jesus depended on the prayers of Simon. To turn away from prayer is to neglect the real sword, to be a coward in a real battle, a deserter. It is to swing wildly. It is to lose your cutting edge. Prayer shapes and sharpens Peter. The Adversary does not only come as a lion, he comes as an angel of light, and as a sword, swinging freely through the air. The Sword of Damocles is always suspended by a hair. It is ready to fall into the open hand which is not at prayer. The real war is staying in prayer. This was the disciples cutting edge. Prayer is mightier than the sword. It has seen more surrender than any sword. This is your weapon of Ephesians 6.

Praying hands

Why do we put our hands together when we pray? Perhaps it is that a sword cannot enter hands which are clasped tightly together around the hands of Jesus? The sword was by Simon's side, but the prayer was in the heart of Christ. Falling asleep once is wearying, but to do it three times is deep sleep indeed. It is the enthroning of the midnight hour, the wasting of the midnight oil. The sword is the easy way out. Jesus comes so many times to this young disciple seeking to strengthen him, to take him on in prayer. Sleepy eyes see but a dim future, the vision is removed as the eyelids close, a veil falls and there is nothing but darkness. We enter a dark world without Jesus. We see, with Peter, through a glass darkly and that glass becomes the blade of the sword reflecting in the moonlight. The heart of the rock named Peter was flinty cold and the sword will be sharpened there until it can cut a hair into fifty parts. Moses, instead of speaking to the rock, smites it and makes it cry rivers of water.[4]

As Jesus prays things around Him begin to grow and blossom. It is prayer which causes growth within. Here was temptation, a stretching of the strength, and if we do not pray then we are weak. 'Behold I stand at the door and knock.' I am standing and knocking even as Peter is sleeping with a sword. Have you tried sleeping with a sword? Not an easy thing to do, but Peter managed it. The sword provides no fence for the disciples. Peter thinks that the sword is a door into something better. Jesus wants the sword to be beaten into a ploughshare. Peter needs to be made fully alive to Christ and His activities. The disciples asked Jesus, Lord teach us to pray in Luke 11:1. Jesus taught them the Lord's Prayer. There is a whole armoury in that prayer and the best dressed army uses it in spiritual conflict.

It is weak Peter who thought sword was word. Let the strength of God begin to do its work, grow up in your faith diminutive disciple, and realise who God is. Let God execute His own plans. This was not the time for scarring faces but for saving souls. The outcome of Peter's action with the sword was to make a hole for Jesus to pour His healing into. Peter was fighting but he was fighting against God. You cannot destroy the weaponry of God with a single sword, yet many try by their own will and power to do so. They face a fully equipped army with a small shield. Jesus overcame the world, and the crowd. When He said, 'I am He', they fell backwards.[5] Peter witnessed what Jesus can do, but in the glitter of the sword, in the confidence he felt when handling it, he forgot.

The things which betray Jesus

Two things in Gethsemane betrayed Jesus; a sword and a kiss. The two extremes of war and peace, yet both, when misused, can do much damage. Vincent, on New Testament Words, says Peter aimed the blow at the head, but missed. The damage was not as severe as it might have been if his eyes had not been tired. We always miss the mark with our own sword. 'I will do what God is not doing,' that is Peter's theology. God touches tenderly the hearts of men. Peter cuts off the instrument of sound. People who do not want to hear cannot receive the teaching of Jesus. Let God lift the sword, let God activate the plans, let go and let God! The helping hand becomes the destroying and crushing hand, hurting and maiming, wielded by Peter. Let Jesus destroy the works of the devil. What is in your hand? Give it to God and see the sword turned into a palm leaf, tears turned into sweat and blood.

Battling through on your own

The temptation for Peter is to battle his own way through. He had seen what Roman soldiers did when they wanted to silence a man, and he says to himself, Be your own man, your own king, carve out your destiny with a sword. The son of Jonas became the master of none, the fool. He would be self assertive, wage a war at his own cost. Converts are not won by these means.

Temptation is a set snare, a ditch digged where we are. Simon can dig his own grave with his sword, stab himself and fall into it, buried with his emotions and his self pity. We too can fall into our own trap and like Peter, attempt to fight our way out. We bring none to us with our barbed approach, indeed we drive them away. We need that trust that Jesus will take us through Gethsemane, through the Cross, through the grave and to the skies. Let the Christ who leads Peter into Gethsemane lead him out. If Peter comes through too early he may be marred. He must not go in his own strength, scarring and hurting. Swords will always be offered, they are the easy option. God's methods are not blade and shaft, He will not destroy the ear which He created. He would rather use it as a channel to the heart. Peter used carnal weapons and carnal weapons will use him. He will find himself swinging on the end of that sword which he sought to swing in the battle. He was too ready to take the sword which went into fat Eglon and the dirt came out.[6]

Why and when we are left alone

Jesus stepped away from the disciples in verse 39. He fought alone that He might always be coming to us and that we might watch and pray with Him forever. Don't cut Him off with a sword. Don't commit suicide on the sword of your own self-will. If you make others into swords life becomes a constant battle. What Peter kills and hurts with will do the same to him. This is the doctrine of living and dying by the sword. If you are bitter, others will be bitter towards you. Peter was sowing what he would reap.

The Statue of Liberty in New York Harbour has a torch in one hand and a tablet in the other on which is written the day, month and year of the Independence of America. Was it such a tablet Peter wanted? Did he want the world to witness his independent action? As Jesus surrendered willingly to the crowd He presented to Peter a melted sword, a ready example for him to follow.

Notes

1 Luke 22:38
2 Genesis 3:24
3 Numbers 20:11
4 Exodus 17:6
5 John 18:6
6 Judges 3:22

19

Overcoming Immaturity

In Mark 14:54, Peter sat with the servants. The Greek word is 'under rowers' meaning whatever he had passed through, whatever the swell or storm, whatever the depths of danger, he hadn't really altered a lot. He certainly hadn't been promoted to First Mate or Captain. There was nothing Admiral or Nelson about Peter's position at this time! Like the leaking vessel of Hebrews 2:1, let them slip. Slip is a nautical term which describes loosing the anchor holding a ship, loosing the securing ropes, to slide as a vessel without an anchor, sail or oarsman. God uses his own characters to illustrate Scriptures. Peter becomes the example to all who fall, despite much effort, many pains, realising that they are not quite there yet.

The term 'under rower' is also used of John Mark in Acts 13:5. We have Mark as our Minister—literally the under rower. The term in the English language used for Minister comes directly from the Latin word Manus (the hand) the one who hands things to another (the handyman) one of low estate or spirit.

When we turn back

Chrysostom referred to John Mark, who turned back from the work of God, as a 'maimed finger'. Mark, remember, means a 'hammer'.

The term 'maimed finger' was used by the Romans to denote a soldier who became a coward. If he would not fight or if he turned his back on the enemy then he became a 'maimed finger'. If one followed afar, as Peter was doing at this time, then he was given the title of 'maimed finger'. With a maimed finger the hammer could not be gripped, the sword or spear could not be handled, the oar, even as an under rower, could not be used as it should have been. The hand was doing less than it was designed to do. It could not carry out fully those things for which it had been created. Peter is both under rower and maimed finger!

There was a certain training which every oarsman had to pass through. They learned their skills in difficult waters and choppy seas, developing their muscles and pulling power in the swell. In the doldrums and occasionally in the 'offing' they found their true manhood. Jesus uses many methods to train Peter, meeting him, developing him, baring his potential to every wind, taking him from Simon to Cephas the rock.

The fact that Peter is still with the servants and has no greater influence tells its own story. It is thought that John, the Apostle of love, brought Peter in. There was a higher station in love. There is always room for Peter in the school of Christ. John had a sharing, caring heart for Peter. Simon, wrecked on the rocks, received a lifeline from John.[1]

Our experiences don't change us

Sometimes even passing through much water does not affect Peter. He can be in the holiest of company, climb the Mount of Transfiguration, see miracles and hear testimonies, yet still remain as solid lead. Those things around him can fail to mould him into the Master's mould. He was as those ever resting on the oars, straining with the little ups and downs of life, making a crutch out of an oar. He was still very much a 'land lubber' when it came to spiritual seas. Maybe he was not with the crowd, not with the soldiers or the men of war, he did not make the Crown of Thorns or bear false witness, but he was still with the under rowers.

The Plimsol Line was introduced to forbid ships carrying more than they were built to accommodate. The word of Christ was that Plimsol Line for Peter, but he ignored it, carried too much and was overburdened. The Man of War became the Frigate, a second class power. His bow was lower than his stern, lower in the water at the front than at the back. The helm surrendered to the stern, the headwind blowing directly across the plotted course.

The requirement for further training

Verse 66 shows that Cephas is still in the shadows, still with the maids of the High Priest, still a tool and not a workman, associated with the immature, with the servant rather than the service. Maturity was available in weeping and repentance. Repentance is the right direction and weeping gives new depths to waters. When will Peter learn to steer the boat, to pull on the oar, to read the Trade Winds correctly? The compass must be in the binnacle, not where he sees and hears only. Which is Starboard and which is Portside? He needs further training, and if that training is done by Jesus then maturity will come to Peter and abide in him. If ever he needed to row in time with the heartbeat of Jesus, it was now. In the shallowness of his life he was made to cry and those tears were added to shallow waters to create a depth in order that he might sail right into the heart of Jesus. He needed the 'helps' of Hebrews 2:18 the frappings passed under the vessel in order to strengthen it. Underneath (no matter how low he falls) are the Everlasting Arms.[2]

Ultimately, it is the immediate presence of Jesus Christ, which causes rivers of water to break from the eyes of Peter. In verse 67 it was as if the eyes of Christ had unstopped the fountains of the deep, melted the ice that Peter was slipping on. The tears streamed down his face, convicting him of so much wrong.

When we follow far behind

Under rowing depicts Peter's attitudes in relation to Jesus Christ. Jesus was not running or moving too fast but as an under rower Peter could not keep up with the Master. There is a great lack in following at a distance. You lose sight of things, cannot hear correctly, a smile becomes a frown, a word of encouragement is misinterpreted, an enquiry becomes a condemnation, a handshake a fist of knuckles. Peter cannot follow Jesus. His own steps do not measure those of the Master. If we are too far behind we are looking yet not seeing, listening yet not hearing. Peter is walking but he makes no progress, the gap between his heart and the heart of Jesus is widening.

In the Garden of Gethsemane Peter had been close enough to hand Jesus a sword. He had rested with Jesus at the Last Supper. He had been so close, yet now there is a gulf, a closed door. 'I taught Ephraim also to go. I taught him to walk. I set Ephraim on his feet, lifting him from his fallen position. I taught him to walk step by step' (Hosea 11:3). This is what the Son of God had sought to do for the son of Jonah.

Peter was following afar off.[3] The tense suggests that he kept his distance. The further he went, the further he moved away. It should have been 'Nearer my God, to Thee'. If we are afar off it is then when the hill, the hedge, the wall will block Jesus from view. Peter, who had been a friend, a disciple, a follower, is suddenly a stranger and as such he slows down the work of Christ in his own life. Natural fires, natural desires will never warm the heart towards God. Peter needs to maintain the spiritual flow, fervent in spirit, serving the Lord.

The prevailing presence of Jesus Christ

The light of another fire was needed, the light of His love and presence, the illumination that such closeness to Christ brings. There is no darkness in Him at all, for He is Light. If there was to be sacrifice and a Holy glow there had to be fire in Peter's own heart. Cephas, Simon, had to go from the Antarctic to the aurora of the sun, gather the garment of grace and the linen of love around his heart, be clothed and warmed in righteousness. Being right, doing right, warms the cockles of the heart! Through Emmanuel Peter is being warned, warmed and filled. There is that fire and sparkle in his own heart which runs right through his body giving him lantern light, electricity encirclement! Sacrifice will always produce its own fire. Notice—he warmed himself. It was an inward, a selfish ministry that he was exercising. There is a certain fire, a certain zeal which will clothe the outward but not the inward. If Cephas carries the Cross there will be wood for a fire! The question that Isaac asked Abraham can be asked again, 'I see the wood and the fire, but where is the lamb?' (Genesis 22:7). A new start, a new fire is needed, kindled by Jesus. There will be the nails of conviction and the blood to cleanse so that Peter can commence afresh with Christ. Peter will always meet with Jesus at the foot of the Cross. If life is shaped by the Cross, and there is self sacrifice, then a fire will be lit which will never go out. Fire kindled by men will die, for it is not zeal but emotion and it does not last. It can be blown out by the winds of change. That which is kindled by God never goes out.

'By' the light but not 'in' the light

Vincent, explaining New Testament words, says, 'By' the fire, 'By' the 'light' of the fire. There had been staves and torches in the Garden. It was by the light of the fire that Peter was discovered and recognised. We are not so lovely in the light of natural fire as we are when filled with Holy zeal. When zeal surrounds us as a cloak it is then that we are warmed. Judas lived for the moment in the glitter of the pieces of silver given to him for his betrayal of Jesus. It was not a lasting glow, but a mere firework sparkle, the smile of the miser with the handful of silver. That silver choked him to death. Many a man has reached for the silvery moon only to discover that, as he reached, he has become a lunatic. In the Garden of Gethsemane Peter had been content to operate within the glitter of a flashing sword as an ear was removed. Lesser love, lesser glow, less show and less know.

'Beneath, and they in a palace' (Mark 14:66,67). Grovelling under the throne, hiding among the palatial. Peter was in the open space surrounding the palace. He was tied up with an earthly palace and from below he was made to look up. Whose flag flew at the palace? Peter's heart was a torn and tattered flag, soon to be stained from the clouds in his own heart as he wept. Half-mast, operating in a different sphere, another level. He found it difficult to understand the movements of Christ. He could not tell how Jesus was responding to His trial. He was at the palace, yet outside of it.

Trying to live two lives at once

It is an impossibility to have one foot in the boat, the other in the depths of the sea. When Peter was lifted from the waves in Matthew 14:31, Jesus said 'Why did you doubt?' The word 'doubt' means to look both ways at once. The man who does that becomes cross-eyed, walks blindly into objects in front of him, looking both ways at once he goes nowhere and sees nothing.

Peter went with them, he sat with them, made himself at home, fellow-shipping and sight-seeing with them. He was left in his coldness in the courtyard. There is no admittance to any palace unless he takes his stand with Christ. If you hang around with the crowd, like Peter did, you will be picked off. He never reached the throne, never reached authority, never came to where the silence of Jesus could speak to him. He was left outside his destiny. The man ashamed to beg, was begging. The man who had known better things was not living at his best. He was asking others what was happening. He was not one of the 'eye-witnesses' of these things. He was not only outside the palace naturally, but also spiritually. Jesus stands accused, that Cephas might never be accused. He stands condemned that Peter might never be condemned. He is 'on' trial in order to help Cephas 'in' trial. When Peter is crucified on his cross in later years, Jesus has already been on that Cross. The trial that Jesus was passing through was happening within the heart of Peter. He was on trial. Judgement was being passed on him. The verdict, readily given, was that of guilty on all counts. There can be death and prison in a spiritual way. Jesus is appealing to Peter, as an under rower and a maimed finger. 'I row the worlds with My little finger', is what He is communicating to Cephas. 'With My hand I uphold all things' (Hebrews 1:3).

What would be left of Jesus? Peter went to see the end and in the end he found a new beginning. Peter felt that the end of Jesus would be the end for everyone else, but instead it was the Omega, and the Alpha.

The signs of the immature and the unstable

In Mark 14:66 and 67 Peter, Simon was with the maids, those who were still serving. There are times when Apostles Designate are no bigger than a little girl, not more than a servant, a Quartus of Romans 16:23. 'A quarter. A portion of the whole.' Manhood and womanhood needs to be developed in everyone.

There are seven stages of growth which it is necessary to pass through in order to reach physical and spiritual maturity. Birth; infancy; childhood; puberty; youth; man; maturity of Age. There are seven men in the one Peter—the man the Apostles know; the man his friends know; the family man; the one the animals know; the man that the maids know; the man Peter himself knows; and the man that Jesus knows. The man that Jesus knows Peter to be is the most important one. Seven aspects of his life, seen as if from seven mirrors—a failure; a fisherman; a convert; a husband; a miracle worker; a preacher; a pillar in the Church.

When Peter was questioned as to his relationship with Jesus Christ he let go of the oars altogether, began to drift towards the waters in which Judas had drowned. We usually speak of drifting 'down' river or 'out' to sea. In Mark 14:54 it is easy to stand and stare, to associate with the servants, but Peter's accent, how he stressed certain words, betrayed his standing in Christ. The tongue is better than the pen though sometimes not as clean. Peter wanted to deny, to get away from the place. He did not want to retain that which linked him to Jesus. Slowly he slipped into the darkness—if you have a cold icy heart there is a danger of slipping. The manner in which Peter spoke had nothing to do with geographical position or where he came from, but it told of where he was going! Language and speech told at whose feet he had been sitting. His tongue gave him away! Our manner and speech tell what garnishes the heart. From the well of the heart the bucket of our speech will be filled. Is this to be another Babel, another confusion of languages? Peter even goes so far as to call on God to smite him if he belonged to Christ! He swears, uses oaths. The fountain is sending forth bitter waters. There is a flood of language. Angels covered their ears, mothers would have dragged their children away. The sweet scent of the Spirit became bad breath, bad language as Peter began to swear. What is bad language? It is when love has lost its alphabet.

The under rower is taking water. The boat is captainless and crewless, nothing but a spinning coracle, heading for the rocks. There is no lifeboat. Peter takes to the coarse fisherman's language again. Our conversation proves our conviction and standing. Manner of language always tells the manner of love. Our language acts as coals and flames from the altar at which we worship.

A simple remark made by a maid found Peter out. Not a great

challenge, not a demonic needing deliverance, not a charge into battle, but a simple word.

Notes

[1] John 18:16
[2] Deuteronomy 33:27
[3] Matthew 26:58; Luke 22:54

20

Repenting and Reinstated

Peter was in a pickle! He had forgotten so much of what Jesus had said to him. In Matthew 26:33 Peter vowed that he would never deny the Lord and Jesus had pointed out that, before the cock crows, he would deny Him three times. The sad outcome is found in Matthew 26:73–75, and Luke 22:61.

The moment the last denial was uttered it was as if an alarm had been activated. The cock began to crow and it led Peter to a well of his own tears. The Lord knew Peter's strengths and weaknesses, his low tide and high tide. He knew the moment when the first faltering steps were taken. He knew when temptation began to arise, small at first, then gathering strength and force, a raging storm beginning its work of uprooting, smashing, devastation. Peter was truly as weak as the water he had once walked on. Having walked on water in the midst of a storm he was about to sink in the measure of his own tears. The words of Peter were so unlike the word of Jesus Christ which was fulfilled in the crowing of a cock. Emotionally the mouth can utter great swelling words bigger than those we can ever swallow, but they need the balance of reality, the reduction of humility. Jesus many times said 'Men say—but I say unto you.'

The word we must rely on

The word of the Lord was not given just as a warning but also for consolation in order for Peter to know that although Jesus was on trial awaiting judgement, His word still held good. He was still very much in charge. Within the body and heart of Jesus was freedom to control, to help, to work things together for good. Jesus never forsook His Kingly authority. The arrangements of God were never plucked from His hands, neither did He lose His grip on them. The Hebrews divided the night into four watches—the beginning of the evening—the First Watch, Lamentations 2:19; the Middle Watch or midnight, Judges 7:19; The Cock Crowing, Matthew 26:34,74,75; Mark 13:35; The Morning Watch or dawning, Exodus 14:24. The Romans divided the night into six watches, each lasting an hour and a half, beginning at midnight. The third of these divisions, at about 3.00 AM they called the 'gallicinium'—the time when the cock begins to crow. The Romans probably sounded a bugle at the time of the cock crowing. Peter had denied his Lord before that bugle finished its note. Mark 14:30 may mean this when Jesus said 'Before the cock crows twice you will deny Me thrice.' Before the cock has crowed, and the bugle which was referred to as the 'cock' has finished sounding, you will have denied Me three times. That would clear up some of the misunderstanding of the number of times the cock was to crow before Jesus was denied. Before the cock crows twice—cock and bugle blowing—you will deny Me three times.

There are others who think that the cock crowed three times during the night. There are differences in the records of the four Gospels, they are not contradictory but complementary, revealing their independence and the fact that the writers of those Gospels did not copy each other. They reveal honesty and integrity.

The call comes to the conscience

The bird's beak, that morning, sounded like the voice of thunder from Heaven into the heart of Peter. The cock crowing was the hammer blows of God. Sinai was here with its flashings of lightning, rolling of thunder into the heart of this feeble Christian. It certainly wasn't the voice of the Beloved. It was the call to war, to be alert. As the cock crowed, apparitions disappeared, the Night Watches stopped, sleeping garments were thrown on one side. The beak seemed to be as a razor blade in the conscience of Peter. It certainly woke him and brought him to a stream of his own tears. Its voice went further than its wings could ever carry it. The cock crow has saved the life of many a man stationed on sentry duty as he was awakened by its clarion call.

This child of Christ was as a soldier in battle. The colours, the flag is in the mud, a carpet spread at his feet. The one who would not fall has taken a nose dive. He had not just lose his balance, he had lost his ground. His was not the falling of the bending reed in the wind, it was that which was about to be cut off at the roots.

There is at this moment in the life of the Apostle to be, the faithful call of a bird which is the herald of a new day. It could have suggested a new start in the things of God. Here was a faithfulness which spoke to Peter's own heart. As it crowed, Peter remembered its Creator, and his own. He recalled the word of the Lord.[1] He had at his fingertips the word of Christ. If this was true, everything else was true and would surely be fulfilled! The cock crow entered the bone and marrow of Peter with its echoing haunting sound. It was the piercing cry which split the heart of Cephas into many pieces. It was the fulfilment of the words of Jesus Christ, an interpretation of the saying 'I told you so'! As it crowed that crow echoed around the heart of this lonely disciple. When everything had fallen apart Peter was brought to remembrance by a cock not having lost the voice which nature had given to it. The cock did not have to change its word or dialect. It did not have to speak in the languages which were placed over the Cross—Latin, Greek or Hebrew. It did not have to go to any College, outside of nature, for it to fulfil its call and role in life.

God uses the useful and useable

The Talmud stated that this type of bird was unclean. If that is true, then Jesus chose an unclean thing to meet the needs of an unclean man. A bird considered unclean speaks to an unclean soul with unclean lips, unclean heart found as part of a swearing man. To the casual listener all it did was to crow. To Peter's heart there was an entirely different interpretation. The echoes of the cock call was the word of God. As it crowed it sang its thankfulness to God for all things. There was a whole choir in its throat performing in the manner best known to it.

It was a combination of cock crowing and Jesus looking which broke the heart of Peter.[2] One came from a distance whilst the look of Christ came from His immediate presence. What the cock said pecked Peter to pieces! There was no defence, no shield for his ears as its cry rang out clear and true. It came to roost sitting on a dying branch in Peter's heart. There was something within him which had dried and withered.

When a child was asked, 'How did Columbus discover America?' the teacher received a reply which made him think. 'Sir,' the child said, 'He sailed Westward and kept going until he got there.' Peter should have done that!

Occasionally when people have been in accidents and are in a coma a well known figure, someone they had looked up to and admired visits and speaks to them, in the hope that the familiar voice will penetrate the unconsciousness, bringing them back to reality. A sudden shock may revive. The voice of love and the familiar can travel down deep mine shafts, raising to the surface things long lost and buried.

What the cock hammered in, Jesus eased into place in the heart of Simon Peter. Only Jesus can 'look' things into place. A mother, when she sees an untidy room looks and suddenly there is movement, action! Jesus looks and stars are placed in the night sky. He speaks and worlds appear. His words become His worlds. He ribbons His Creation with a rainbow. After a storm of tears He provides a multi-coloured handkerchief in the shape of a bow to wipe the tears away. Men can only provide an umbrella whereas God provides a rainbow! He says nothing yet accomplishes everything. His Look is the crowning point. He says, 'Fight under My friendship; Battle with Me wherever I go.' Where He looks, whatever He looks at, His gaze becomes the pointed finger of Light. I must look where He is looking and see what He is seeing.

Hearing and obeying the word of God

It is not enough to hear the word of God, we must know that we are under the gaze of Jesus Christ. Everything said, known and done is under His gaze, stretching back into our youth and forward into the future of our mature years. Peter must have seen that look for it to be recorded. He saw forgiveness, love, help and kindness in that glance. Did ever eyes talk like His eyes? Was there ever so much promised in a single glance? They were eyes of refuge for Peter. 'He remembered the word of the Lord' suggests a mental grasp. His mind became a mirror and the words of the Lord were reflected on its surface. Suddenly the word of the Lord became something that mattered, a master of action. There was instant recall, instant replay. That word, like particles of gold in a stream, rested in Peter's heart. He remembered a promise given, a promise forgotten. Jesus had not forgotten Peter, nor had He forgotten how to forgive.

Memories can melt or move us

When Peter remembered, he burst into tears. His heart sprung a leak! The pain translated into tears. There are moments of darkness, hours of uncertainty for all until the word of the Lord begins to crow like a cock. The word brought Jesus back into the daylight.

Did Matthew 10:33 spring up from that word of the Lord? 'Them that deny Me before men, I will deny before My Father.' Was it the word which spoke of putting hand to plough and turning back? Was it the word of the parable where the sun scorched the plant causing it to wither because of persecution, or that which fell by the wayside? Was it only the word spoken about the cock crowing? I think many of the words of Jesus, the teachings of Christ came flooding into Peter's heart even as the dove in Genesis returned to the hand of Noah in the Ark. The word broke Peter, turning him into a fountain of tears.

The cock had been the throwing of stones into the water and as Jesus looked to calm those troubled waters they burst their banks in grief. Peter remembered all that needed to be remembered. The original Peter with all his youthful zeal and desire stepped back into life. There was something which flew in with the cry of the cock. It was a new day dawning after an endless night of trial. It is the word and the eye of God which moves us if we are to be moved. That look of Jesus so full of compassion did its work. It took hold of Peter's heart.

God places and pieces us back together

God took all Peter's failings, like pieces of broken glass that were jagged and, in grace, He pieced them together, removing all evidence of cracks. That heap of denial, the cursing and the swearing had to be flushed out through real tears. The look of Jesus which said 'Will even you Peter, My dear companion and friend, deny your Lord?' Peter, probably still with the bloodstained sword at his side, was looked upon with pity. The word came to remind, to caution, to tell and be repented of. Jesus walked along that look using it as a pathway right into the heart of Peter. It was the white beam of Holiness, more startling than the rays of the dawn.

Peter needed the cock to arouse him. Cocks call people from their beds, from their shades of darkness, into light. The cock was the herald of the sun, the new day. It was the messenger of the Lord as much as ever John Baptist was. It was the Lord's feathery trumpet. Peter needed the word to remind him, the look to break in. The cock, the Christ and the command of the word will always do their greatest work when we allow them to take their place. Every feather and crow of that bird was in the realm of Christ's influence. The cock awoke; the Look softened; the Word directed. There were three denials and there were three elements in Peter's repentance.

That look of love melts, moves, manipulates. From the mess there arises another of rock nature, the repentant. In that look was an appeal of the open door, of better days, of a new start and a new life. As the cock crowed the dawn came into this disciple. Each spear of light entered into his darkness and led to the fullness of light. We say, 'If looks could kill.' These looks made alive! As Jesus looked and as Peter caught hold of that glance, some of the servant's heart and the beauty of Jesus humbly subjecting Himself entered into Peter. It was as if the look brought with it the servant heart. It was but a reflection of the heart of Christ.

Parkhurst says, 'Jesus looked at Peter with steadfastness and attention. That look was the shining of the sun on the remote summit of his heart. It melted both snow and ice that were to run out in tears as he wept with bitterness. The weeping washed away the works of the night.' Weeping may endure for a night, but joy comes in the morning! Jesus kissed Simon better with His eyelids as

He gazed upon him. It was the same look Jesus gave to the Rich Young Ruler in Mark 10:21. Jesus, beholding him, loved him as if he was the only one who existed. He loved him with all and loved him as if he was all. The intensity, the durability, coupled with the availability of the love of Christ was in that one look.

Repentance as deep as the love of God

In Mark 14:72, the tense means, 'He kept on weeping.' Roll after roll of weeping, wave after wave washed over his soul, as a boat out at sea drifting. One difference between Judas and Peter was that Judas never wept in repentance, he never called Jesus 'Lord'.

Some of the last words before the Cross and some of the first words after the Resurrection were to Peter. It was only an eclipse which happened to this Disciple, not an extinction of faith. He stumbled to find his feet and he wept to find his heart. The tears which came from it also led to it.

Of all those who were in that hall, from the officials and the trial personnel to the onlookers, and John was probably there as well as Peter, it is Peter that Jesus turns to look upon. Shivering with cold, empty of inspiration, Peter finds fulfilment in just one glance from the Lord. Those on whom the eyes of Jesus rest find rest indeed. There was light and a new day in those eyes as all the love of every dawn sparkled. The love of Heaven looked at Peter as if searching and finding that for which it had searched. The quickening eye moved across a slumbering spirit like sunlight gently tapping on closed eyelids, moving across the face of the deep and the distraught and said, 'Let there be light!' Peter was never where Jesus could not see him, never where Jesus could not find him. He was never too far removed from the Son of God. Cephas, wherever he was, whatever he was, wherever he went, was always in the centre of the Kingdom of Jesus.

When Jesus looked he did not see Peter as he was. Jesus never does. He saw him as he could be, should be and would be! In that look the grace of God went to the aid of Simon. That look said it all.

The things which cause us to remember

Peter long remembers what happened, for later in his Epistle he speaks of 'remembering things' (2 Peter 1:12). Verse 13—'Stir you up as a dying ember into a flame by bringing these things to your memories.' Verse 15, 'Always have these things in remembrance.' 'I want to stir up your pure minds by way of remembrance' (2 Peter 3:1). Remember as I did and repent as I did. He becomes the memory man. From every word written a face was formed and each letter was the eye of Jesus looking out at them again from Holy Writ. Those eyes were as the sparks from a flint. There is a sense, as Peter writes to those scattered abroad, that his eye was never totally wiped dry. He was never totally free from the pain of denying Jesus. 'I remembered to forget and I forgot to remember. Now I must remember to remember.' The Holy Spirit will be my Remembrancer' (John 14:26). Those things which did not mean much were forgotten and those Eternal realities were given a permanent residence in the recesses of the mind of Peter. Every time he heard a cock crow in the future he was reminded of the forgiveness of God!

The Weather Vane was first produced by a Minister who had been speaking about Peter's denial. He wanted to remind the people to keep true, to remind them of Peter's forgiveness, so he had a weather cock placed on the Church. Whichever way the wind blows, the cock remains. God is like that. The love of God is always facing in the right direction. Don't let yourself be blown hither and thither by every wind of doctrine. When the winds of adversity blow, treat them as the breath coming from the mouth of God in a kiss.

Part of the growing pains of Peter is the pain of repentance, of accepting that he was wrong, needed to make it right. Peter went out and wept. All the swearing, the denying, the cursing left him in those tears. Each tear had a sin harnessed to it and as they flowed the sins were washed away. Small pieces of grit were turned into pearly tears as he wept. That crying was the repenting, the sobbing heart a soul wrestling to victory. Those tears were Peter's soul sweating in the conflict. He not only had a tear-stained face but a blood-washed heart. Love, a look of love, had conquered to crying. It was remembering unto repentance for Peter.

Notes

1 Luke 22:61; Matthew 26:75
2 Luke 22:61

CHAPTER

21

The Quantity and Quality of Love

In John 20:1–6 Peter had witnessed the empty tomb and knew that the Lord had risen from the dead. The women also had seen the angels and witnessed the empty tomb, but to those who heard the news it seemed but idle tales. The word 'idle' was used by the medical writers of the day to describe delirium, hysteria and the mentally sick, and even after the Crucifixion and Resurrection when Jesus appeared so many times they did not yet understand the Scriptures. There were other things Peter did not understand. He did not understand that as the fish might fit into the sea so he was being fitted into a plan and part of that plan was the love of God. Peter's heart needed to be enlarged. The sun needed to rise again over the sea of his thinking, never to set, so that he never again asks the question 'Who is it?' when he sees Jesus in all His glory. He needed to see Jesus in the light of a new day. The call of God had to be more than the constant repetition of the sea bird call, the faint echo had to become a clear sound so that he could prepare himself to battle.

When Peter went fishing again the love of God flowed with him, more love than could be navigated, completely surrounding him. Peter could never be in any place where the sun of God's love did not shine.

Understanding what God is saying

Did Cephas understand what Jesus was seeking to do in his life? Every time they met there was an impartation of the Life of Love seeking to produce a lovely life in Peter. Sometimes that love appeared in a word, a parable, a story, a miracle, a glance or even in a fish, but it was met with a closed door, a shuttered mind. This follower of Jesus must understand that he cannot fight in two armies, cannot arrange his life under two commanders. He must hate the one and love the other. It has to be all one. There can be no Time Out. The life of following Jesus and Cross-bearing is daily and it is for ever. There were new depths of love which a night spent toiling and taking nothing would release into the heart of Peter. Jesus was waiting for the ship to be empty, the activity to cease. At the end of Peter's toiling the love of God is just beginning. There is a side to life, the right side, which Peter had not yet discovered, but where he must cast his nets for a draught.

Peter had decided that it was better to fish than to simply do nothing.[1] His strong personality and fisherman's heart was loosed into the sea. All his capabilities were sailing these waters. All that was fisherman was in Peter, while all that is love was in Jesus Christ. Peter returned to fishing like a fish being released into water after captivity, back to his original place and same circumstances as when he was first called some two years previously.[2] What had two years ministry and miracles done for him? How had his life changed? He is still toiling, still taking nothing, like the athlete running and never reaching the end of the race or the footballer who never scores a goal.

But it will happen…it will come to pass in the time of Jesus Christ. The words 'and it came to pass' are written over Peter's life. The Lord of Love waits many days, months and years but at the end of the allotted time He triumphs. The footsteps of Christ may seem to disappear in the sea but actually they walk on the water and Peter is in training to follow those footprints. There may be hours and days when it seems as if this work of art is untouched, but dormant under the canvas nature is doing her blending work, ripening the colours which no brush could add. Nature is signing the masterpiece.

A new burning love and devotion

Peter has been through so many trials. At the end he wept bitterly. Then Jesus appeared on the shore with a fire and fish.[3] The last time we really saw Peter he was warming himself by a fire, but the ashes had appeared. Now here is Jesus with a new fire and newly caught fish wanting the fire to be in the heart of Peter. Jesus wants Peter to reclaim that which fell into the fire as he denied his Lord, wants him to be aglow with God and the purposes of God. It was with a draught of fish that Peter had been called originally. He lost his office by a burning fire and here he must regain that flame and inner glow that only Jesus Himself can restore.

John 21:10 shows Jesus wanted Simon in partnership, not puzzled and in pieces, hence His words 'Bring the fish which you have caught.' He wanted Cephas to understand that working with Him would bring success.

The threefold challenge

Peter has denied the Lord three times and there must be a threefold challenge as to the real nature of the love in the heart of this disciple. That love has diminished but it must grow, and it does so as it is challenged afresh. Like all who follow Jesus, Peter did not want his love to be challenged, yet it had to be to change it into true love. It had to go from toiling, sailing, rowing and casting to catching by being on the right side. When Simon loves Jesus he is casting his nets on the right side. The salt water had to be replaced by water from the pure spring. It was not to be a cock crow but Christ Himself who reinstated the wanderer. He met Peter on the seashore. Jesus is waiting, always tenderly waiting. He has great patience, eternity spans the area before Him. Jesus is expecting visitors! He has the two emblems of Christianity in His hands, both fish and fire. Have you any meat? He asked. The Prodigal Son began to be in want and was ready to perish in hunger. When they were invited to dine it is the same word as in Matthew 22:4, where the king is inviting to a wedding feast. Jesus is to Peter and the other disciples as one who serves. John Trapp, in his Commentary, remarks 'The Greek word used for this meal comes from a word which means prayers.' There is a little altar on the beach and the fish is laid on the fire. Jesus fed Peter before He challenged him, fulfilling His own words through the Apostle Paul, 'If your enemy hunger, feed him' (Romans 12:20). In so doing you will heap coals of fire on his head. He will be melted, he will have his mind filled with desire towards you, not to kill you but to help you. All that anger, jealousy, malice and pride will be turned and he will love and serve you forever. You will be together as flame in a fire. Jesus had to bring Peter out of the sea before He could teach him. Not by drawing in the soil or the sand as with the woman taken in adultery, but in the make up and manner of Peter. Salt had to be taken from his nature and replaced by love. There was something better in Jesus than ships and sea, there was that which would remain forever sailing, forever voyaging, forever catching. Peter must never be the one in the proverbial fisherman's story—the one that got away!

Love is tested in trials

Peter, do you love Me more than these? More than the other disciples? More than the fishing boats, more than the miracles? Do you love Me even having cursed and sworn that you do not know Me? Immediately one of the other disciples had pointed out that Jesus was on the shore, Peter had leapt into the sea! Do you love Me like that? Jesus was to ask him. Will you plunge into all that I am and have for you? Only Jesus can piece together the broken parts of a life and make them as if they had never been broken. In fact a life can be better arranged after the breaking than before, if Jesus does the work. There were more baskets left over after feeding five thousand than the few loaves and fishes they commenced with in Mark 6:43.

The speaking, loving Saviour

It was to the Sea of Galilee or Tiberias, the place of the harp, so called because of its shape, that Jesus came and spoke to Peter.[4] Tiberias is from a Hebrew word meaning 'twang'. There was more twang, more salt and sting in what Jesus had to say than in any sea. He had more fish and had caught more fish with one word than all the nets put together! When you hear the 'twang' you know the arrows of the Lord have been released and will strike their targets. What a lovely song of love He sang into the heart of this man who followed afar. Jesus used sea and situation as angelic ministries and messengers. A hundred best tunes in one melody! It was heart music which came into Peter's soul. Here is Jesus, striking up the band and all that is brass responds to the call and becomes silver and gold. It reminds one of Scarborough where the organist appeared to come up out of the water on an island in the middle of a lake!

When Peter heard it was the Lord he jumped into the water.[5] Was it not depth that Jesus had been seeking during the past three years? There had been that urging for Peter to get out of the boat, that trying for so long to get him to go over the side, to drop the net on the right side, to do the right thing. Full commitment and dedication was the demand and order of the day.

He makes all things new

It was the beginning of a new day, a new fire, new challenge, new love. After toiling all night and taking nothing it is good to meet with Jesus who toiled in the darkness which enveloped the Cross and in doing so gained the world.[6] The Man who has everything meets the man who has nothing. Jesus gave the son of Jonas what he wanted, then told him what He wanted! Jesus believed that if you give, it will be given unto you, pressed down, shaken together and running over.

In the days of love and deep fellowship they had walked on the sea together, but now Jesus is on the shore and Peter goes to toil, as a son of Adam. He seemed to have all the right equipment, he did all the right things, but there was no success story to tell. He toiled all night but had no bread, fish or fire. How different when, restored and in love, he preached as in Acts 2 and three thousand were added to the Church!

The potter knows that one touch is not enough. One blast of wind does not blow far enough. One fishing trip does not catch all the fish. When Jesus was included, then they caught fish. The boat, low in the water was filled with fish. It took another miracle touch, another exercising of Lordship to bring Peter to the shore.

John 21:2 describes how the seven were gathered together—

Peter, Thomas, Nathaniel, James, John and two others, all needing the love of God. They needed a new direction, injection and a rejection of that which surrounded them. On this tide came the love of Jesus Christ. To catch Cephas was the purpose of the exercise, to get Peter walking on everyday water, not to sink. All the doubts of Thomas, some of the betrayal nature of Judas and some of every other disciple was in Peter.

Where the emphasis should be

It is the Simon of pre-conversion days, the flesh and blood failure that Jesus comes to speak to.[7] He was on the shore while Peter was all at sea. A new anchor, the love of God, was required.

The very word Jesus uses for love would immediately change Peter as to the depth, height, length and breadth of that love. Here we see Jesus slipping 1 Corinthians 13 as a chapter into the book of the growing pains of Peter. There was a certain emphasis in the Greek language which does not appear in our own English tongue. FEED my lambs, Feed MY lambs, Feed My SHEEP. A lot of love was needed to do that, and Jesus must see that His relationship with Peter is secure. Love must come in before it can be given out. Peter needed to take another look at the Saviour of men, listen to His voice afresh, letting it fall as dew onto the early Spring grass. Love must be fed and refreshed. Love must be as a foundation before you can build on it. Jesus did not challenge Peter as to how he caught his fish or handled the nets. He did not question why Peter did not keep a true course or how he strained at the oars. He challenged his love. He went to the root cause, to the motivating power, what was in the heart. There need not be any toiling all night. There can be the light of love into the night. Paul and Silas sang a love song at midnight in Acts 16:25. There need not ever be a time when we toil all night and take nothing. Love stamps us with usefulness.

There are four words for love in the New Testament. In the English language there is but one word which means all manner of love—love for friend, for partner, for God. It is the remarkable exchange of these words, two of them used in Jesus meeting with Peter, which makes it so beautiful and challenging. There is an interchange between the words Agapao and Phileo. The four Greek words are:

1. *There is Eros,* the love between the sexes.

2. *There is Storge,* the love between families, brother, sister, mother, father, uncle. Love for King and Queen. Love for a leader.

3. *There is Philia,* the love of friends or for friends, meaning to cherish. It is that which is found in any human friendship. It knows its limits. There is an end to it.

4. *There is Agape,* the love of God and love for God. It can describe the love for only riches, wealth and pleasure. It is a love to the exclusion of all else, yet it includes all else. If you love the Lord your God with all your heart then you will love your neighbour as yourself. It is a much stronger word than the others. This word demands the whole man. It has to do with the heart, is to have a throb in what we do and is connected with the will.

Affection or devotion?

When Jesus came to Peter He said, Do you LOVE Me more than these? Jesus uses the strongest word for love. Here we have the science, the service and the strength of love. Love in all its beauty and essence of depth. Many streams cannot wash it away, much water cannot overcome it even if those waters be found in the Sea of Tiberias. Love needs a partner, needs someone to love. It is love designated, love in its fullest conceivable form. It is so big that God needed a world to love. This love is the very nature of God.

Peter's reply is in the lesser word—Phileo. I love You. I love You as a Friend. I love You as I love my fishing and my home. I love You enough to kiss You but not to die for You. I love You enough to follow You but not to worship You. I don't mind having You as one of my friends, even my best friend.

Peter has the kind of love which does not mind watching the miracles happen but he needs that love which creates miracles in himself. It is a love based on friendship, grows out of a relationship.

It is self interest love, personal relationship love. Jesus is demanding a love which not only makes a fire and places fish on the coals but, during the enforced absence of the Messiah, will continue as if He is present.

The strength and length of love

Then Jesus takes Peter's words and gives them His interpretation.... Do you MILDLY love Me? Do you love Me as a mere reflection? Do you love Me with a measured, cold, calculated love?

Peter is found out! 'You know that I love You with such a depth, with the love of God. I love You with the Cross love. I love You with every ounce of my being. You are in my thoughts morning and night. I cannot get You out of my mind. That is the sort of love I have and love You with. For You, Jesus, have weighed me in the balances of love and You have found me wanting. The measure in the glass has not been a full measure. The measuring rod I have used has been a short, broken rod.' Peter uses the word Agapao, the same word that Jesus used at the beginning of the conversation! Jesus has brought Peter from human love to Divine love, the love of God, filled with unfathomable depths. He has brought Peter from the shallow waters into the plunging depths, from the stream of his own thoughts to a vast ocean. There needs to be fish offered and fire kindled before the feast can begin. Peter steps from simply loving the home to loving the whole world. Jesus was leading Peter from a love without arms to a love which throws its arms around the Universe, a love which is warm, obeying and yielding, as wax before a fire. This sort of love cannot be cast in bronze or marble as some Buddha, it is a love which rejoices to run the race in serving other people with no thought of gain or reward. It is not to the love of Sinai that Peter is brought but to Mount Zion, the love of the Heavenly people, the Church of the Firstborn. It is a love which needs more than the Sea of Tiberias to express itself fully and freely.

John Bunyan describes Christian as having a book in his hand, weeping. He depicts Christian running, walking, stumbling, crawling on all fours. He might have thus been describing the son of Jonas. The reason why Christian found himself stumbling and falling into the Slough of Despond was because he did not see the steps which ran right through the middle! For there to be steps, there had to be a builder!

The conversation between the Resurrected Lord and the limping soldier went rather like this:

> Jesus: Do you love Me with a warm, deep and everlasting love? Is it deep enough for a whale to swim in?
>
> Peter: I love You dearly.
>
> Jesus: Feed My lambs.
> Do you love Me with a love of great depth?
>
> Peter: I love You dearly.
>
> Jesus: Shepherd My sheep.
> Do you love Me with a warm, longing love?
>
> Peter: I love You with an everlasting embrace, beyond the measure of depth. I love You with every part of my past, as if it were the whole.
>
> Jesus: Feed My little sheep.

Although He knows all, He loves all

Cephas is brought to the place of accepting the true, deep full and rich love of God and in John 21:17 confesses, 'You know all things, yet You still love me with an everlasting love, with a sincere love, a love which is undying, which cannot decay.' If that is put in its correct setting then all things work together for good. My life, every life, must revolve around the fact that Jesus knows all things, does all things, works all things together. If Peter can understand that, then life will be so much easier. The Cross will feel lighter and the growing pains will not seem so painful since they are cushioned by such deep love. Tiberias, the place of the harp, was the scene of placing the harp into the heart of Peter. He was to be a true mistrel of the love of God, sounding out through vale and hill and across the surface of the sea.

The Peter who is revealed later is the powerful Pentecostal preacher. A giant has been born in the land. The growth now appears above the surface of the earth. He has caught many fish, but not those swimming in the sea, they are those things which bring wholesome character to his life. There has been transportation and transformation. It has taken a long time but now we find

Peter fully formed, no longer a child. The pains have been many, sometimes he has been stabbed through as with a dagger, but he is now growing from youth to manhood, a giant leap. He comes to the richness of experience through his growing pains which have worked for him a more exceeding weight of Eternal glory.

After many trials iron has been placed in his soul and he writes his Epistles full of maturity and sensibility. Jesus has never left him, and he is now ready to become Peter, the Pastor, Preacher, Teacher and Miracle Worker. The growing pains of Peter have been worth it all.

Notes

[1] John 21:3,15–19
[2] Matthew 4:18–22; Luke 5:1–11
[3] John 21:9
[4] John 21:1
[5] John 21:7
[6] Luke 23:44
[7] John 21:15